I0810394

IMAGES of America

Chilton County

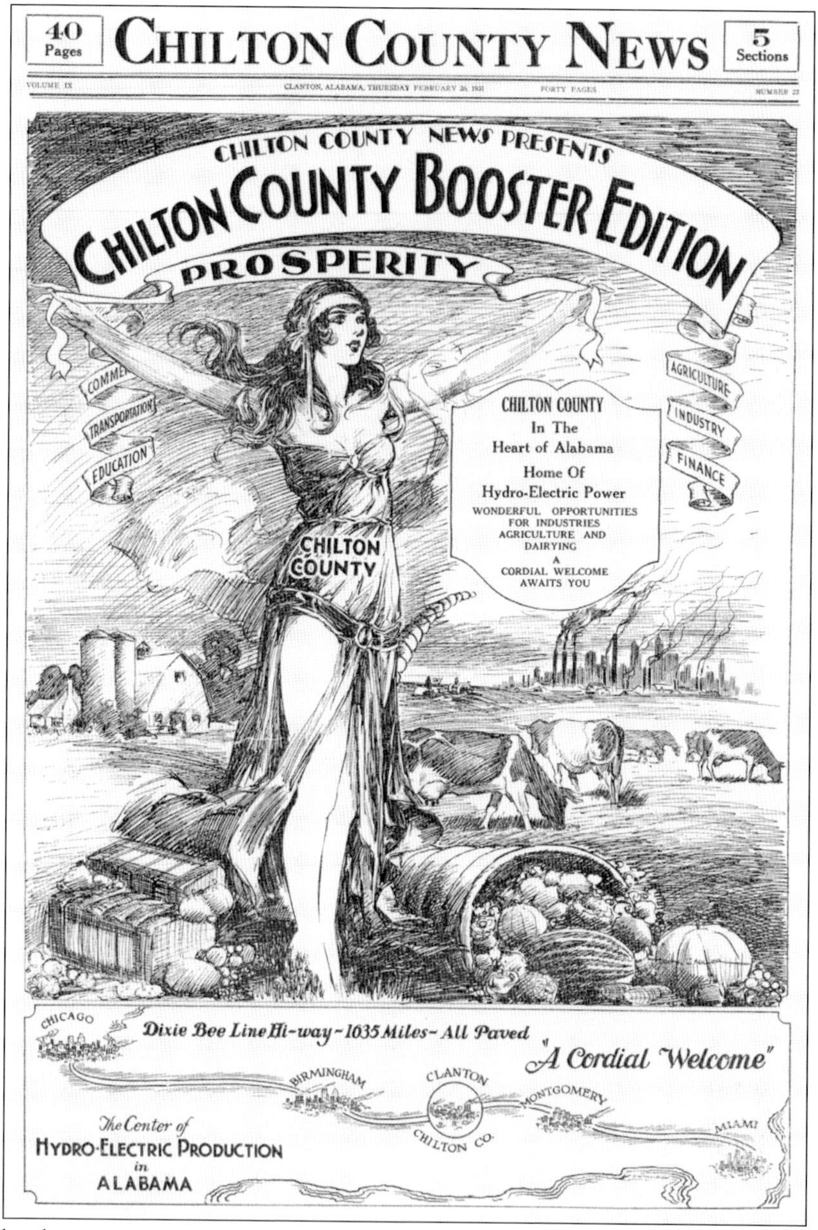

A cordial welcome awaits you in Chilton County! The front page of the February 26, 1931, issue of the *Chilton County News* features the wonderful opportunities for industries and agriculture in the Heart of Alabama, including commerce, transportation, education, and finance. The all-paved, 1,635-mile Dixie Bee Line Highway extending from Miami to Chicago provided access to Chilton County from major cities along the route. (*Chilton County News*.)

ON THE COVER: Seventeen-year-old Barbara Burnette, Chilton County High School senior and contestant in the 1948 Peach Queen competition, provides an attractive invitation to the annual Peach Festival under one of the large signs on the highways leading into Chilton County. The second annual festival included the crowning of the Peach Queen, a peach auction, a street dance, a concert, and a parade. (Chilton County Extension Office.)

IMAGES
of America

CHILTON COUNTY

Billy J. Singleton

ARCADIA
PUBLISHING

ISBN 978-1-4671-2518-5

Published by Arcadia Publishing
Charleston, South Carolina

Printed in the United States of America

Library of Congress Control Number: 2017932815

For all general information, please contact Arcadia Publishing:
Telephone 843-853-2070
Fax 843-853-0044
E-mail sales@arcadiapublishing.com
For customer service and orders:
Toll-Free 1-888-313-2665

Visit us on the Internet at www.arcadiapublishing.com

For the people of Chilton County, Alabama, who welcomed my family into their home

Contents

ACKNOWLEDGMENTS

Images included in chapter 1, "Peach Capital," are provided courtesy of the Chilton County, Alabama, Extension Office except as noted. The author gratefully acknowledges the contributions of Gay West, Chilton County Extension coordinator, for her support and dedication to the people of Chilton County.

Images for chapter 5, "Maplesville," are provided courtesy of Joel Atchison and Clement Clapp of the Maplesville Historical Society except as noted.

Images for chapter 6, "Thorsby," are provided courtesy of Glenn Littleton and the Thorsby Historical Preservation Museum except as noted.

Images for chapter 7, "Verbena," are provided courtesy of Chuck Rice and Betsy Hornady of the Verbena Historical Society except as noted.

The author is deeply indebted to the following individuals and organizations for their contributions and support of this project: Arcadia Publishing title management coordinator Jeff Ruetsche; Meredith McDonough and the Alabama Department of Archives and History (ADAH); Thorsby Historical Preservation Museum; Maplesville Historical Society; Verbena Historical Society; Mayor Billy Joe Driver, Debbie Orange, and Susan Rickles of the City of Clanton; Superintendent Tommy Glasscock and Kim McKinney, Chilton County Board of Education (CCBE); Janice Hull and the Chilton County Chamber of Commerce; William Tharpe, Alabama Power Company Archives (APCA); Bill Rambo, director, Confederate Memorial Park; *Chilton County News*; Rex Bittle; Douglas and Janice Cleckler; Betty Giles; Kim Gillespie; Betsy Hornady; Steve Langston; Richard Moore; Lacey Newman; Connie Powell; Chuck Rice; Derek Scott; Becky Tucker; and Robert Tucker.

The author is especially grateful to Semmie E. Scott of Scott Studios for his passion in recording the history of Chilton County through his photographs.

The author gratefully acknowledges the patience, understanding, and assistance of the director and staff of the Chilton County Public Library.

INTRODUCTION

Located at the geographic center of the state, Chilton County has maintained the distinction of being the "Peach Capital of Alabama" for more than 100 years. The mild climate and gently sloping terrain at the southern point of the Appalachian Range create an ideal environment for cultivation of numerous varieties of the county's principal agricultural export. Each year, Chilton County peach orchards produce more than two-thirds of the total yield of Alabama's leading commercial fruit.

For the people of Chilton County, the peach represents more than an agricultural and economic staple. In many ways, this humble fruit has become symbolic of a way of life. The theme of pageants, festivals, and parades, the iconic peach is prominently displayed on buildings and billboards throughout the county. The water tower in Clanton, designed to resemble a large peach, is affectionately known by residents as the "Big Peach." A familiar landmark that welcomes travelers along Interstate 65 to Chilton County, this unique structure provides subtle encouragement for visitors to exit the interstate to sample peach ice cream, peach pie, and other specialties offered by local vendors.

The most prominent display of civic pride relating to peach production in Chilton County is the annual Chilton County Peach Festival. Held during late June, the festival includes pageants, parades, and other events that culminate in an annual charity peach auction and crowning of the Chilton County Peach Queen.

First held in July 1947, the Peach Festival was organized to promote the Chilton County peach industry. The festival theme "Chilton County Peaches Are Tops" adorned advertising, parade floats, and window displays of local merchants. During the inaugural peach auction, state representative Lee Hornsby was the high bidder on a bushel of Hale Haven peaches produced on the farm of W.H. Lenoir of Maplesville. The following day, the award-winning peaches were transported to Washington, DC, by Eastern Airlines and presented to Pres. Harry Truman during a ceremony at the White House.

The story of Chilton County is not limited to its most famous agricultural export. Established during the most turbulent period in the history of the United States, the 65th Alabama county was originally known as Baker County. Created through a reallocation of land from Autauga, Bibb, Perry, and Shelby Counties, Baker County was established on December 30, 1868, less than one year after the state of Alabama was readmitted to the Union following the War between the States.

One of 14 counties formed during the period of Reconstruction that followed the war, Baker County was named for Alfred Baker (1828–1896), a prominent resident of the former Autauga section. Although Baker opposed the act of secession that led to Alabama being the fourth of 13 Southern states to secede from the United States, he enlisted in the Autauga Rangers Home Guard as a second lieutenant. After the war, Baker was appointed postmaster of Grantville, a small settlement located on Walnut Creek.

In accordance with the act of establishment, Grantville was selected as the county seat of Baker County. Five commissioners conducted the business of the new county in a one-room log cabin located approximately three miles northeast of the present Chilton County Courthouse. In

1870, the original courthouse was destroyed by fire. The county seat was subsequently relocated to Goose Pond, a small village adjacent to the South & North Alabama Railroad being constructed to link Montgomery with Decatur in north Alabama.

Established in 1868, Goose Pond was founded by county namesake Alfred Baker. In late 1870, shortly after becoming the county seat, Goose Pond was renamed in honor of James Holt Clanton (1827–1871), a brigadier general of the army of the Confederate States of America. Born in Columbia County, Georgia, Clanton was eight years old when his family moved to Macon County in central Alabama. Clanton would later enroll at the University of Alabama to study law but soon withdrew to serve in the US Army during the Mexican-American War (1846–1848).

Clanton returned to Macon County after the war to complete his study of the law. He attended the law school of William Parish Chilton, future chief justice of the Alabama Supreme Court. Admitted to the Alabama bar in 1850, Clanton established a law office in Montgomery. In 1855, Clanton was elected to represent Montgomery County as a member of the state legislature.

On January 11, 1861, the Alabama Legislature approved the ordinance of secession to dissolve the union between the state of Alabama and the other states united under the Constitution of the United States of America. Clanton opposed the ordinance of secession but remained steadfast in his support of Southern unity, a conviction that led him to join the 1st Alabama Cavalry. Clanton served with distinction as a military officer until March 1865, when he was seriously wounded and captured at Bluff Springs, Florida. After the war, Clanton returned to his law practice in Montgomery and resumed his position as a leader of the Alabama Democratic Party.

On December 17, 1874, in response to a petition submitted by residents, the Alabama Legislature approved a measure to rename Baker County in honor of William Parish Chilton. A history of Chilton County produced in 1927 by the Clanton Study Club suggests an indiscretion by Alfred Baker created sufficient moderation of public opinion to cause the people to seek a new honoree. The indiscretion may have been related to a belief that Baker had become overly cooperative with northern business interests to further his political and financial affiliations.

A native of Kentucky, William Parish Chilton (1810–1871) moved to Talladega in 1834 to establish a law practice. In 1848, Chilton was appointed associate justice of the state supreme court. In December 1852, he succeeded Edmund Strother Dargan as chief justice. Like James Holt Clanton, Chilton opposed the ordinance of secession but remained loyal to his adopted state. From 1861 to 1866, he served as a member of the provisional legislature and permanent congress of the Confederate States of America. Chilton personally escorted Jefferson Davis to the provisional capital in Montgomery for his acceptance speech as president of the new confederation of states. Although Chilton resided in numerous locations in Alabama, he never lived in the county that bears his name.

Throughout its history, advances in transportation have been a significant influence on the economic and demographic development of Chilton County. Early roads and stagecoach routes facilitated a migration of settlers to the central region of the state. As the efficiency and popularity of rail transportation brought about the decline of travel by the stagecoach, construction of the rail system created the framework for the early development of Chilton County. Following the Second World War, the affordability of mass-produced automobiles prompted the decline of the railroad as a system of mass transportation and created an immediate need for more highways and roads. Each advance in transportation technology had a direct effect on the towns and communities of Chilton County.

Access to transportation was a primary consideration in the establishment of the communities of Clanton, Maplesville, Verbena, Thorsby, and Jemison. The original town of Maplesville, founded in March 1829, was located at the junction of two heavily traveled overland routes, the Fort Jackson Road and the Selma-to-Elyton Road. Named for early merchant and postmaster Stephen W. Maples, the town was surrounded by abundant farmland, timber for construction, and fresh water from nearby streams.

During the period when Tuscaloosa served as the capital of Alabama (1826–1846), Maplesville experienced considerable growth, expanding to include a post office, inn, taverns, and horse racing tracks. A stop on the first postal route between Montgomery and Tuscaloosa, the inn at

Maplesville served as a changing station that provided fresh horses for stagecoaches as well as food and lodging for passengers.

In March 1848, legislators in Montgomery approved the formation of the Alabama & Tennessee River Railroad Company, an event that had a significant impact on the future of Maplesville. The new rail service was established to connect the city of Selma to the Tennessee & Coosa Railroad at a point along the Tennessee River. The section of rail line from Plantersville to Montevallo was routed through the small community of Cuba, three miles west of Maplesville. As the efficiency and economy of rail transportation increased, passenger travel along stagecoach routes began to decline, a trend that had an adverse effect on the growth and prosperity of Maplesville.

In August 1853, surveyor William H. Wilson established the boundaries for a new town in proximity to the Maplesville Depot, which had been constructed to serve the new rail line. In 1856, the post office was relocated to a site near the depot to allow convenient access to the railroad. To take advantage of opportunities created by the railroad, Maplesville merchants began moving to locations more convenient to this modern transportation system. Over time, the town of Maplesville was reborn adjacent to the new railway that traversed the western portion of what would become Chilton County. The former townsite was slowly reclaimed by nature as Maplesville, a town older than its county, began a new chapter in its history.

The intersection of two well-traveled stagecoach routes was also a significant factor in the establishment of the town of Verbena, originally known as Summerfield. The name was changed when residents learned of another community of the same name located near Selma. Local history suggests the name Verbena was favored due to the abundance of the verbena plant native to the area.

Rail service provided by the Louisville & Nashville Railroad (formerly the South & North Alabama) brought growth and prosperity to Verbena. An early railroad brochure describes Verbena as having the advantages of an altitude well above sea level with fine water and no mosquitoes, providing priceless features of health and comfort.

The convenience of rail travel allowed prominent residents of Montgomery to escape the oppressive summertime heat of the city to enjoy the cool, fresh air prevalent in the higher elevations of Verbena. Considered a resort area, the town could boast of a number of modern conveniences, including a post office, rail depot, school, and hotel. A haven for the well-to-do of the Montgomery River region who sought refuge from recurring epidemics of yellow fever, Verbena became known as a town born of this often fatal disease. The Verbena climate was considered so recuperative that American poet and author Sidney Lanier resided for a short time near the town in an effort to alleviate the symptoms of tuberculosis he contracted while a soldier during the War between the States.

A mild climate and convenient access to transportation were also factors in the establishment of the town of Thorsby. Born to Scandinavian parents in Minnesota, Theodore Torkel Thorson traveled by train to Alabama in 1895 seeking a region of temperate climate and land more suitable for the cultivation of fruits, vegetables, and vineyards than his home state. Thorson was accompanied on his journey by his brother Sam Thorson, John F. Petersen, and K.G. Faegre.

Arriving in Birmingham, the group made an acquaintance who suggested that Thorson consider an area near the town of Jemison, a small community located on the Louisville & Nashville Railroad in Chilton County. Unable to locate sufficient property to meet its needs, the group continued south to inspect parcels of land near the depot at Strasburgh, approximately three miles north of the Lomax community. After evaluating the climate, the length of the growing season, the availability of land, and its strategic location between two of the largest cities in Alabama, Thorson concluded that the area north of the Strasburgh Station was well suited for his purposes.

Thorson formed the Concordia Land & Improvement Company to market 5- and 10-acre lots to families of Scandinavian heritage being recruited from the upper Midwest. A modern hotel was constructed to provide temporary lodging for new arrivals. Families could also rent a boxcar on the Louisville & Nashville Railroad for $30 to ship household furnishings to their new home.

The founder's vision of a community that consisted of craftsmen, merchants, and farmers became a reality as the town grew to include two hotels, a school, and five churches. Industry also expanded with the construction of a sawmill, cotton gin, blacksmith shop, bakery, flour mill, bank, and two wineries.

The first stop in Chilton County for Thorson and his fellow travelers, the town of Jemison, was originally known as Langstonville and, later, Langston Station. The settlement was near the stagecoach route that led to Montevallo and was named for pioneer and prominent landowner Louise Langston.

The arrival of the railroad in 1870 served as a catalyst to attract additional settlers to the area. In 1871, a post office was established in the general store of postmaster D.A. Aliston. The following year, a railroad depot was constructed to accommodate passengers and mail on the north-and-southbound service.

At the suggestion of railroad developer John T. Milner, Langston Station was named in honor of state senator Robert Jemison Jr. of Tuscaloosa (1802–1871). Jemison was a founder of the Jemison, Powell, Ficklen & Company Stage Line, which traversed north and central Alabama. A pioneer industrialist and entrepreneur, Jemison was instrumental in the development of the city of Birmingham and the mineral district of Alabama.

Like other early transportation systems, the system of roads and highways has significantly influenced the development of communities throughout Chilton County. In 1914, construction of the Montgomery-to-Birmingham Road commenced along a route that paralleled the Louisville & Nashville rail line. Paved in 1926, the route became a section of US Highway 31, which connected the cities of Miami and Chicago. Known as the Dixie Bee Line, Highway 31 became the first modern highway in Chilton County and the main thoroughfare through Verbena, Clanton, Thorsby, and Jemison. Increased traffic along the Bee Line Highway supported the economies of towns and communities in Chilton County, as automobile service stations, restaurants, and motels created jobs and tax revenue.

Although the establishment of transportation systems has traditionally been the catalyst that creates and sustains local economies, the evolution of these systems often has the opposite effect. The emergence of the automobile and airplane soon relegated the railroads primarily to the carriage of freight. As travel by rail peaked in popularity, Chilton County was served by no fewer than eight railroad depots. Today, only two remain, and neither serves in its original capacity.

As early roads and railroad systems contributed to the founding and economic expansion of communities along their routes, the emergence of the interstate highway system would have a similar effect on the future development of Chilton County. Opened in 1960, the first completed segment of Interstate 65 in Alabama originated four miles south of Clanton and extended to a point two miles north of Calera. Interstate 65 has become the most heavily traveled highway system in the state and provides a direct connection between the four largest cities in Alabama. Until the next milestone in transportation systems becomes a reality, the Interstate 65 corridor will be the dominant factor affecting the future development of Chilton County.

Created amid unprecedented change, Chilton County has been transformed by the events of a rapidly changing world. Through it all, the people of Chilton County have remained steadfast in their commitment to their families, communities, and the county that is their home. As Chilton County crosses the threshold into its second century, the communities that are the heart of Alabama—Clanton, Jemison, Maplesville, Thorsby, and Verbena—will continue to evolve as they have through generations. But the history of a county is more than a time line of events. The history of Chilton County is the story of its people. It will be the people who ensure the legacy of Chilton County as the history of our future is written.

One

Peach Capital

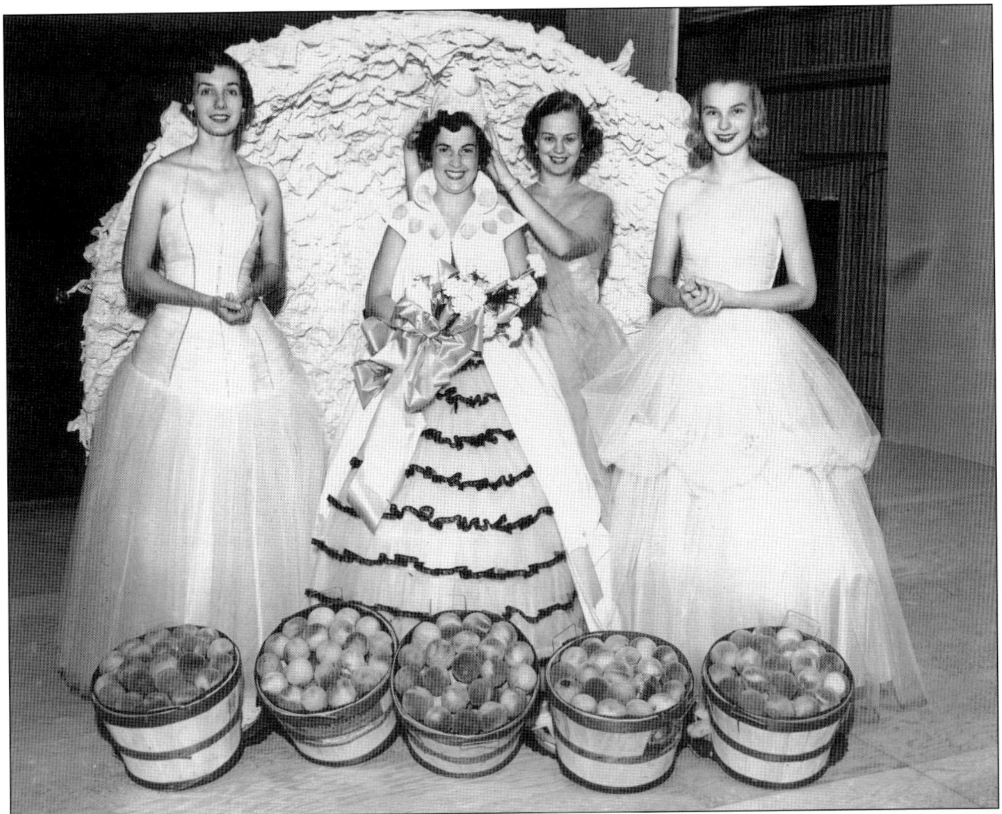

First held in July 1947 at Thorsby, the Chilton County Peach Festival was organized to promote the local peach industry. The theme, "Chilton County Peaches Are Tops," adorned parade floats, banners, and the storefronts of local merchants. Today, the annual festival is held during late June and features parades, pageants, and other community events that culminate in a charity peach auction and crowning of the Chilton County Peach Queen.

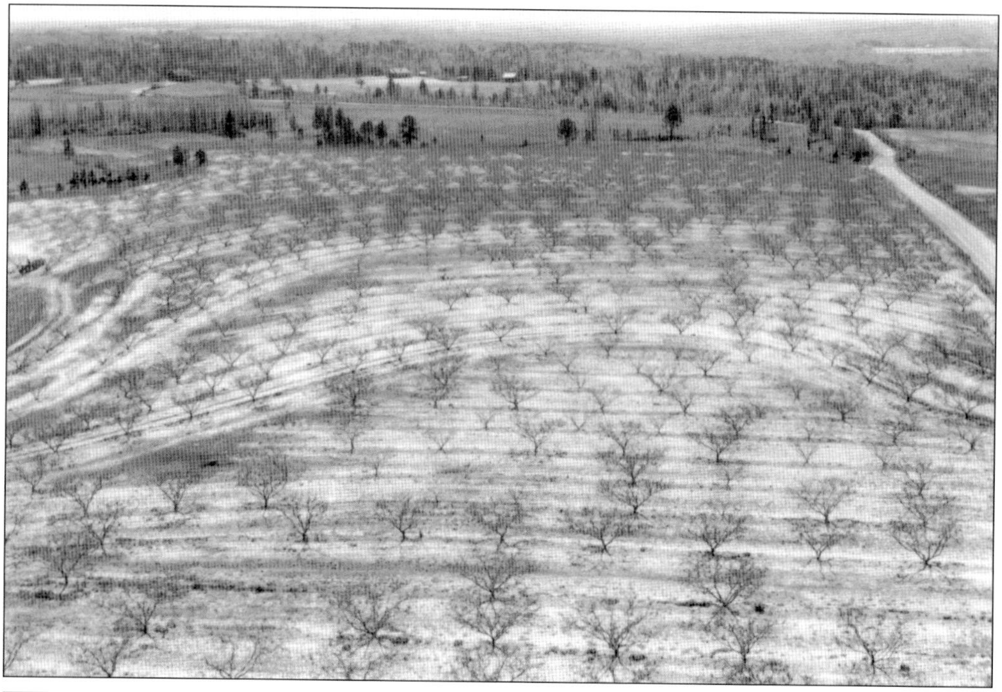

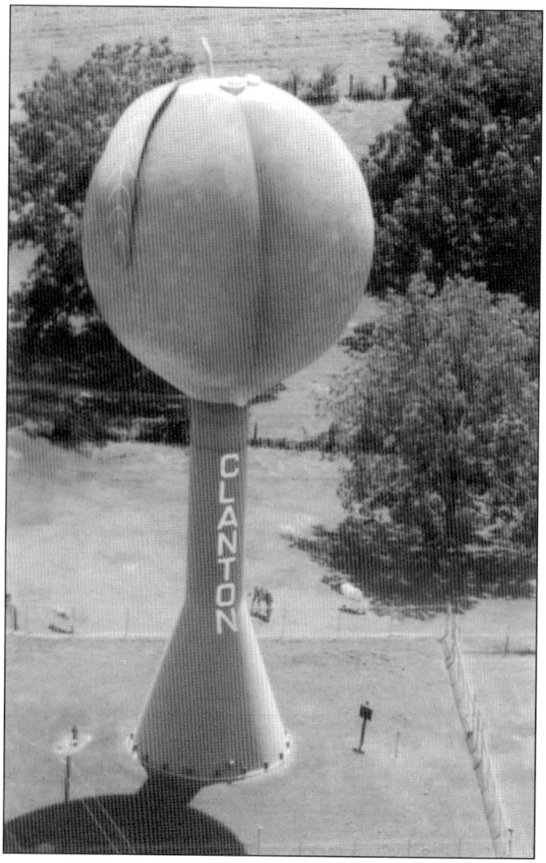

Chilton County earned the distinction as the Peach Capital of Alabama during a resurgence of the peach industry during the years following the Second World War, as orchards in Chilton County produced more than two-thirds of the state peach crop. In 2015, Chilton County accounted for 72 percent of peach production in Alabama, the state's leading agricultural export. Approximately 35 different varieties of peaches are produced in Chilton County.

Known by locals as the Big Peach, the 500,000-gallon water tower at Clanton is a tribute to the Chilton County peach industry. Constructed in 1992 by the Chicago Bridge & Iron Company, the tower is a familiar landmark that welcomes travelers on Interstate 65 to Chilton County. This unique structure also provides subtle encouragement for visitors to exit the interstate to sample peach-flavored specialties offered by local vendors. (Author's collection.)

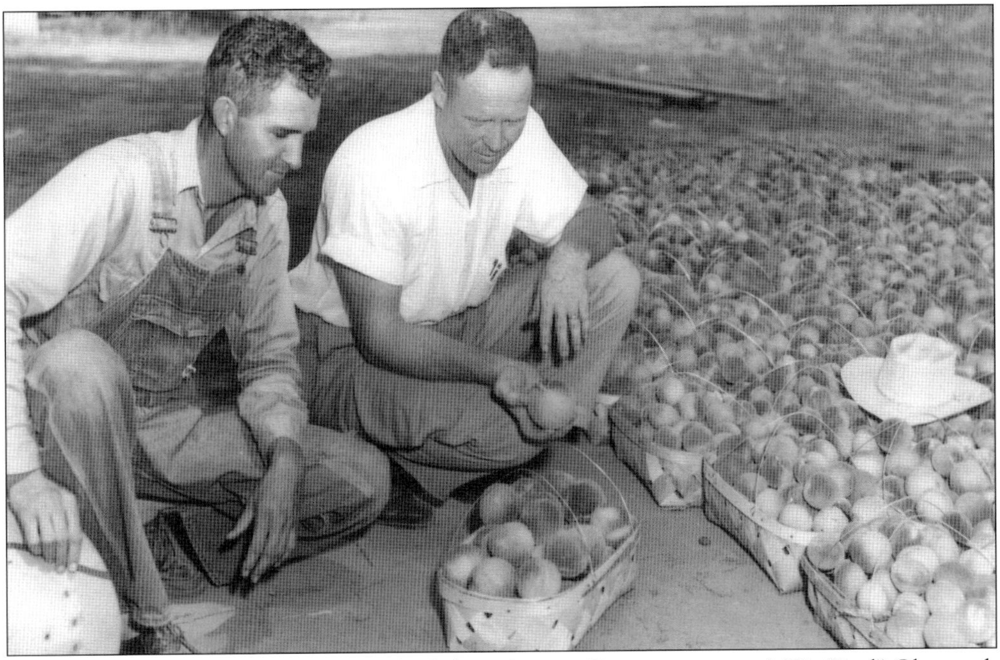

Peach grower H.O. Headley (left) and Chilton County Extension agent M.R. "Red" Glasscock inspect baskets of peaches bound for sale at local markets. Although many Chilton County peach growers sell their produce to local markets, the largest producers also pack and ship peaches to out-of-state markets. As the county extension agent, Glasscock worked with peach growers to develop methods to maximize production.

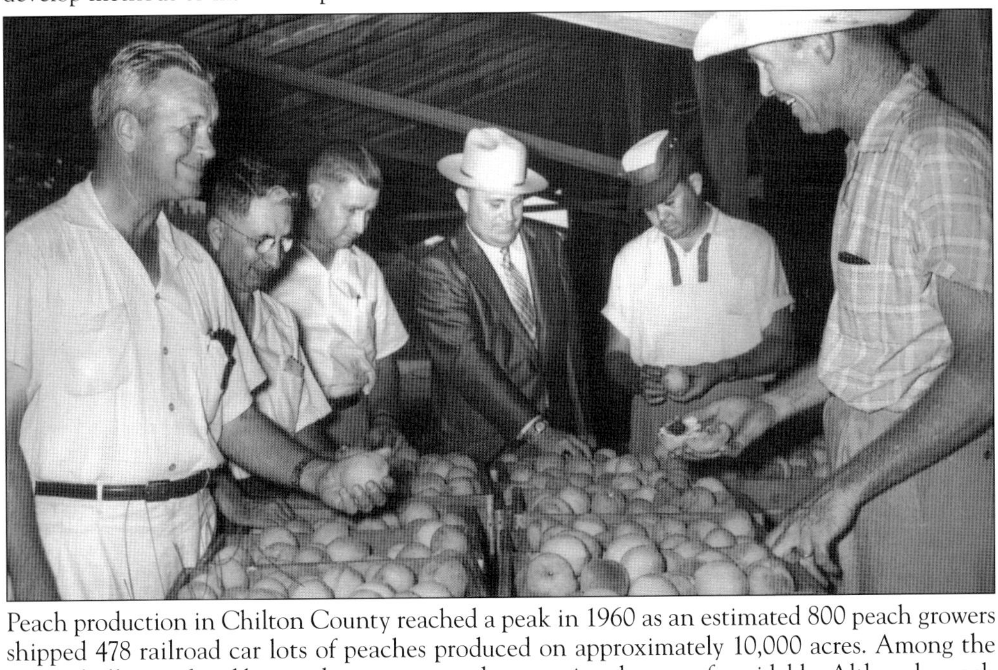

Peach production in Chilton County reached a peak in 1960 as an estimated 800 peach growers shipped 478 railroad car lots of peaches produced on approximately 10,000 acres. Among the many challenges faced by peach growers, weather remains the most formidable. Although peach trees require a chilling period during the winter months, the entire 1955 crop was lost due to the devastating effects of a late frost.

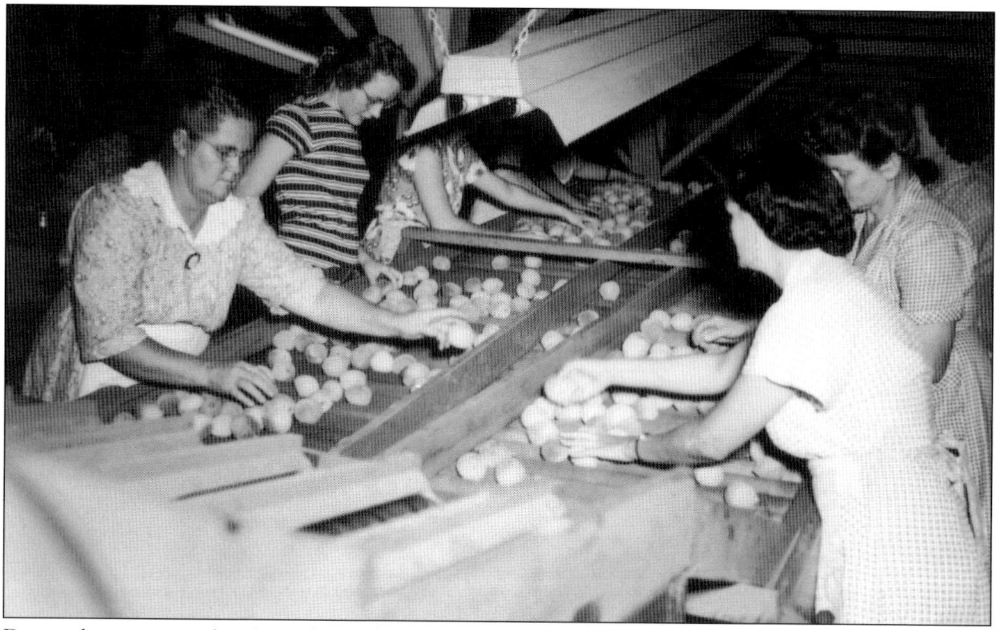

During harvest, peaches from the orchards were transported to the packinghouses to be sorted and graded. Sorted by variety, the peaches were then inspected to ensure they were mature, but not soft or overripe, and free from decay, damage, worms, or wormholes. The peaches were then placed in crates for shipment out of state or in baskets for delivery to local outlets. Sorting and grading peaches required sharp eyes, quick hands, and concentration. The seasonal work afforded students and homemakers the opportunity to earn extra money for school or the household. According to news reports, only the best Chilton County peaches were being shipped to larger markets in Detroit, Chicago, Dayton, New York, Saint Louis, and even Atlanta, capital of the Peach State.

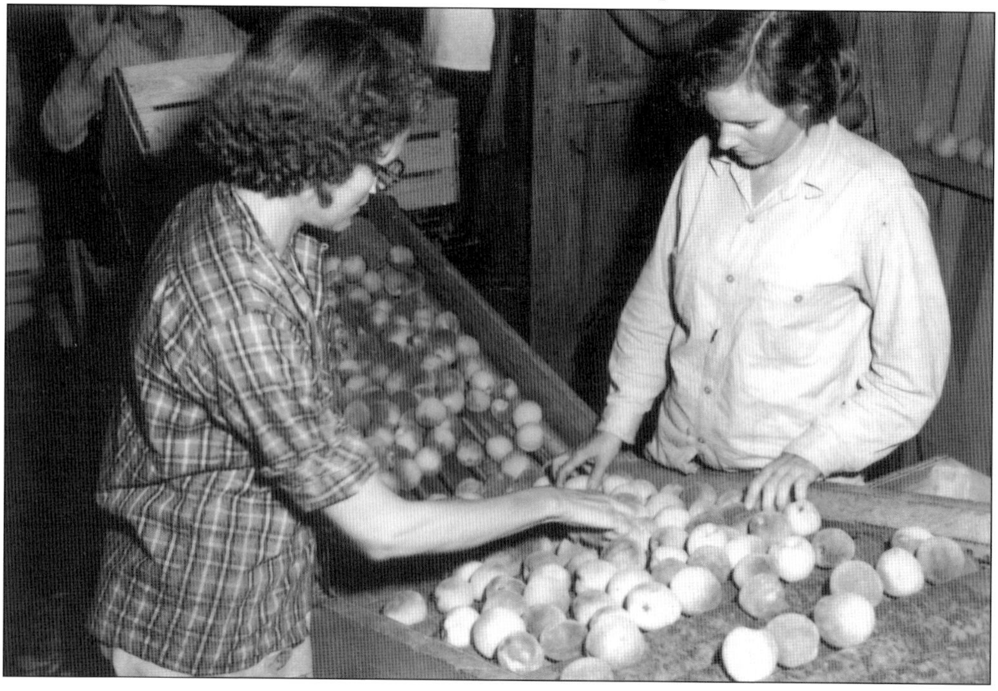

In a 1952 publicity photograph, Marie Shaw displays new packaging to be used by the Chilton County Fruit and Truck Growers Association for the transport of peaches to markets outside of Chilton County. Instead of the traditional wood packaging, the new packing crate was made of cardboard and could support the weight of a 200-pound man.

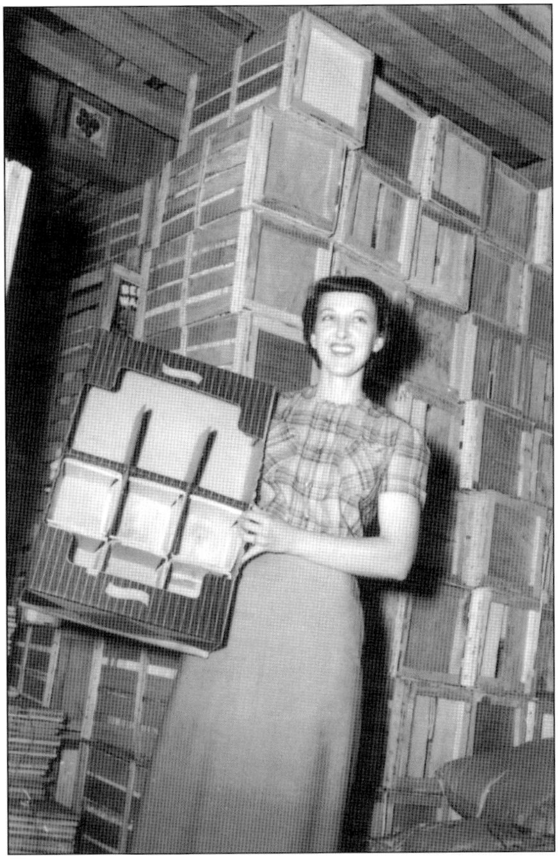

Although Chilton County peaches are shipped throughout the United States, individual baskets are still sold through local markets, roadside stands, and the beds of pickup trucks. During peach season, trucks loaded with baskets of Chilton County peaches traveling to markets in Birmingham and Montgomery are a common sight during the early morning hours along the interstate, highways, and county roads.

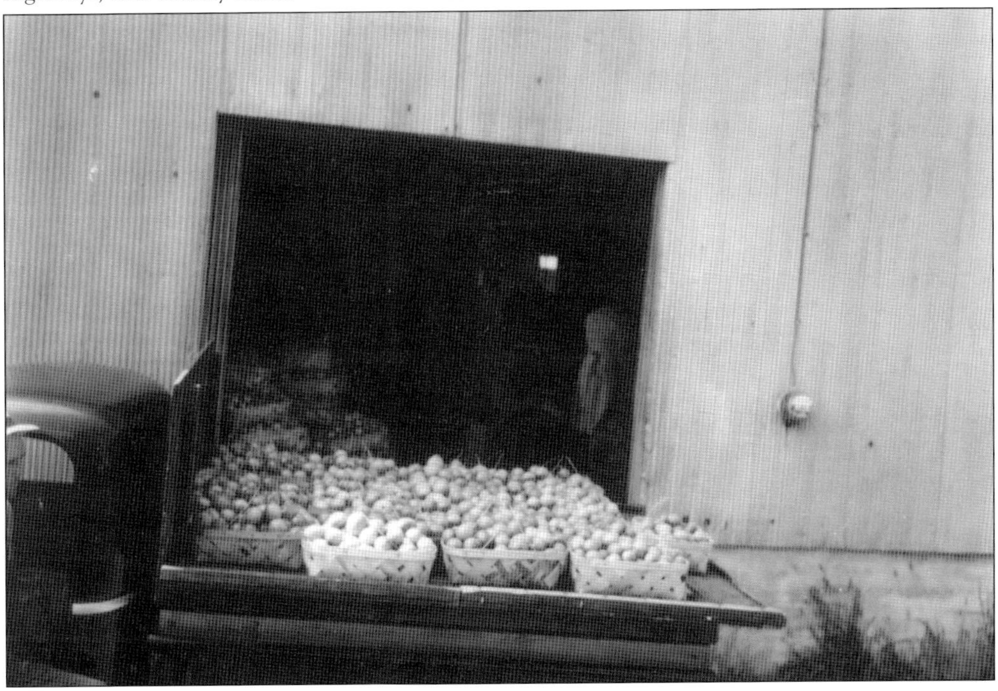

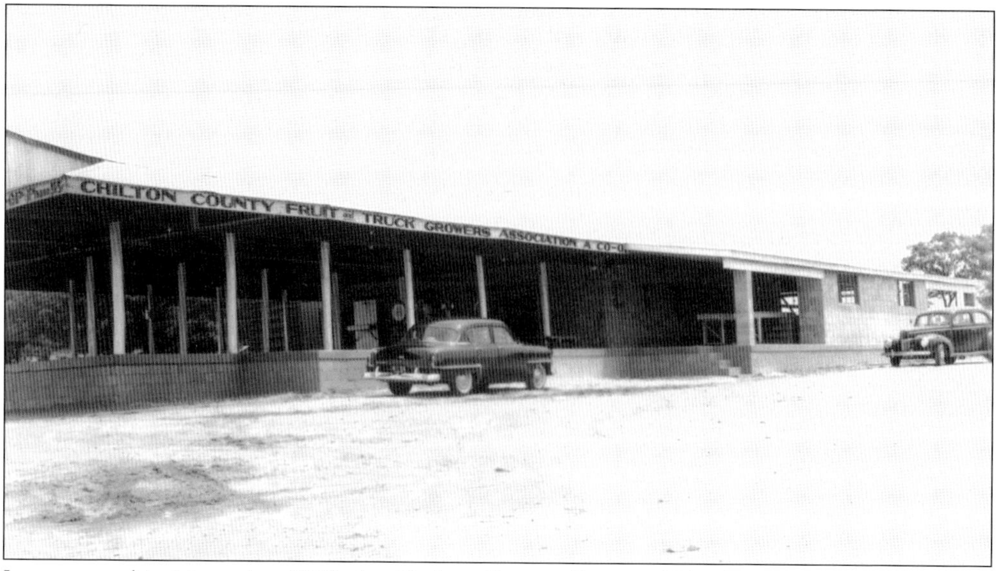

Incorporated in November 1925, the Chilton County Fruit and Truck Growers Association in Thorsby was established as a cooperative to create a more efficient marketing and distribution system for locally grown fruits and vegetables. Truck growers are farms that produce one or more varieties of seasonal crops on a large scale for shipment to distant markets where cultivation might be limited by the local climate.

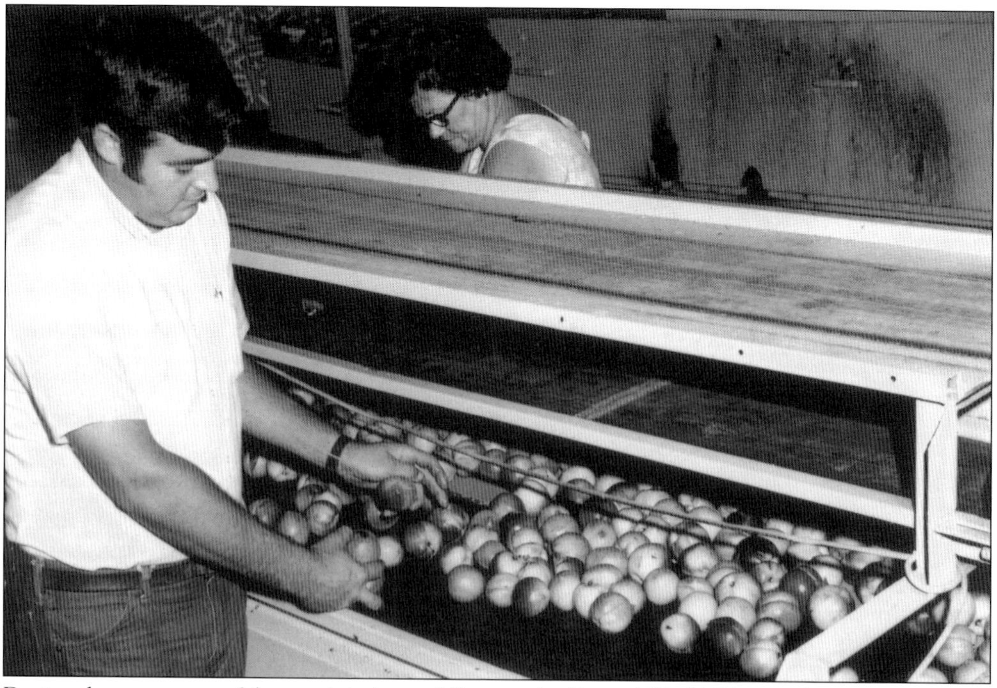

During the resurgence of the peach industry following the Second World War, modern packinghouses capable of handling large quantities of peaches were constructed in Chilton County. The peaches were processed by means of conveyor lines, washed and chilled with cold water, and graded for size and quality before being packed in wooden hampers for shipping. These hampers were later replaced by cardboard packaging.

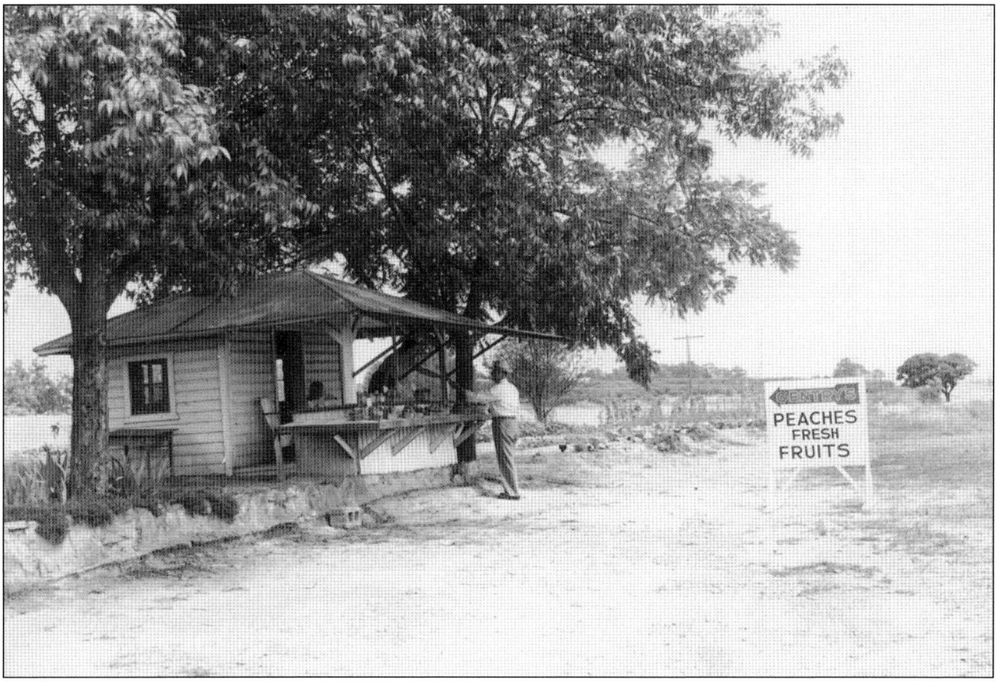

Roadside fruit stands like Gentry's Peaches and Fresh Fruits were a common sight along US Highway 31 from Verbena to Jemison. In many cases, these stands were built near the orchards and farm fields, providing customers with a supply of freshly picked peaches and other produce. Cash-only businesses, fruit stands eliminated the costs associated with transporting produce to markets, allowing growers to sell their produce at a reduced rate. The fruit stand was a place not only to purchase fresh fruits and vegetables but also to discuss politics, current events, and local gossip. For the children of growers, the long, lazy, carefree days of summer vacation were spent working at the family fruit stand.

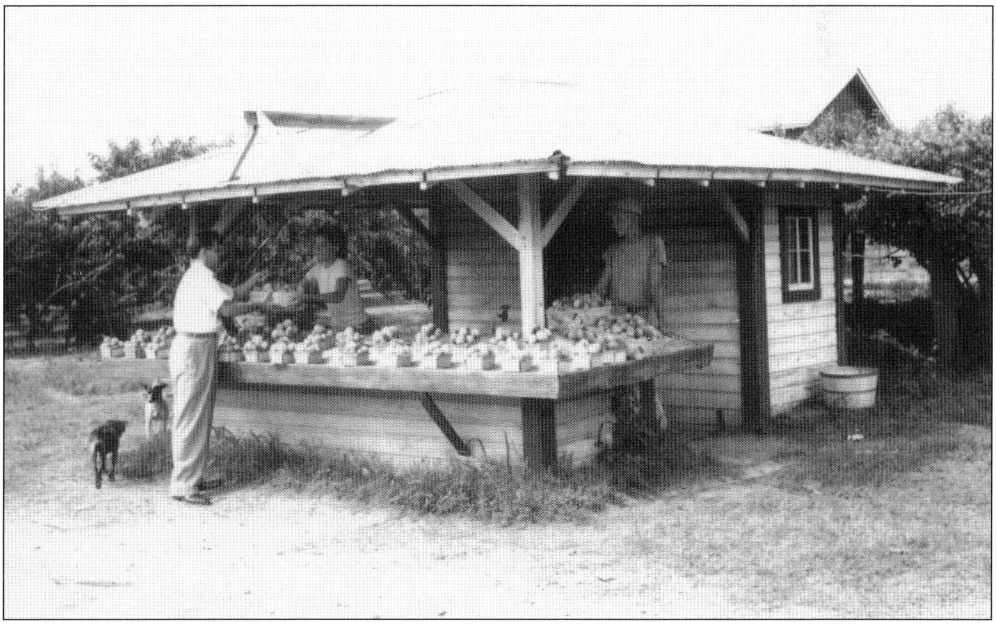

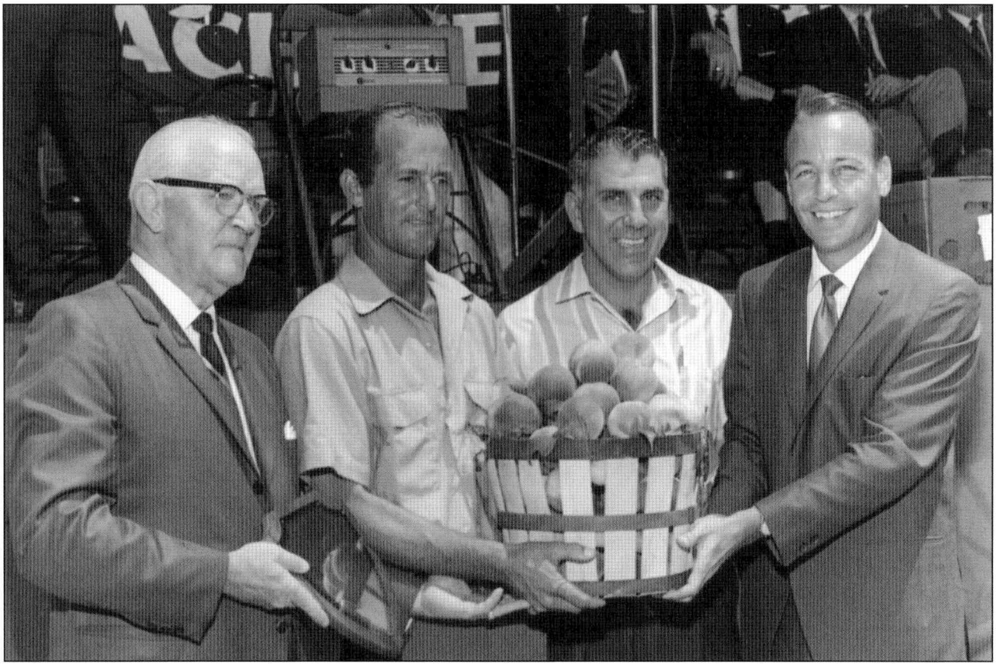

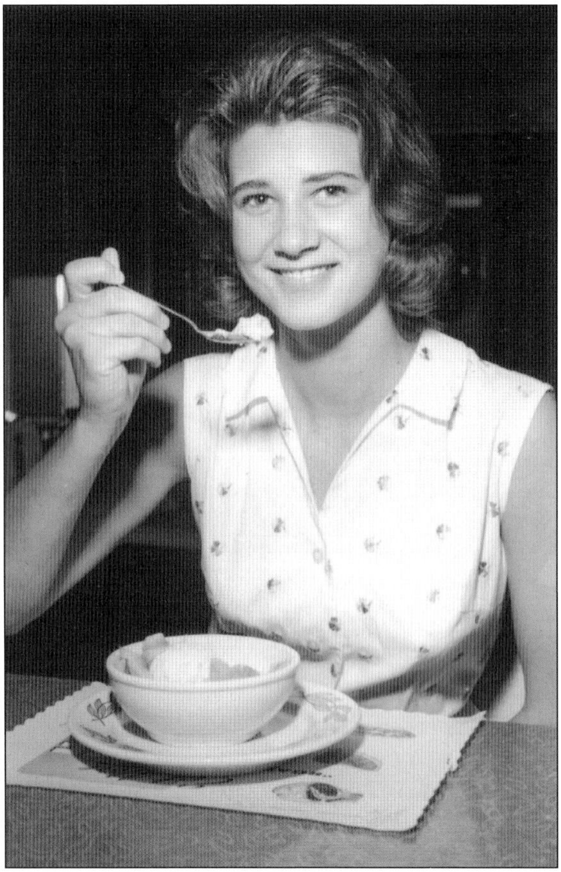

Each year, a basket of prizewinning peaches is traditionally presented as a gift to politicians, notable personalities, or charitable organizations as a gesture of goodwill. In 1967, Lt. Gov. Albert P. Brewer (far right) accepted a basket of Chilton County's finest peaches on behalf of Gov. Lurleen Wallace. Accompanying the lieutenant governor are, from left to right, Commissioner of Agriculture Richard Beard, Horace Easterling, and Pat Ferlise.

A young woman enjoys the fruits of a successful Chilton County harvest. A local favorite, a bowl of peaches and ice cream always provides refreshing relief from the summer heat. Chilton County's principal agricultural export can be enjoyed in many forms, including pies, ice cream, shakes, tarts, in a bowl of milk, or sprinkled with sugar. Regardless of how they are enjoyed, Chilton County peaches are tops!

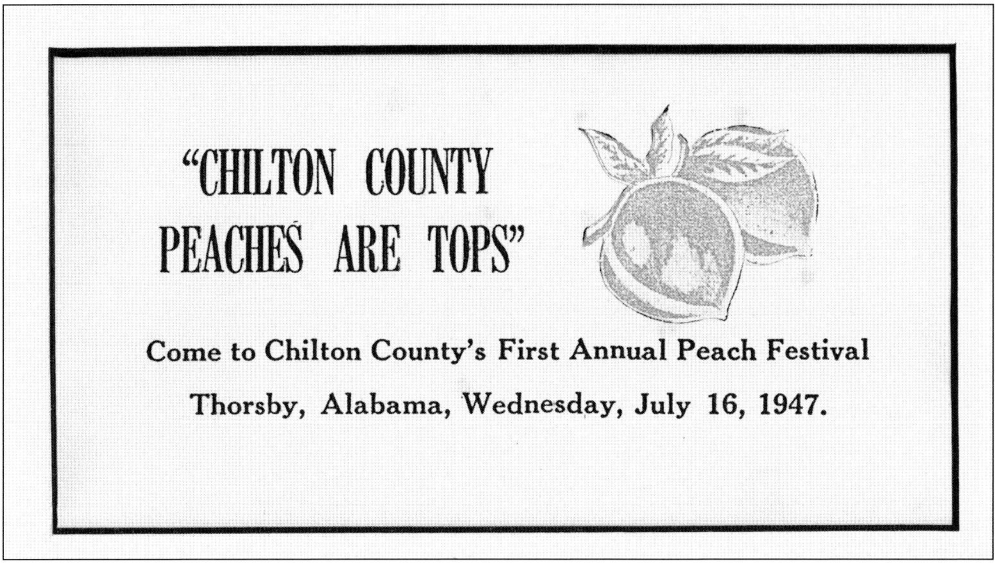

An ad for the inaugural Chilton County Peach Festival proclaims "Chilton County Peaches Are Tops." The one-day festival began with a parade from Clanton to Thorsby. The parade included so many participants that more than two hours were required to travel the seven-mile route. Festival activities included an all-day picnic, a baseball game, and a dance with music provided by the Lewis Simpkins Orchestra (Thorsby Historical Preservation Museum.)

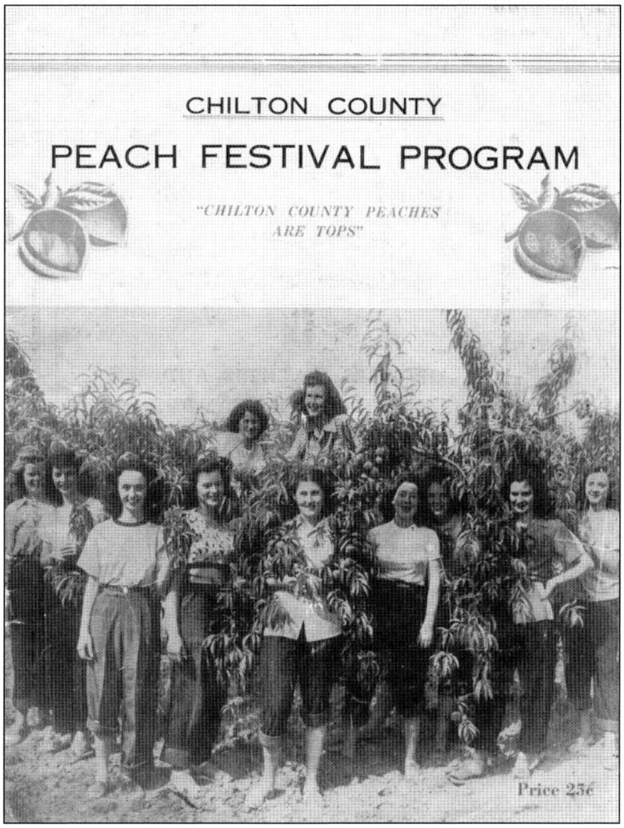

The program for the inaugural Peach Festival features contestants for the title of Chilton County Peach Queen. To be eligible, a contestant had to be unmarried, between 15 and 25 years of age, and the daughter of a Chilton County peach producer. The 1947 Peach Queen was selected at a banquet held at Thorsby Institute on the evening preceding the festival. (Thorsby Historical Preservation Museum.)

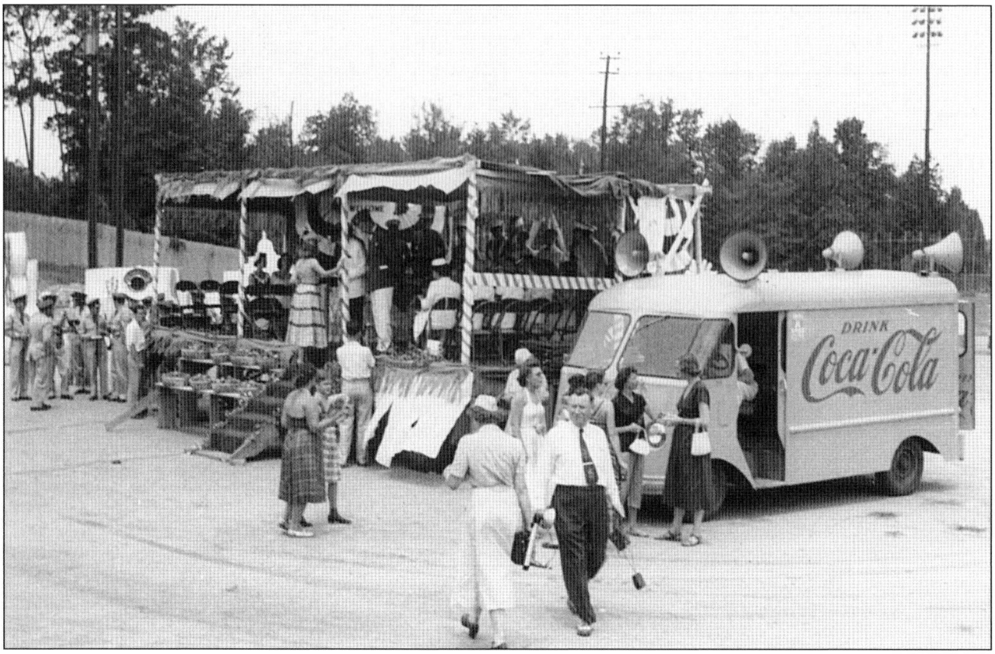

The 1947 Peach Festival parade included automobiles and trucks loaded with peaches to add color to the parade. Participants assembled at the Chilton County High School in Clanton. The Maxwell Field military band from Montgomery (left) led the assembled vehicles on the seven-mile parade route to Thorsby. Traffic control was provided by the Alabama Highway Patrol and local law enforcement with the assistance of the Thorsby Boy Scouts.

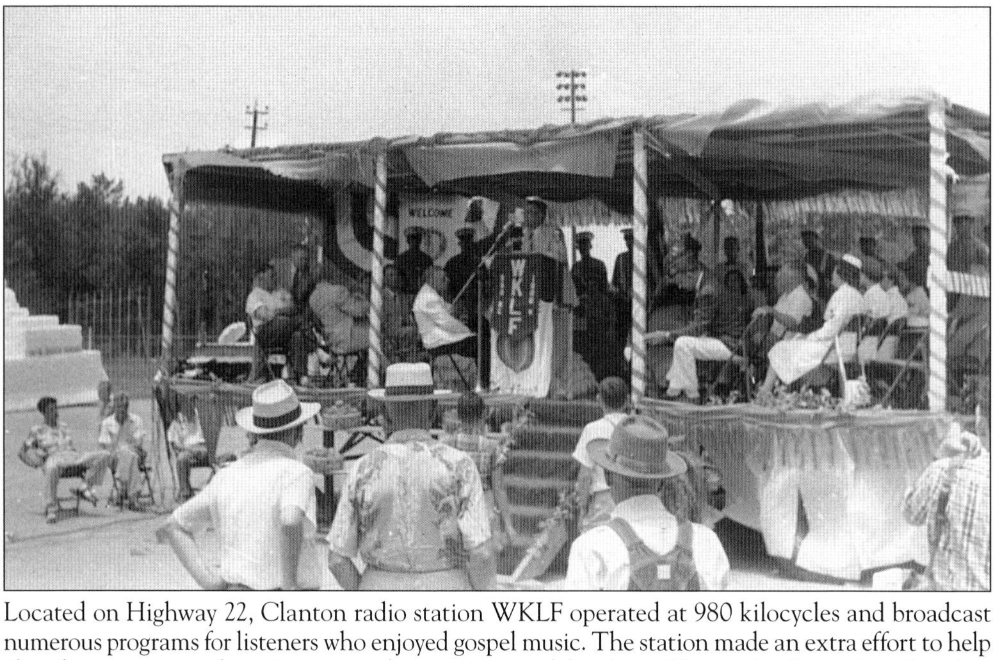

Located on Highway 22, Clanton radio station WKLF operated at 980 kilocycles and broadcast numerous programs for listeners who enjoyed gospel music. The station made an extra effort to help churches announce their singings and anniversary celebrations. The station began broadcasting in 1947, the same year as the first Chilton County Peach Festival. Dignitaries for the 1947 festival included Lt. Gov. J.C. Inzer representing Gov. "Big Jim" Folsom.

In a publicity photograph for a special Peach Festival edition of *Alabama Magazine*, contestant Edna Lane Johnson is shown picking one of Chilton County's world-class peaches. The daughter of William and Marion Johnson of Clanton, the five foot, five inch graduate of Chilton County High School was described as having black hair and blue eyes. At the time of the competition, Edna Lane Johnson was 18 years of age.

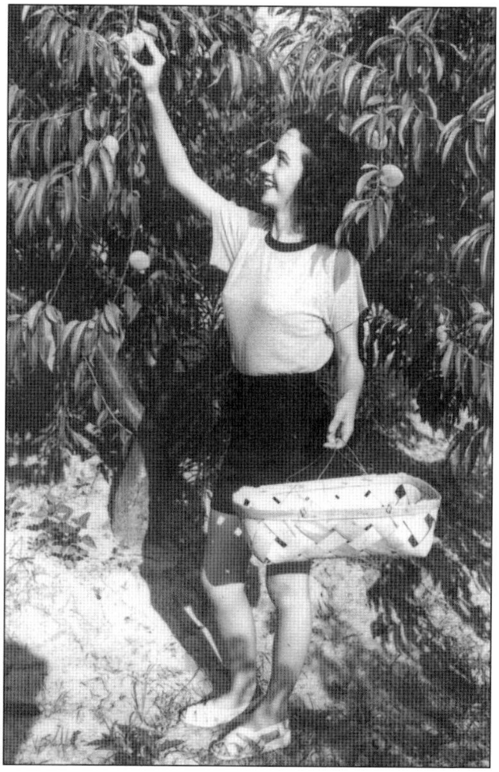

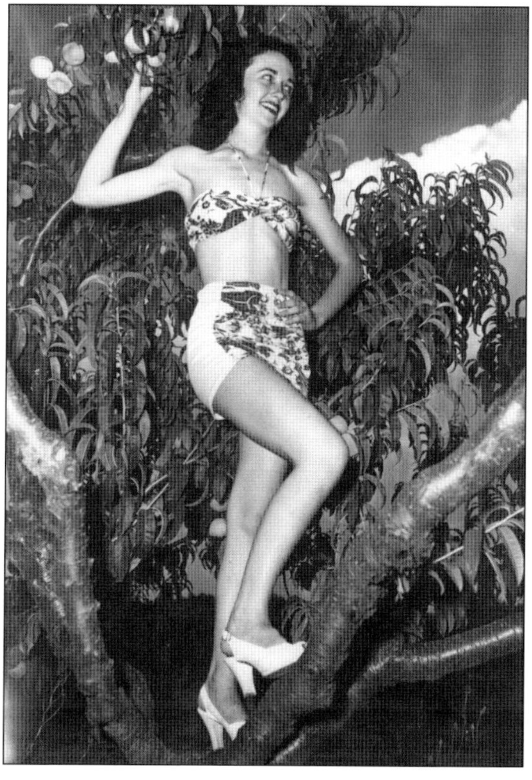

Edna Lane Johnson, a 1947 Peach Queen contestant, prepares for the swimsuit competition. Twelve young women competed for the title. In addition to a personal interview with the judges, contestants participated in evening gown and swimsuit competitions. The young woman selected as Peach Queen received her crown from Lt. Gov. J.C. Inzer. Unlike current competition winners, the 1947 Peach Queen ruled for only one day.

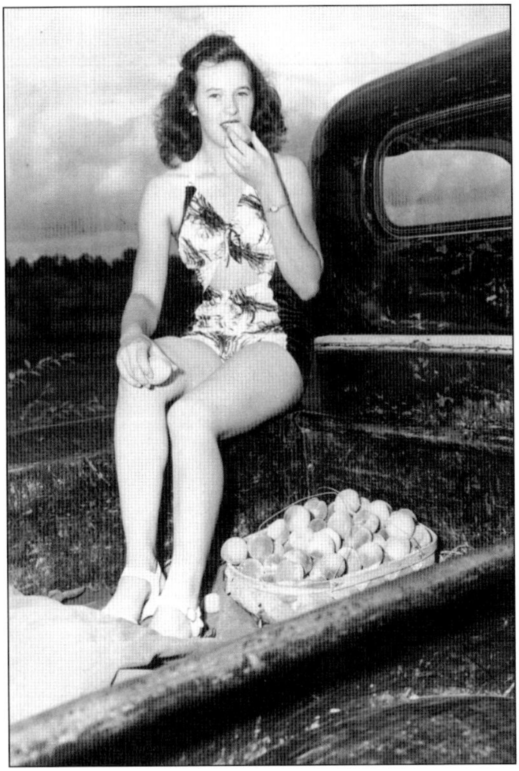

At 15 years of age, Essie Lou Jones competed for the title of 1947 Peach Queen. The daughter of Arthur and Gladys Jones of Stanton, Essie Lou was five feet, seven inches in height with brown hair and brown eyes and attended school at Stanton. The youngest of eight children, Essie Lou was given the nickname "Chick" by her father.

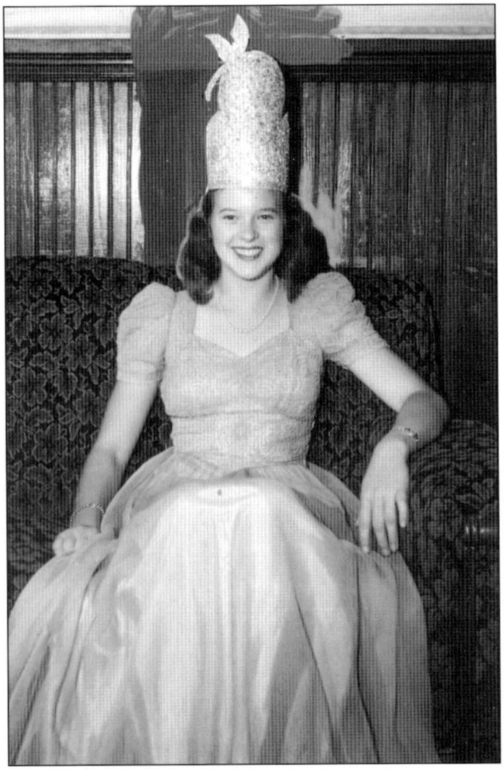

Essie Lou "Chick" Jones was selected 1947 Peach Queen by a panel of judges during the competition held at the Thorsby Institute. Ironically, a young man of the same nickname, Cecil Clark "Chick" Carlton, was named king of the festival. At the time, Carlton served as assistant Chilton County Extension agent. Marjorie Bentley of Thorsby was runner-up for the title.

A young woman poses near the railroad depot in Thorsby during the 1947 Peach Festival. The parade originated in Clanton and concluded in Thorsby and was described by the *Union Banner* newspaper as "a mile in length and a gorgeous sight to behold." Local rain showers did not dampen the enthusiasm of the participants. Many of the events were held on the grounds of Thorsby Institute. (Thorsby Historical Preservation Museum.)

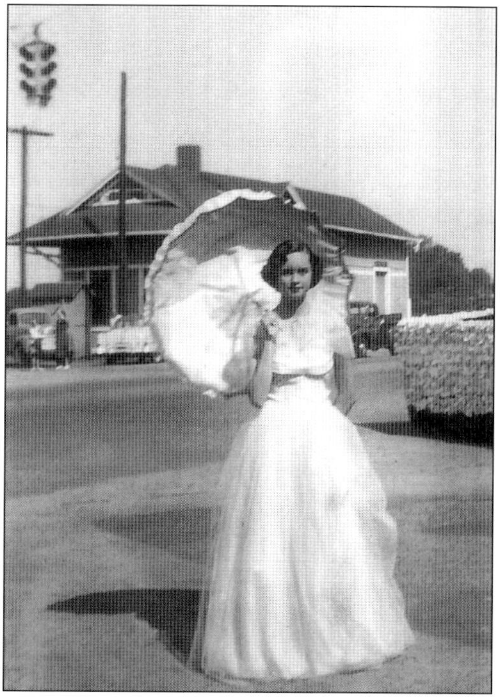

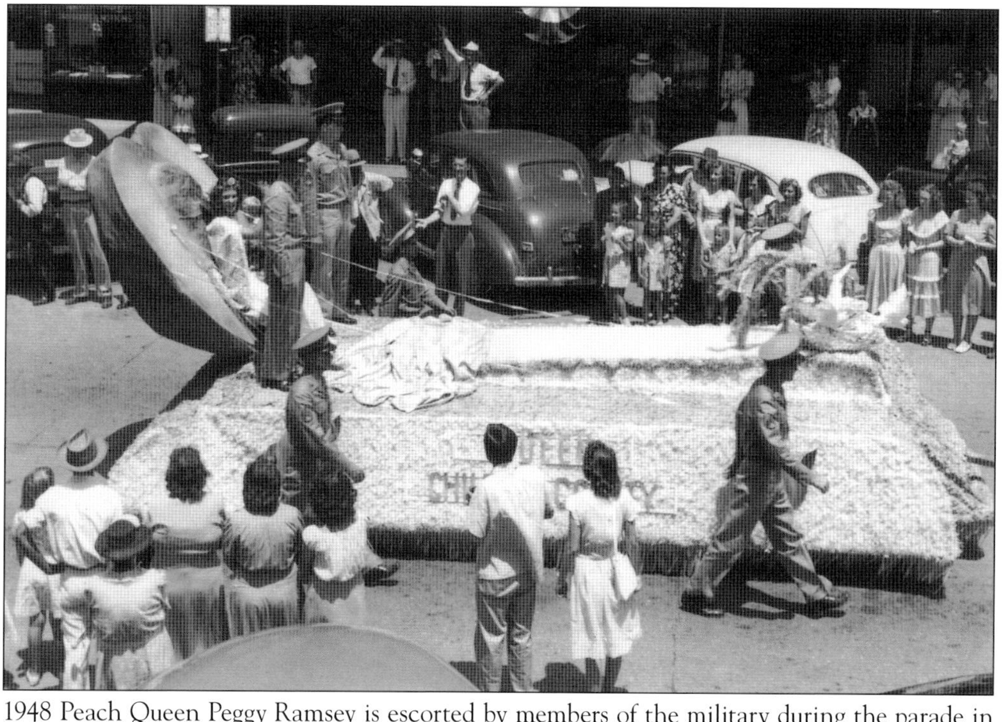

1948 Peach Queen Peggy Ramsey is escorted by members of the military during the parade in Clanton. The countywide celebration is held on an annual basis and has become the region's most eagerly anticipated community event. Originally, the festival was hosted by Thorsby and Clanton. In 1952, the festival was moved to Clanton and contests for Little Miss Peach and Junior Miss Peach were added.

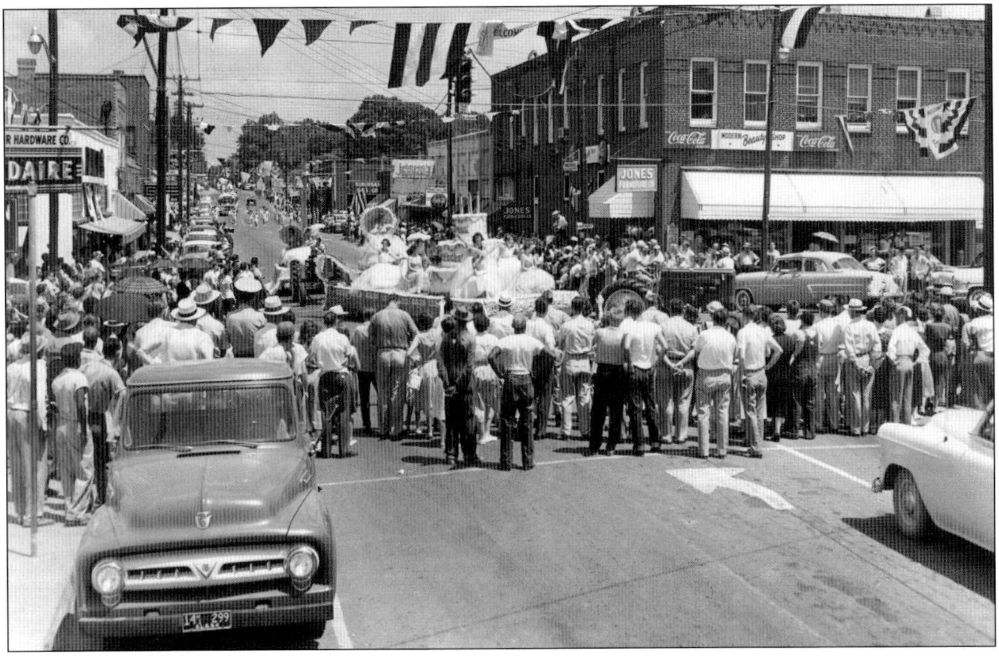

The 1954 Peach Festival parade is pictured on Seventh Street in downtown Clanton. The 1954 celebration was slated to conclude with a concert by the Blackwood Brothers Gospel Quartet at the airport. Shortly before the concert was scheduled to begin, quartet members R.W. Blackwood and Bill Lyles were fatally injured in an aircraft accident at the airport. Johnny Ogburn of Clanton, a last-minute passenger on the aircraft, also perished in the crash.

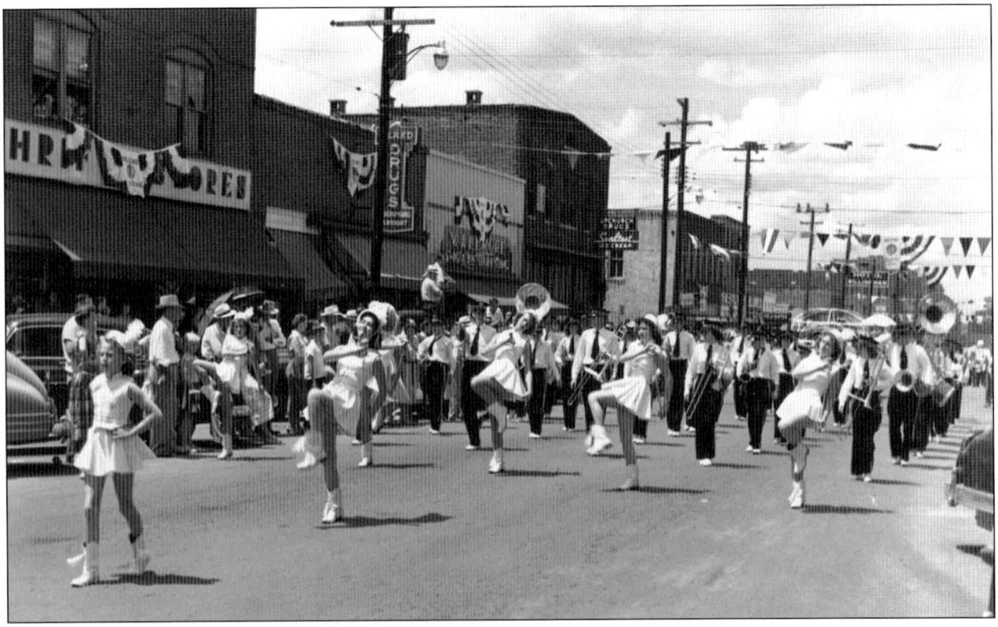

Majorettes lead the 1954 Peach Festival parade on Second Avenue North in Clanton. After the parade, parents could treat their children to Sealtest ice cream at the Upchurch Drug Company or spend a few minutes shopping for dry goods at the V. J. Elmore store. In 2008, the Hotel Willingham, visible in the background, was placed on the Alabama Register of Landmarks and Heritage.

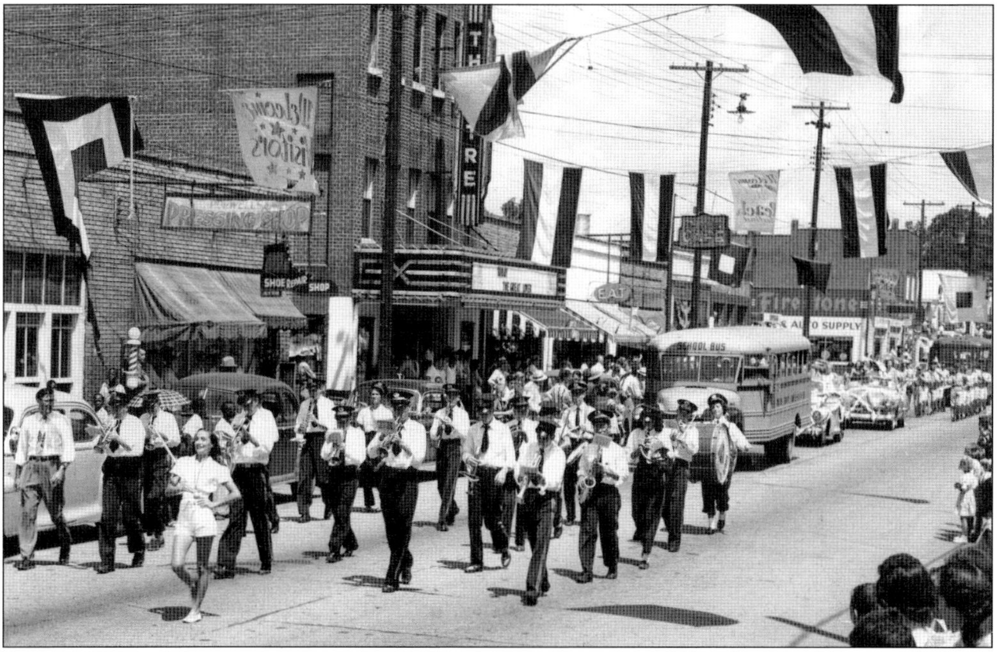

The 1949 Peach Festival parade passes the Wadesonian Theater on Seventh Street in Clanton. Opened in May 1936, the facility could seat 576 people. The marquee advertises the movie *The Great Lover*, starring Bob Hope, Rhonda Fleming, George Reeves, and Jim Backus. Next door, the owners of the Dixie Café boasted, "Your appetite demands the best, your stomach deserves it and the Dixie Café serves it."

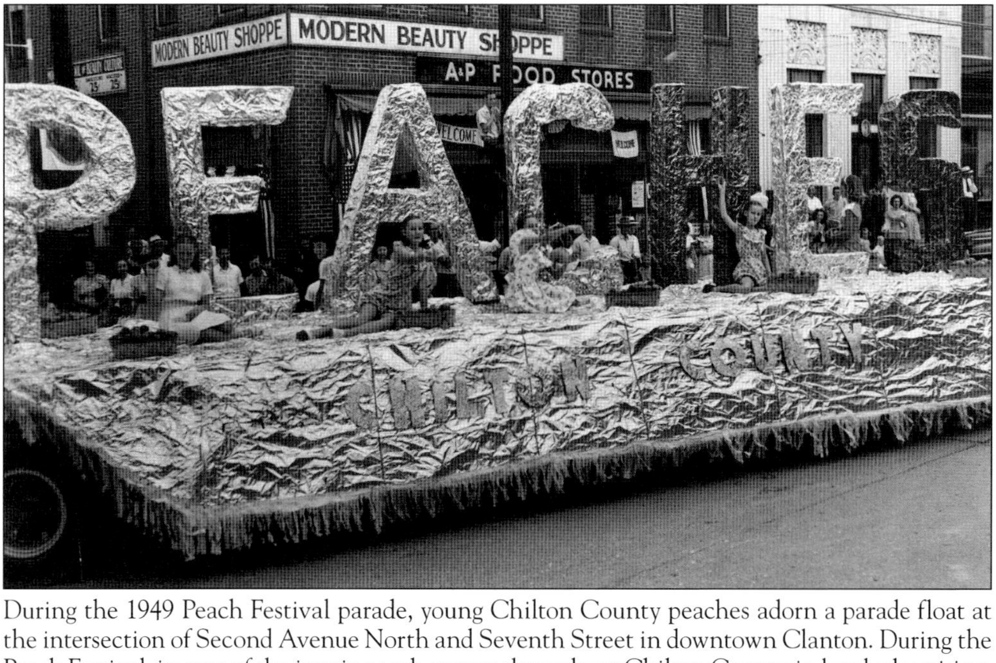

During the 1949 Peach Festival parade, young Chilton County peaches adorn a parade float at the intersection of Second Avenue North and Seventh Street in downtown Clanton. During the Peach Festival, images of the iconic peach appear throughout Chilton County in local advertising, window displays of merchants, and advertisements in local media. In the background, the Modern School of Beauty and Culture advertises manicures for 25¢.

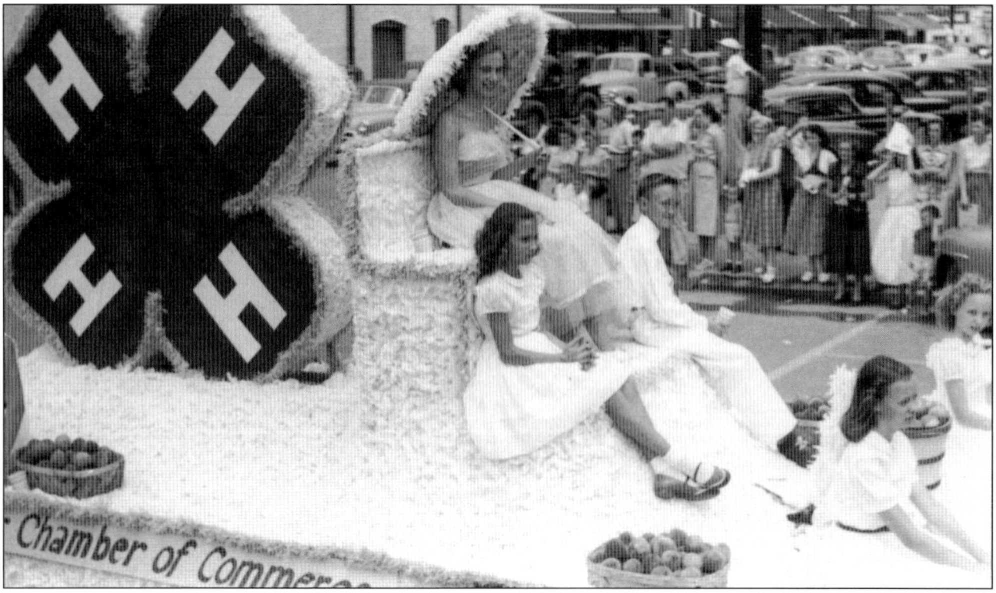

A 1954 Peach Queen contestant and her attendants greet the crowd from a float decorated by the 4-H clubs of Chilton County and sponsored by the Chilton County Chamber of Commerce. Organized in March 1951, the mission of the Chilton County Chamber of Commerce is to advance economic growth and prosperity, to promote a healthy business climate and to enhance the quality of life for all citizens.

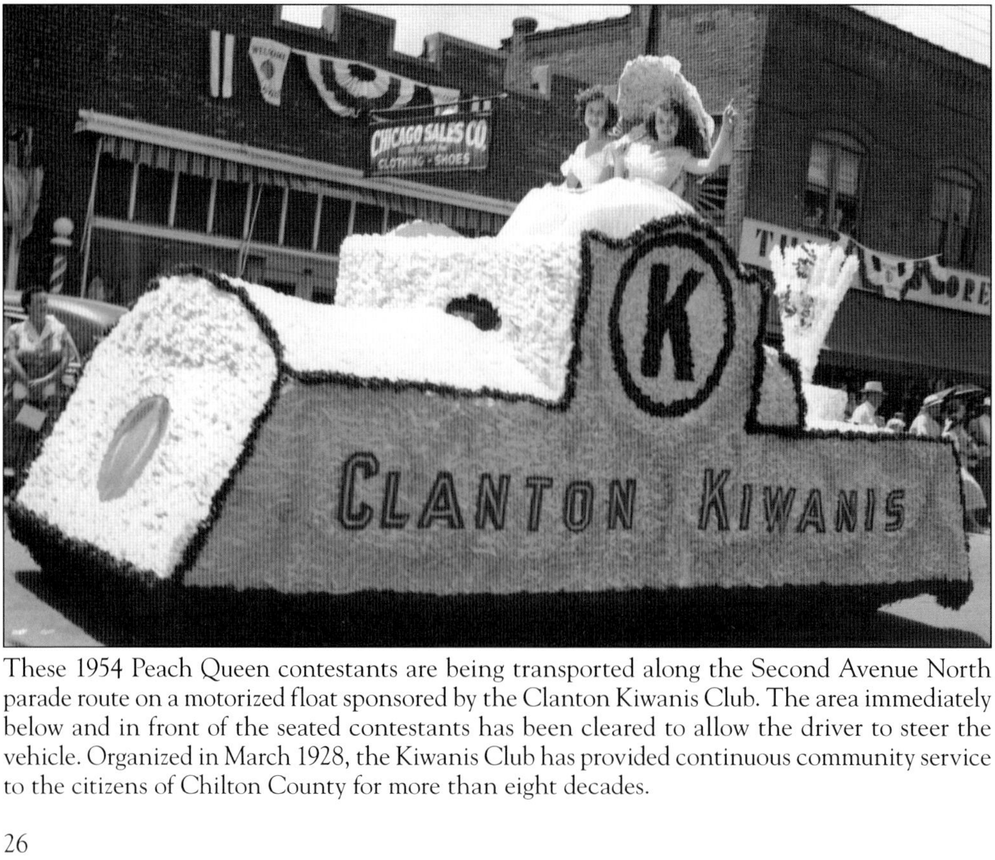

These 1954 Peach Queen contestants are being transported along the Second Avenue North parade route on a motorized float sponsored by the Clanton Kiwanis Club. The area immediately below and in front of the seated contestants has been cleared to allow the driver to steer the vehicle. Organized in March 1928, the Kiwanis Club has provided continuous community service to the citizens of Chilton County for more than eight decades.

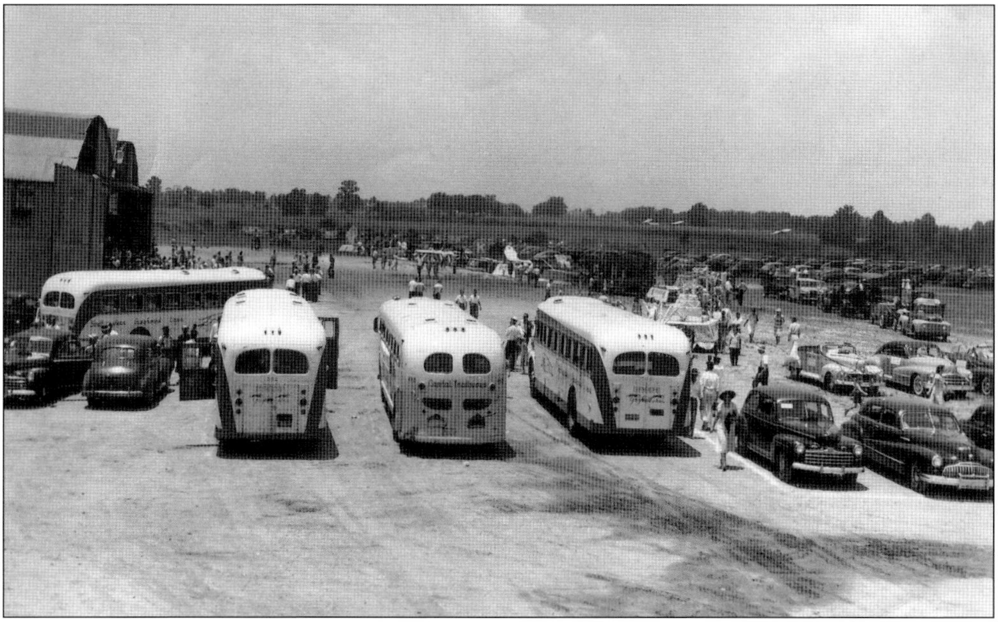

For many years, the Chilton County Airport served as the location of numerous Peach Festival activities, including concerts, dances, and auctions. In 1948, the festival parade originated in Thorsby and terminated at the airport. The hangar shown in this image is in the final stages of completion after being transported from the Tuskegee Army Air Field to the Chilton County Airport.

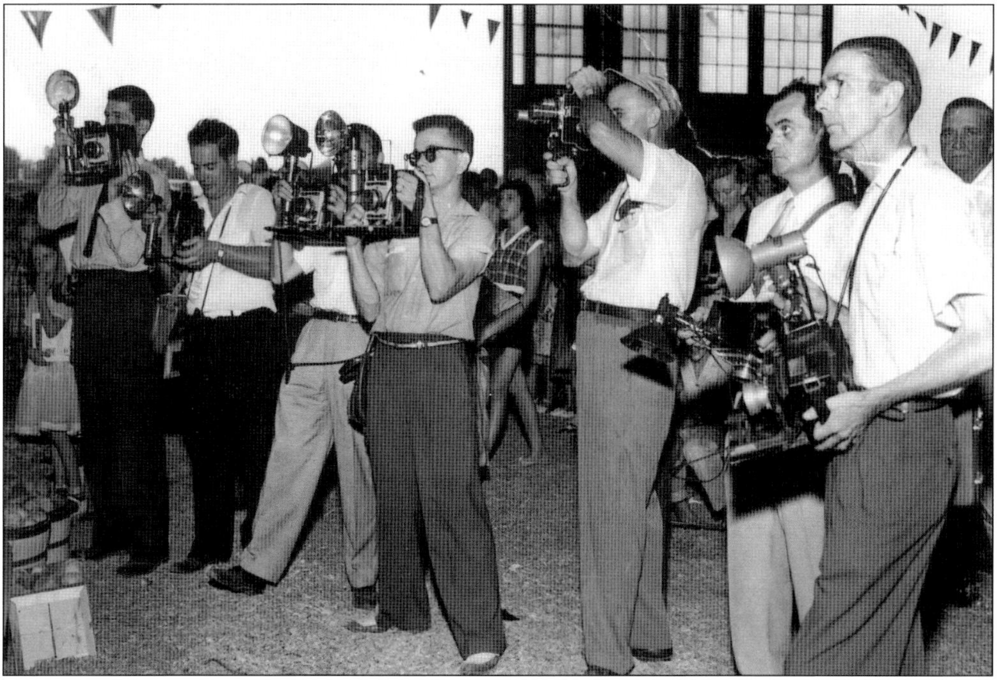

Photographers from media outlets throughout the state record festival activities in the large hangar at the Chilton County Airport. Relocated to Chilton County at a cost of $10,000, the surplus military hangar was obtained in 1948 through the War Assets Administration. For the festival, the dirt floor has been covered with wood chips to minimize dust.

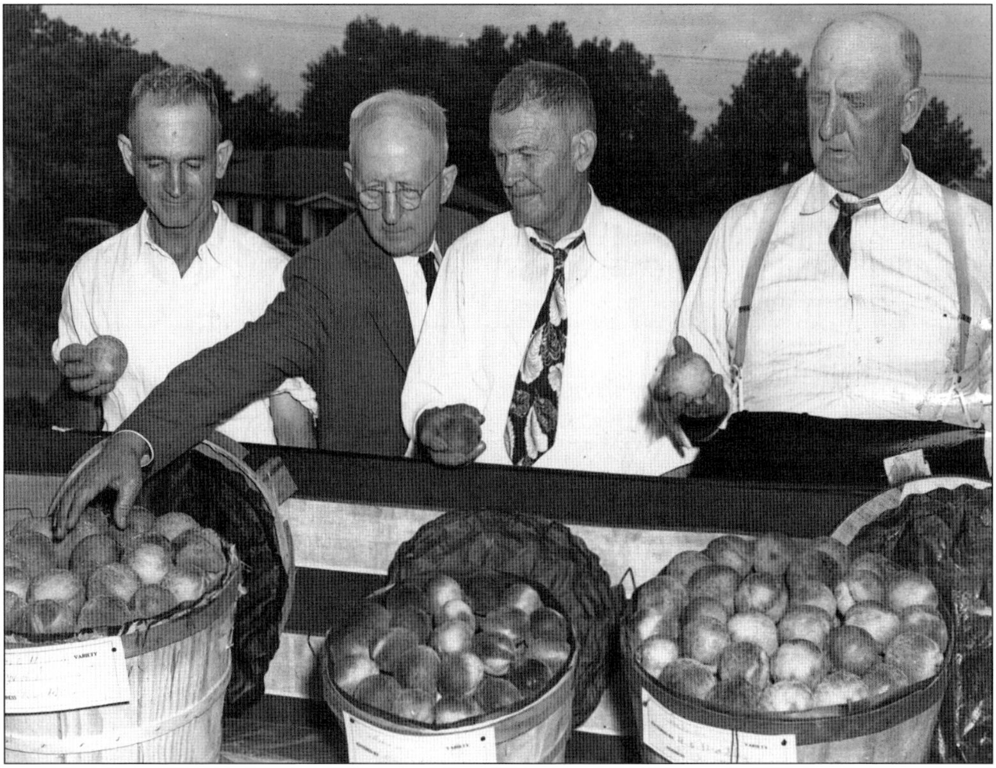

Shown from left to right, W.H. Lenoir, Sen. W.A. Gulledge, A.B. Jones, and A.D. Headley view the prize peaches of the 1947 festival. For first place, Lenoir was awarded a cash prize of $25. The peaches of A.B. Jones of the Alpine community placed second, while those of Houston Headley (A.D.'s son) of Clanton placed third. A.B. Jones was the father of festival queen "Chick" Jones. (ADAH.)

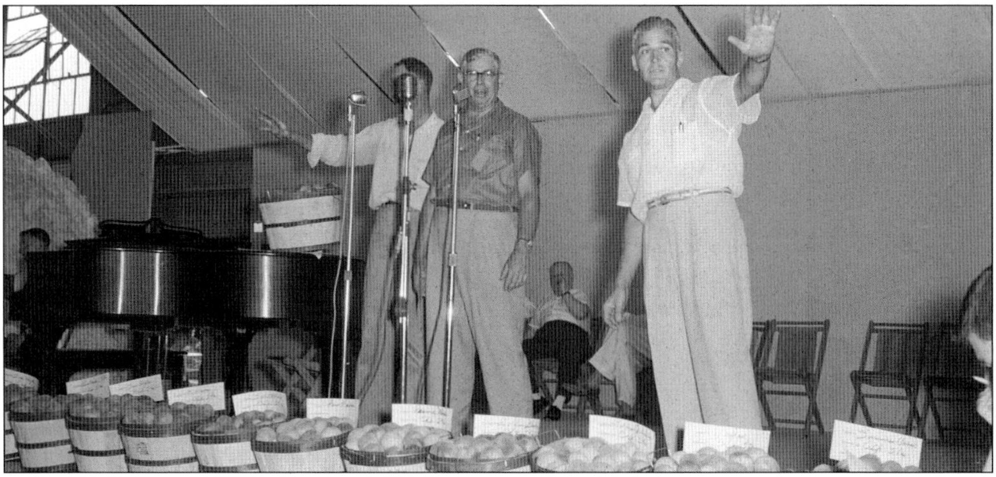

The peach auction of 1947 was the first to be held in Alabama. Sponsored by the Clanton Lions Club, the peach auction has become an extremely popular event to raise funds for community service efforts. In 2016, twenty-six baskets of peaches produced on 14 farms were sold. The proceeds of the auction, more than $27,000, were utilized for service projects in and beyond Chilton County.

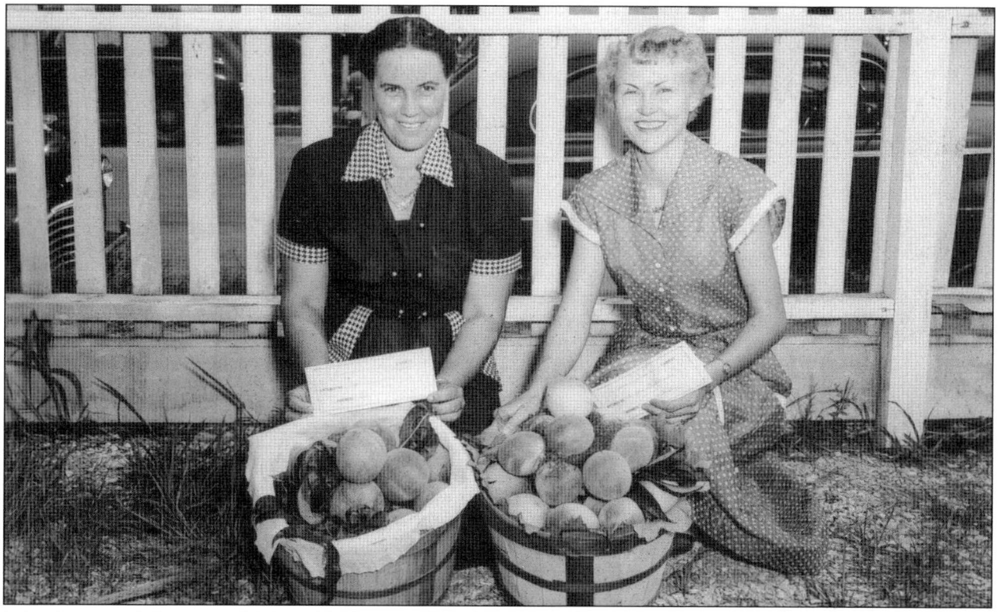

Mrs. Lonnie Minor and Mrs. Clyde Headley display baskets of prizewinning peaches. Producing the best peaches in Chilton County affords peach growers bragging rights for the year. At the first peach auction in 1947, the award-winning Hale Haven peaches sold for $250. In 2016, the basket of blue-ribbon peaches sold for $4,600.

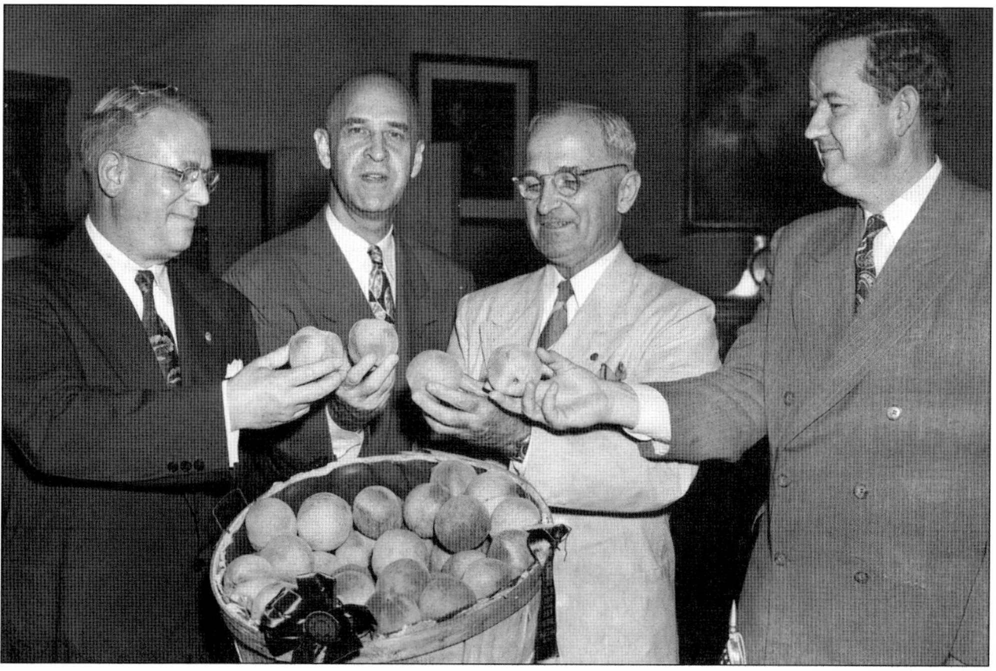

The prizewinning Hale Haven peaches of the 1947 Peach Festival were escorted to Birmingham by the festival queen and king. Flown to Washington, DC, on Eastern Airlines under the personal supervision of company president Eddie Rickenbacker, the peaches were presented to Pres. Harry Truman in a ceremony at the White House. Attending the presentation are, from left to right, Rep. Pete Jarman, Sen. Lister Hill, Truman, and Sen. John Sparkman. (ADAH.)

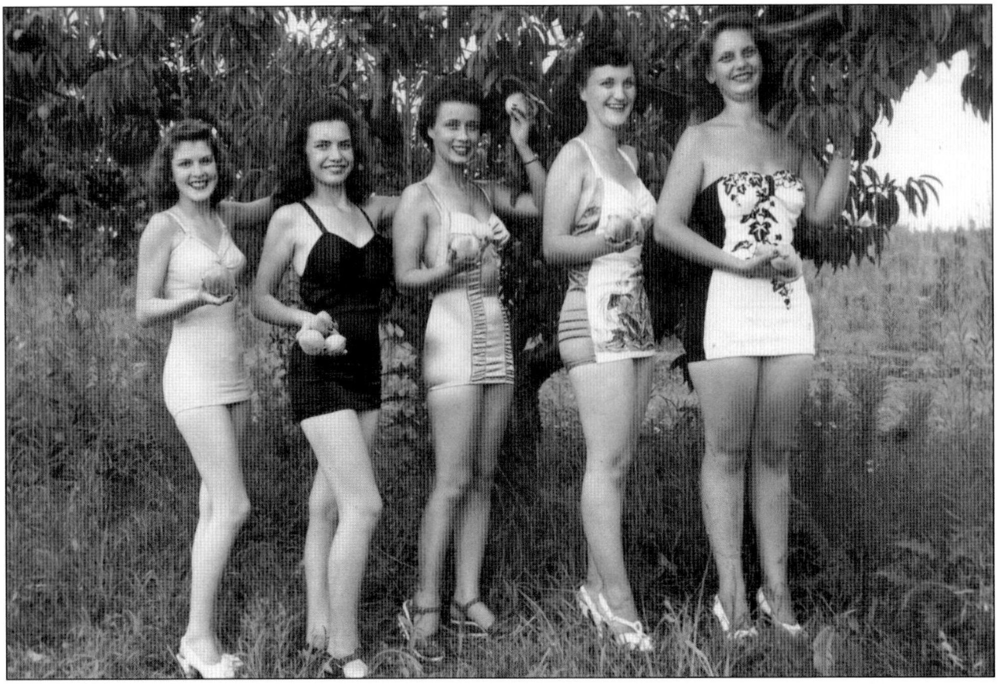

For more than 70 years, the Peach Queen pageant has been one of the most anticipated community events in Chilton County. In preparation for the pageant, contestants participate in a series of events that include interviews, talent development, and presentations. Contestants also pose for publicity photographs to be distributed in local and state publications. Young women participating in the pageant are photographed at various locations throughout the county, primarily in or near the peach orchards. Because the swimsuit competition represented an important and popular aspect of the competition, appropriate images of the contestants were included in pageant promotion material. In 2015, the swimsuit competition was eliminated from the Peach Queen pageant and replaced with a casual wear category of competition. (Above, ADAH; below, Chilton County Extension Service.)

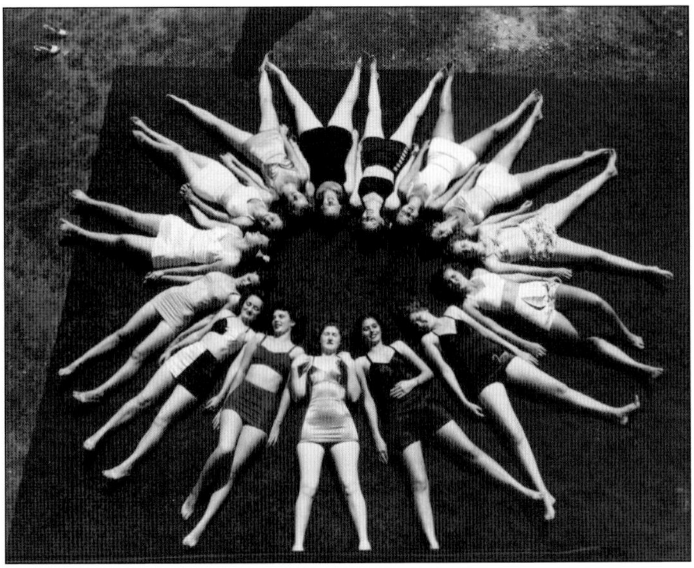

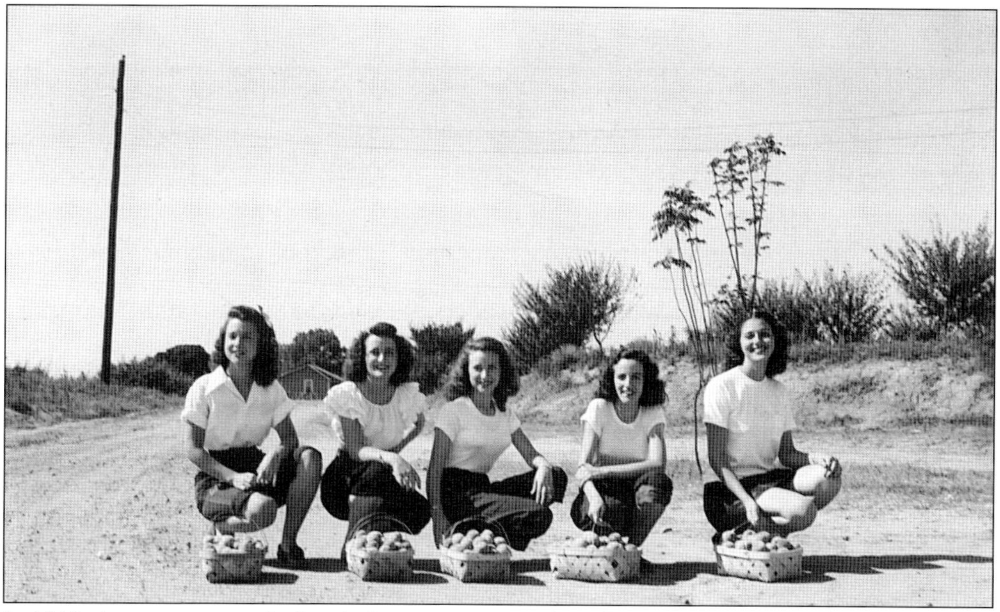

In 1948, the competition for Peach Queen was opened to all unmarried young women, as the rule restricting the competition to daughters of peach growers was eliminated. Sixteen contestants competed for the honor of representing Chilton County, including, from left to right, Barbara Burnette, Eva Jo Bean, Sarah Nell Williams, Imogene Williams, and Betty Jean Gore, shown at the Cox Fruit Stand on Highway 31 in Thorsby.

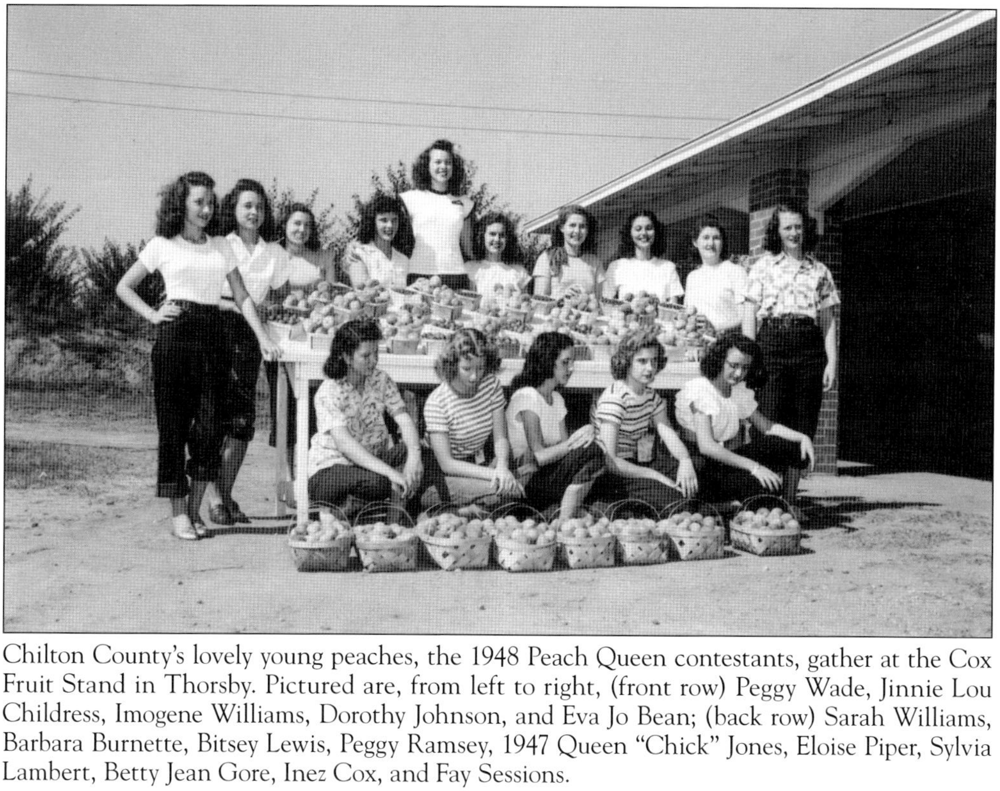

Chilton County's lovely young peaches, the 1948 Peach Queen contestants, gather at the Cox Fruit Stand in Thorsby. Pictured are, from left to right, (front row) Peggy Wade, Jinnie Lou Childress, Imogene Williams, Dorothy Johnson, and Eva Jo Bean; (back row) Sarah Williams, Barbara Burnette, Bitsey Lewis, Peggy Ramsey, 1947 Queen "Chick" Jones, Eloise Piper, Sylvia Lambert, Betty Jean Gore, Inez Cox, and Fay Sessions.

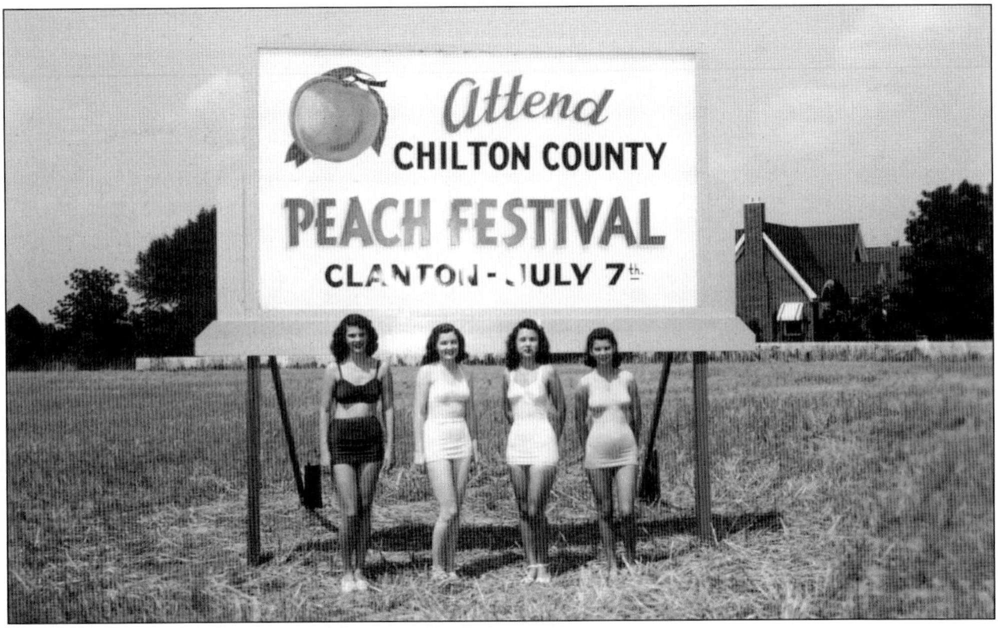

Above, from left to right, 1948 Peach Queen contestants Peggy Ramsey, Bitsy Lewis, Barbara Burnett, and Peggy Wade prepare for the swimsuit competition as they pose in front of one of the large signs advertising the festival on the highways leading into Chilton County. A graduate of Chilton County High School, Ramsey was selected queen of the festival. A graduate of Linden High School, Lewis worked as a stenographer in Clanton. Seventeen-year-old Burnett was sponsored by the Clanton Veterans of Foreign Wars and enjoyed playing the piano and swimming. Wade attended Chilton County High School and was sponsored by the Clanton Pilot Club. Below, from left to right, contestants Lewis, Burnett, Ramsey, and Wade pose in their casual wear.

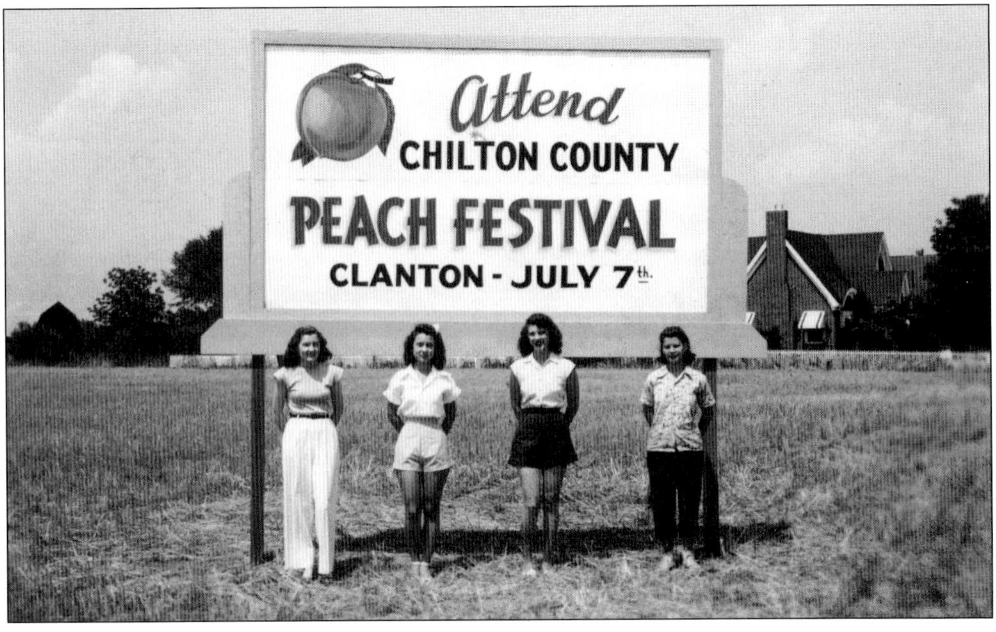

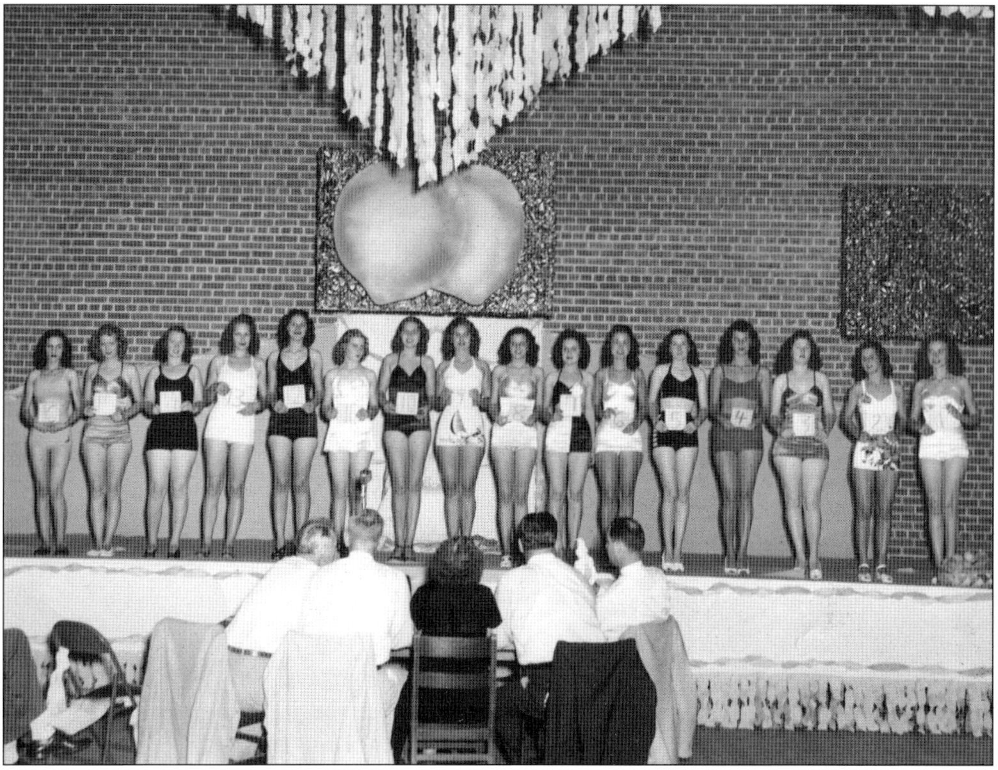

The Parade of Peaches is seen at the Chilton County High School gymnasium during the 1948 Peach Festival competition. Judges for the competition included Birmingham mayor Cooper Green, Clara Burleson of the *Birmingham News*, T.W. Lumpkin of Auburn, Col. T.M. Farris of Atmore, and Jesse Oldacre of Cullman. The previous evening, contestants were presented to the public at the Wadesonian Theater in Clanton.

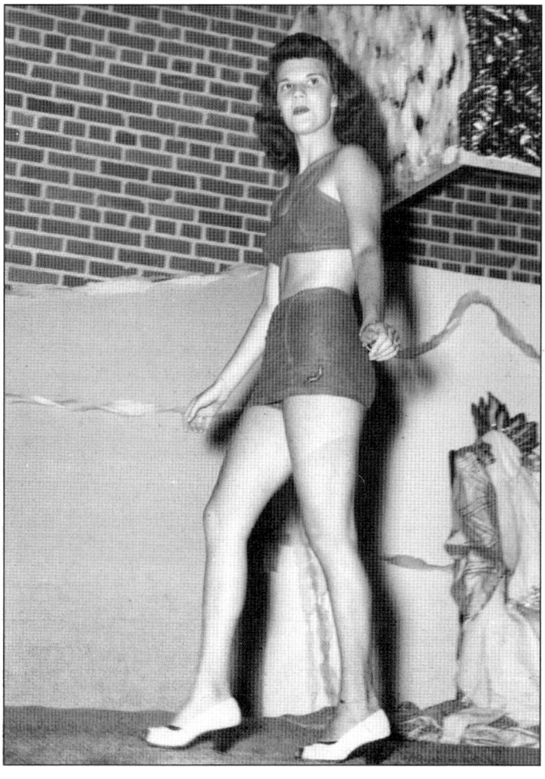

1948 Peach Queen contestant Peggy Ramsey passes in review during the Parade of Peaches held at the Chilton County High School auditorium. A graduate of Chilton County High School, 18-year-old Peggy was sponsored by the Clanton Kiwanis Club. The daughter of Cecil and Pauline Ramsey, Peggy was a majorette in the high school band and enjoyed swimming as her favorite hobby.

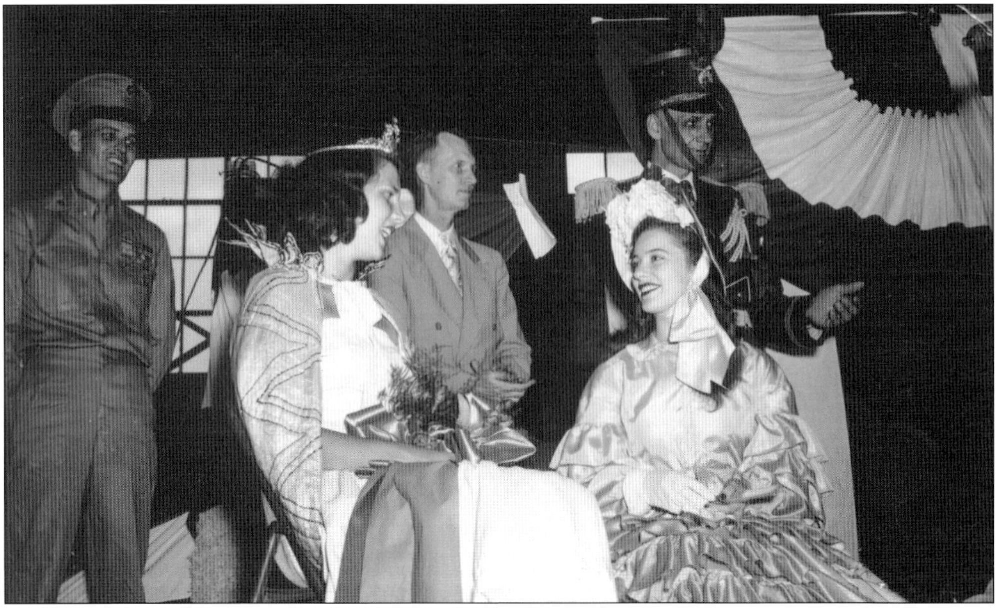

Held only three years after the end the Second World War, the 1948 Peach Festival was supported by personnel of the armed forces of the United States. The Clanton National Guard provided the color guard, while a US Air Force band from Maxwell Field led the parade. In this image, a US marine adorned with an infantry badge and multiple overseas campaign ribbons participates in the festivities.

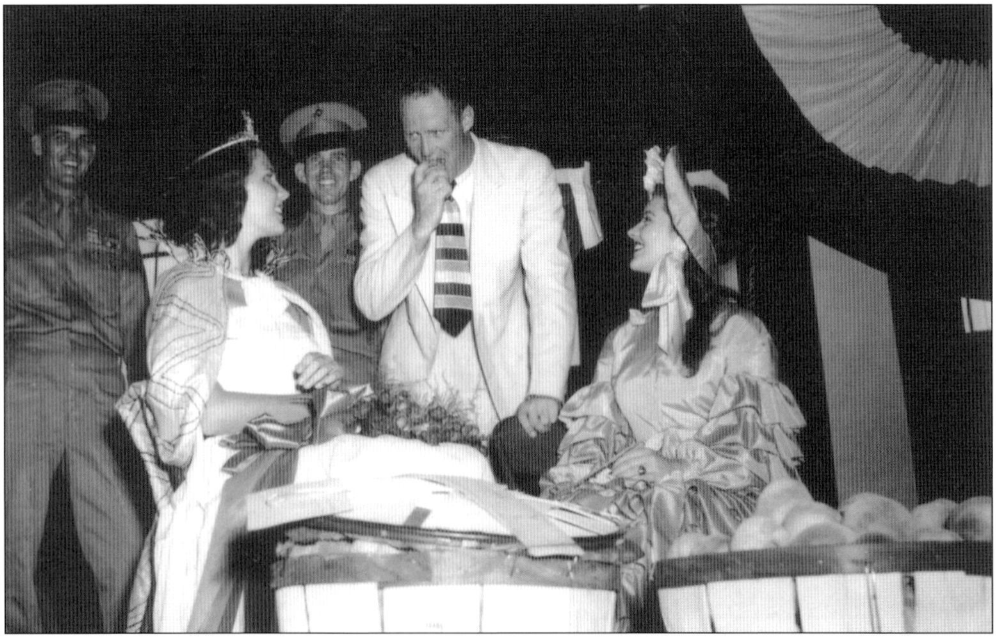

M.R. "Red" Glasscock, chairman of the 1948 Peach Festival, samples one of Chilton County's prizewinning peaches, presented to him by Chilton County's prize peach, festival queen Peggy Ramsey. Immediately following the parade, the coronation of the queen was held in the hangar of the Chilton County Airport. Later in the evening, a street dance featuring Buck Littleton and his Rainbow Serenaders was held in downtown Clanton.

Hugh Webb (seated), manager of Clanton radio station WKLF, served as master of ceremonies for the 1948 Peach Queen competition in which 16 young women competed for the title. Peach Queen Peggy Ramsey (seated) is accompanied by (standing, left to right) Eloise Piper and Sarah Williams, contestants representing Thorsby Institute. Since the festival was financially self-supporting, members of the public were charged a 50¢ admission fee.

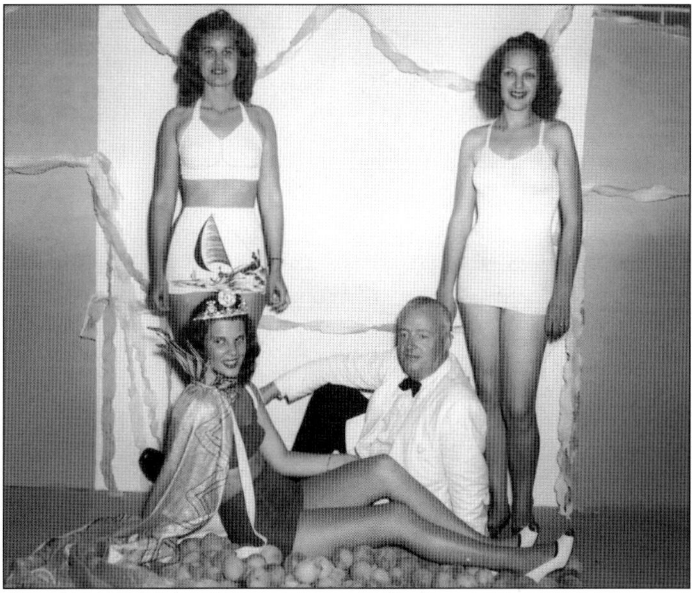

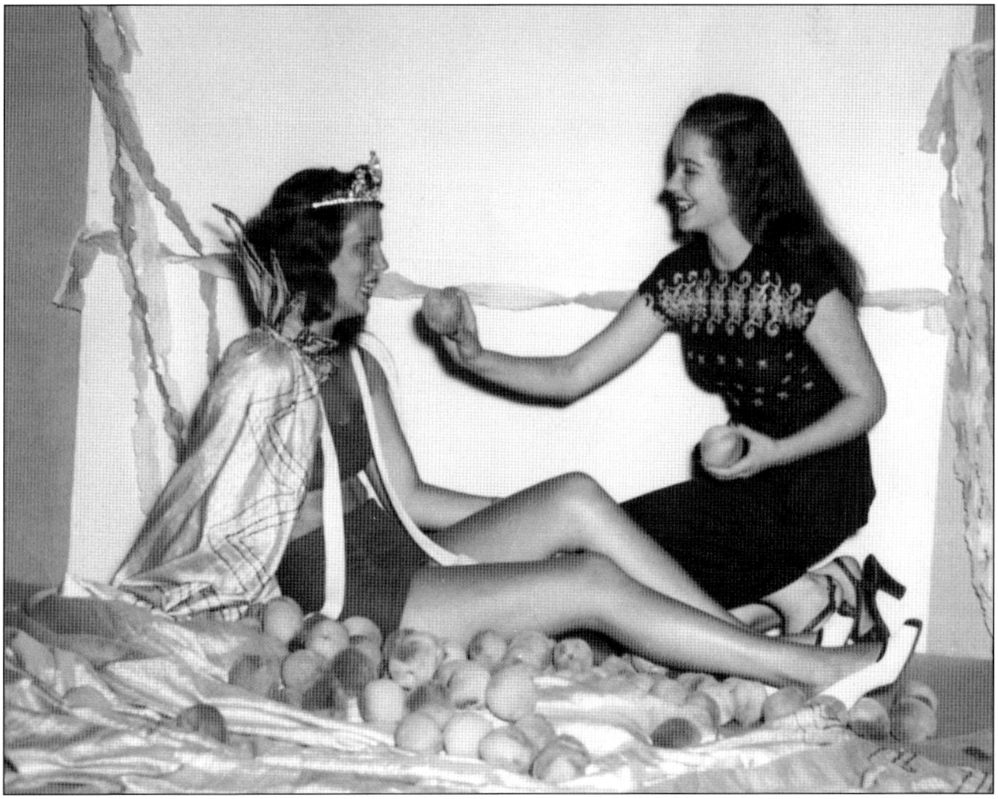

Peggy Ramsey, 1948 Peach Queen, is offered a symbol of the harvest over which she reigns. In recognition of her selection as queen of the Peach Festival, Ramsey earned a trip to Miami, Florida. The 1948 festival was advertised as one of the biggest events ever witnessed in the county. Civic organizations, merchants, and peach growers contributed their time, talent, and resources to make the event a success.

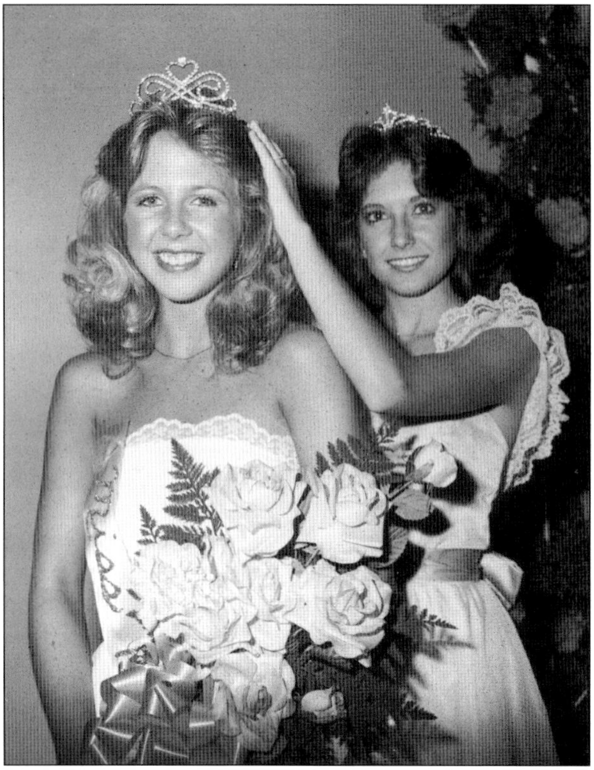

Seventeen-year-old Wendy Jill Forrest (Bryan) is crowned the 1982 Chilton County Peach Queen by the reigning 1981 queen, Nancy Carmichael. Through the years, Chilton County Peach Queens have devoted their efforts and, in many cases, their lives to the betterment of their community. After completing college, Wendy Bryan returned to Thorsby and influenced the lives of thousands of young students during more than 20 years as a teacher.

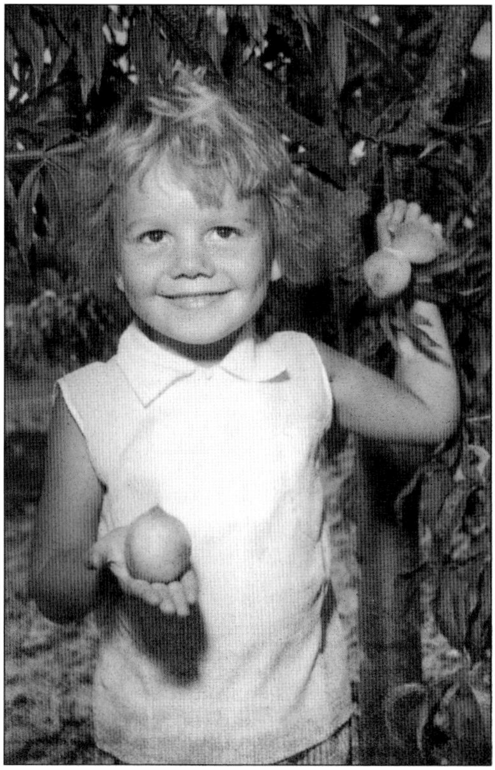

In Chilton County, the dream of becoming a Peach Queen begins at an early age. In recent years, the pageant has been expanded to include the titles of Junior Miss Peach, Young Miss Peach, and Little Miss Peach. Unlike early Peach Queens who reigned for only one day, Peach Queens now represent Chilton County at community events throughout the year.

Two

Reconstruction County

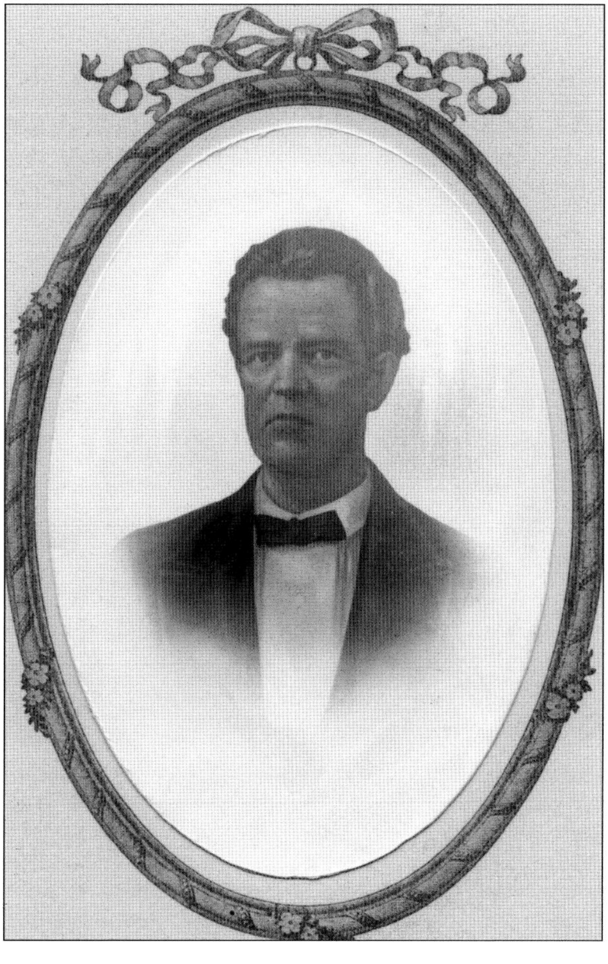

A native of Kentucky, William Parish Chilton (1810–1871) moved to Talladega, Alabama, in 1834 to establish a law practice. Appointed an associate justice on the Alabama Supreme Court in 1848, Chilton became chief justice in 1852. An early opponent of secession, Chilton later served as a member of the provisional and permanent congresses of the Confederate States of America. In 1874, Baker County was renamed in his honor. (ADAH.)

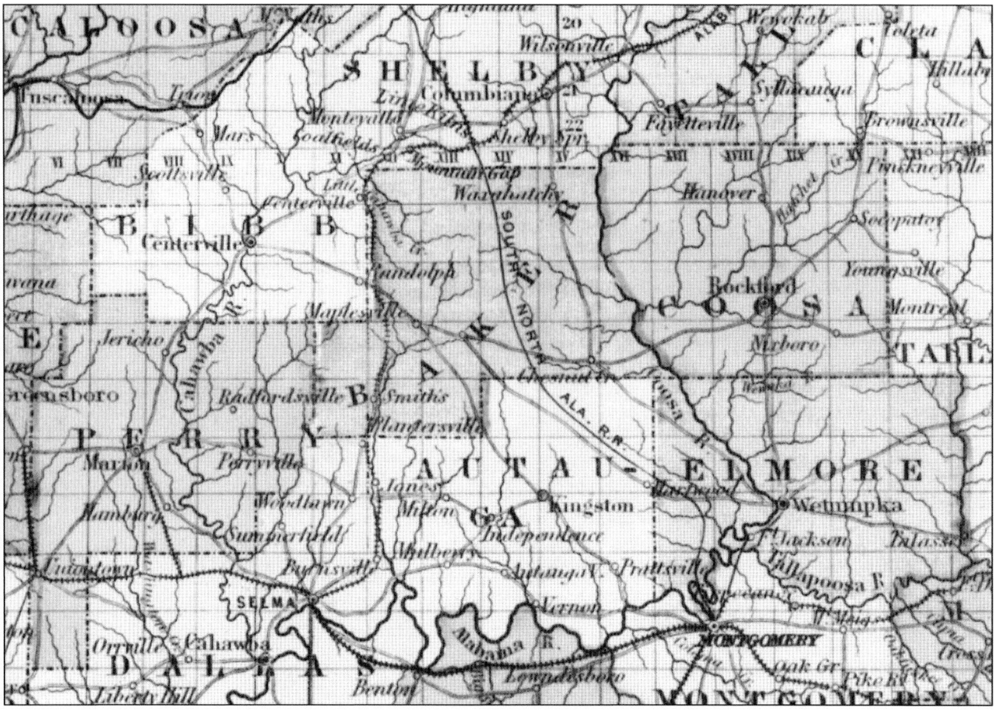

On December 30, 1868, the new county of Baker was established by the Alabama Legislature. Named for prominent resident Alfred Baker, Alabama's 65th county was created from land obtained from Bibb, Autauga, Perry, and Shelby Counties. In December 1874, the name was changed to honor Alabama Supreme Court justice William Parish Chilton (W.S. Hoole Special Collections Library.)

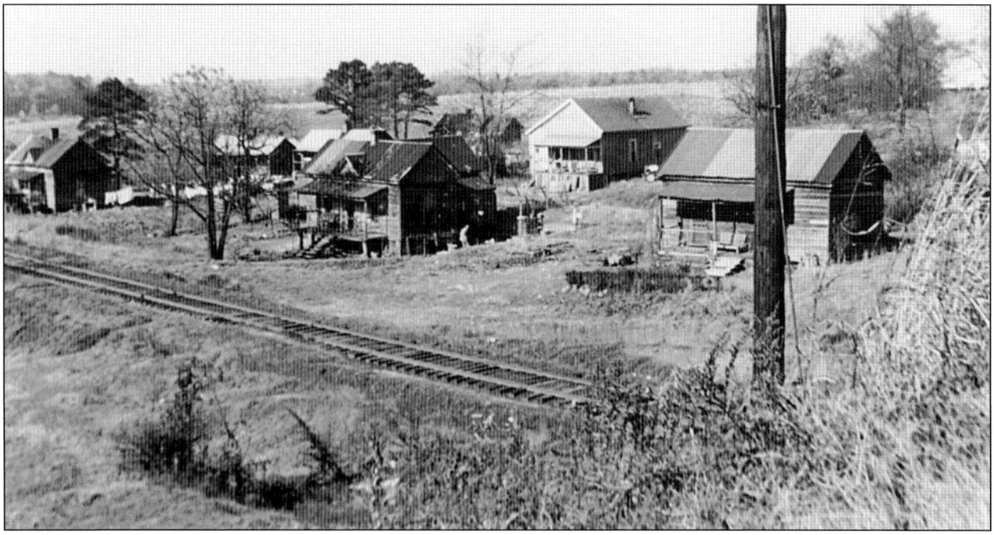

Construction of railroad systems in Chilton County established the framework for the county's development by creating new markets for agricultural and timber products and increased accessibility to the region. Rail systems fostered the development of Verbena, Clanton, Lomax, Thorsby, Jemison, and Maplesville. More than 15 timber companies in Chilton County also utilized rail systems to transport harvested timber to finishing mills. (ADAH.)

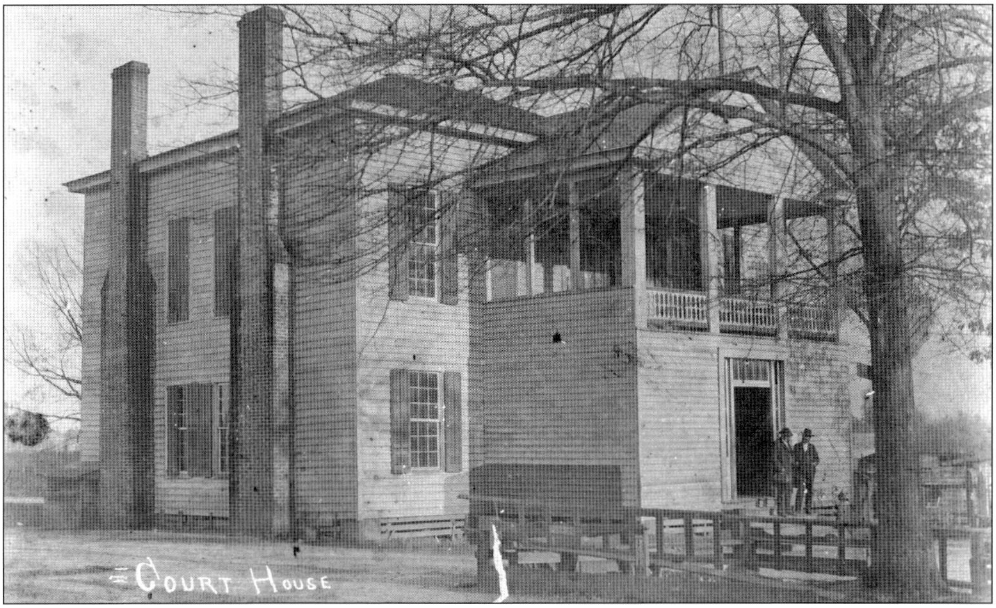

In 1870, fire destroyed the one-room courthouse at Grantville. The county seat was subsequently moved to Clanton. The first county courthouse to be constructed in Clanton was a two-story wood-frame building located near the intersection of Second Avenue North and Sixth Street. This building was used until 1896, when it was replaced with a modern two-story brick structure. (City of Clanton.)

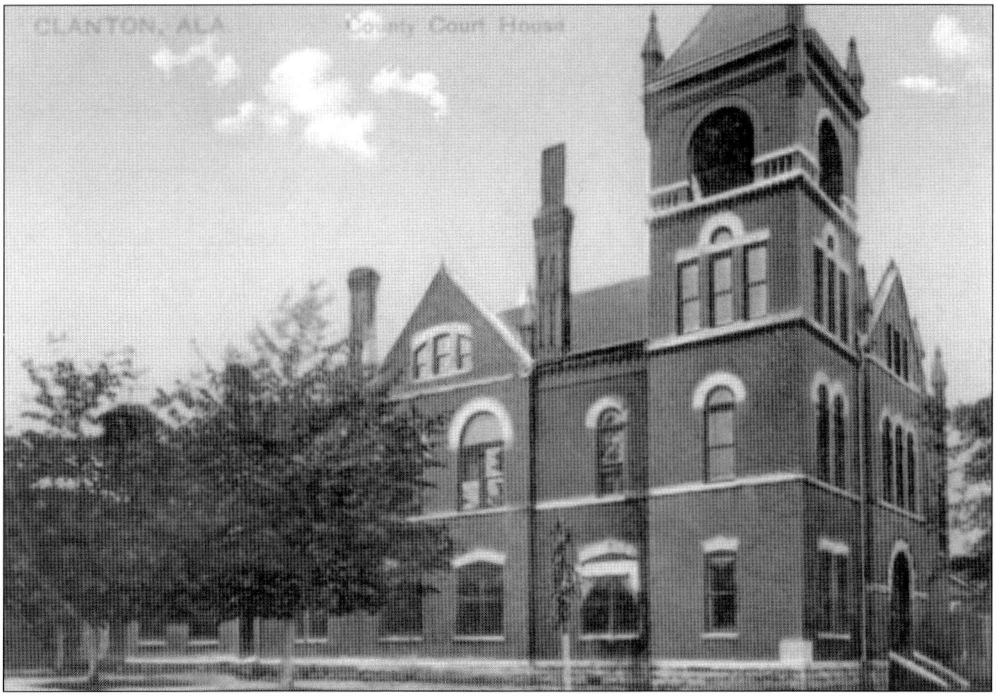

In 1896, construction of the second Chilton County Courthouse was completed. The two-story brick structure was located on the site now utilized as the west parking lot of the current courthouse. The building was extensively damaged on September 5, 1918, in a fire of suspicious origin. Many early education and tax records of Chilton County were lost in the blaze. (Kim Gillespie.)

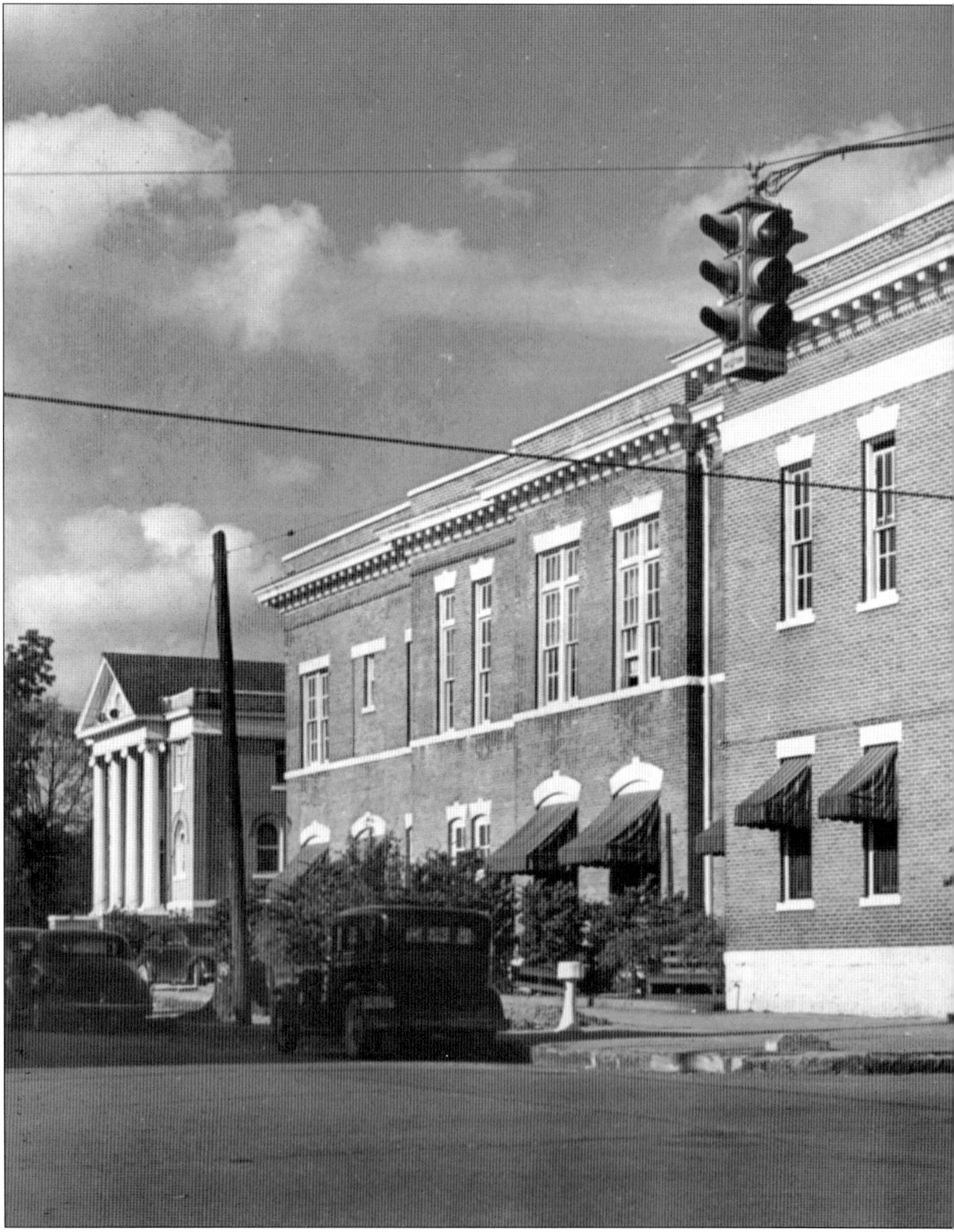

In October 1919, the first session of the commissioner's court was convened in the new Chilton County Courthouse. The new building was located on the corner of Second Avenue North and Sixth Street on the same site as the former courthouse. This building would serve as the seat of Chilton County government and as a gathering place for dignitaries, local officials and residents for more than 40 years. By 1954, the structure of the building had deteriorated significantly. Following

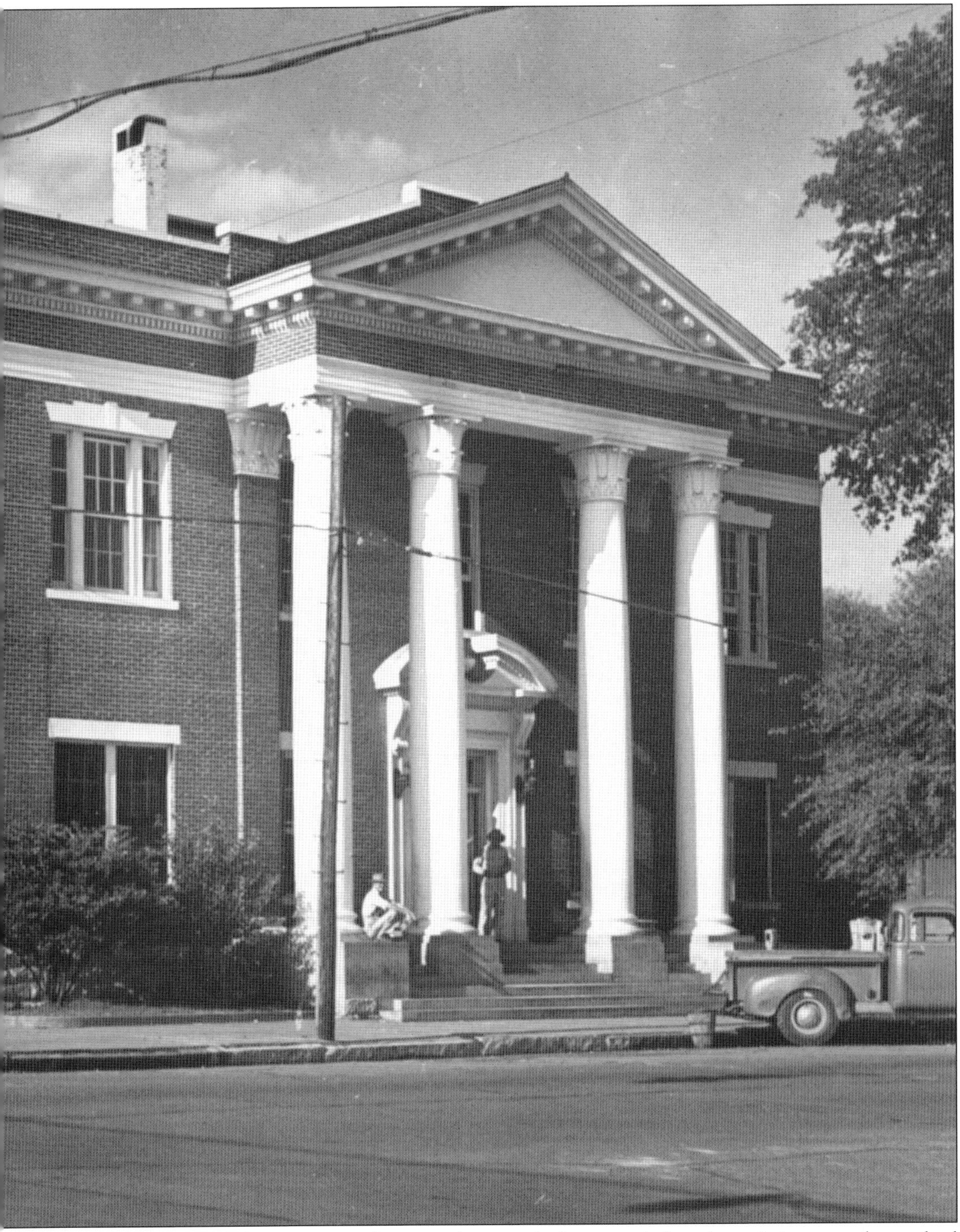

an inspection of the structure, the state fire marshal reported that the existing courthouse had served beyond the economic and efficient life of such a building in a growing and progressive county. Probate judge Maynard D. Tingle then initiated the effort to construct a new courthouse facility. (Author's collection.)

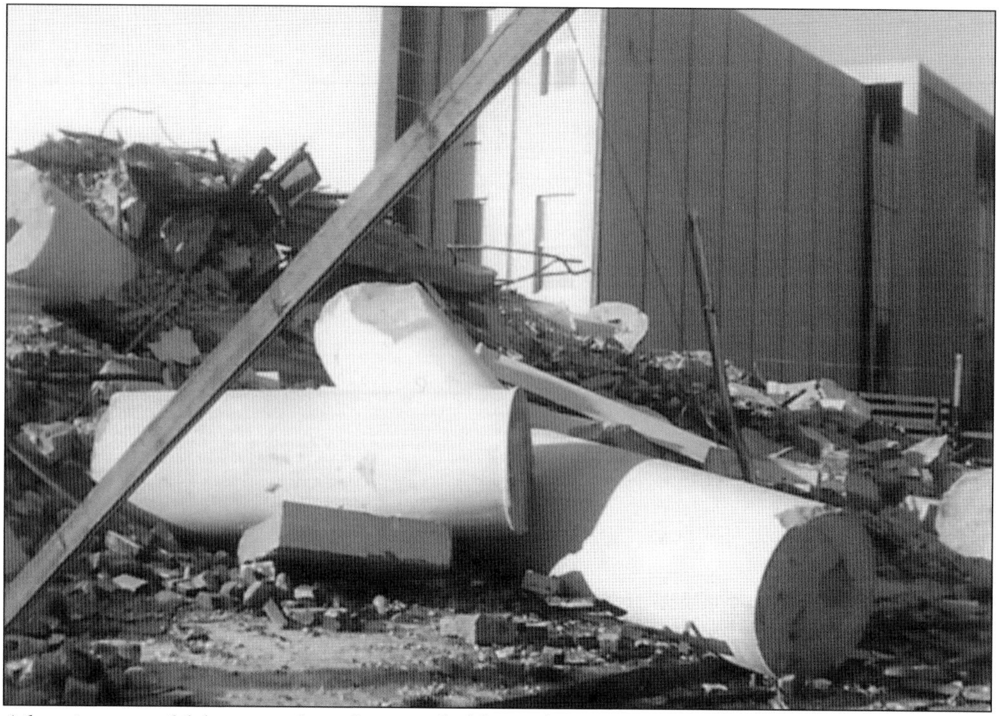

After six years of debate, a referendum was held in February 1960 to allow the citizens of Chilton County to determine the issue of constructing a new courthouse. The ballot also included the question of where to locate the new structure. Voters overwhelmingly approved construction of a new building at the same site. The columns of the former courthouse are visible to the left in this image. (Kim Gillespie.)

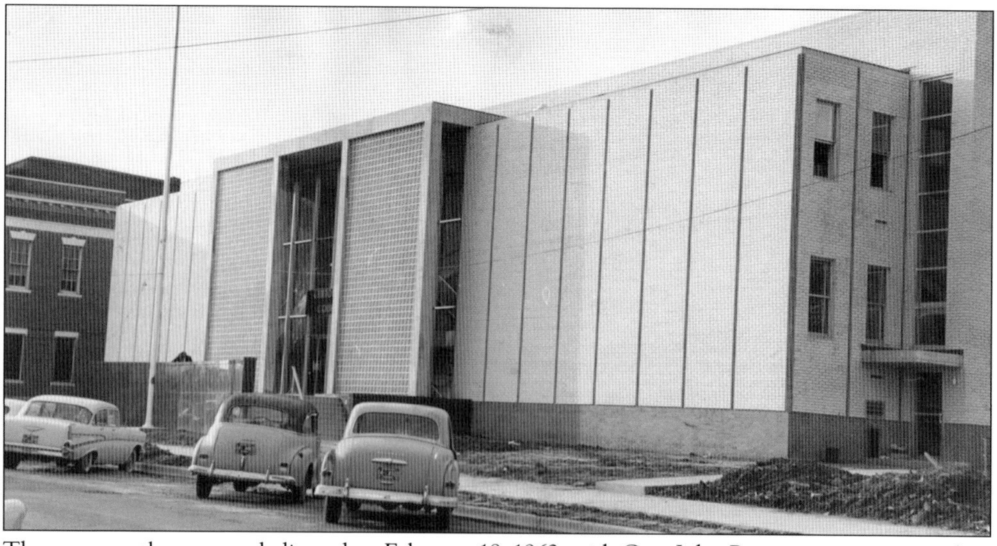

The new courthouse was dedicated on February 18, 1962, with Gov. John Patterson as guest speaker. Prior to construction of the new building, the Chilton County Board of Revenue purchased a parcel of property adjacent to the former courthouse. This provided additional space to allow the new structure to be built slightly east of the former building. A parking lot was constructed on the site of the old courthouse. (ADAH.)

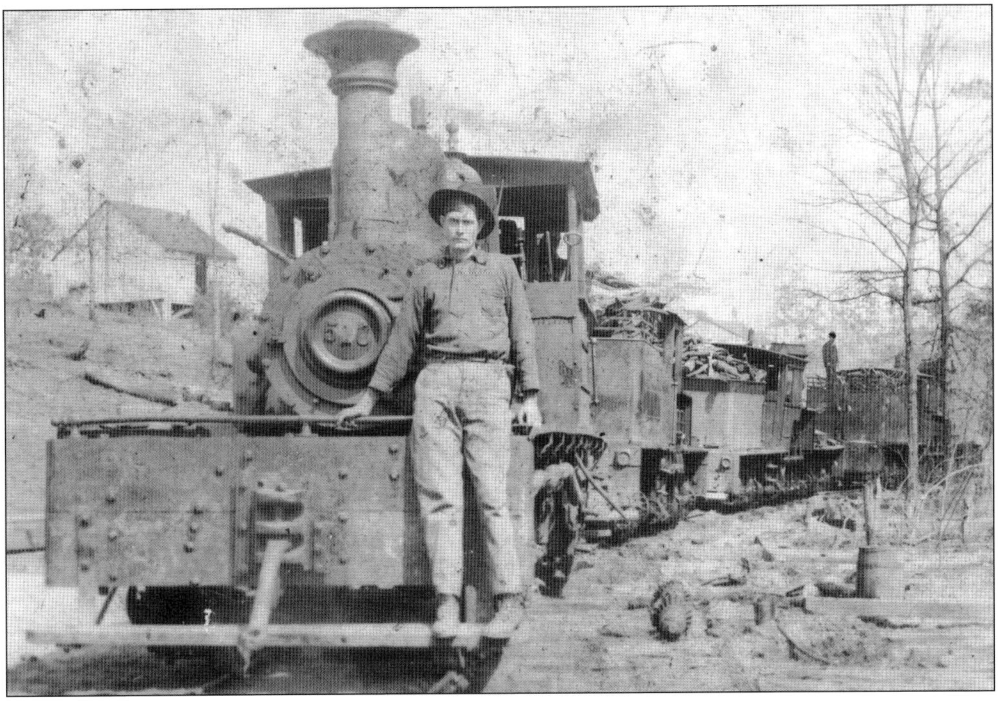

In 1896, the E.E. Jackson Lumber Company began operations in Chilton County. The company operated a sawmill at Riderville, a small settlement north of Plantersville. The Riderville, Centerville & Blocton Railroad utilized eight locomotives and 30 railcars to support logging operations in Chilton, Dallas, and Perry Counties. The company ceased operations in Chilton County in 1915, relocating its operation to Choctaw County. (ADAH.)

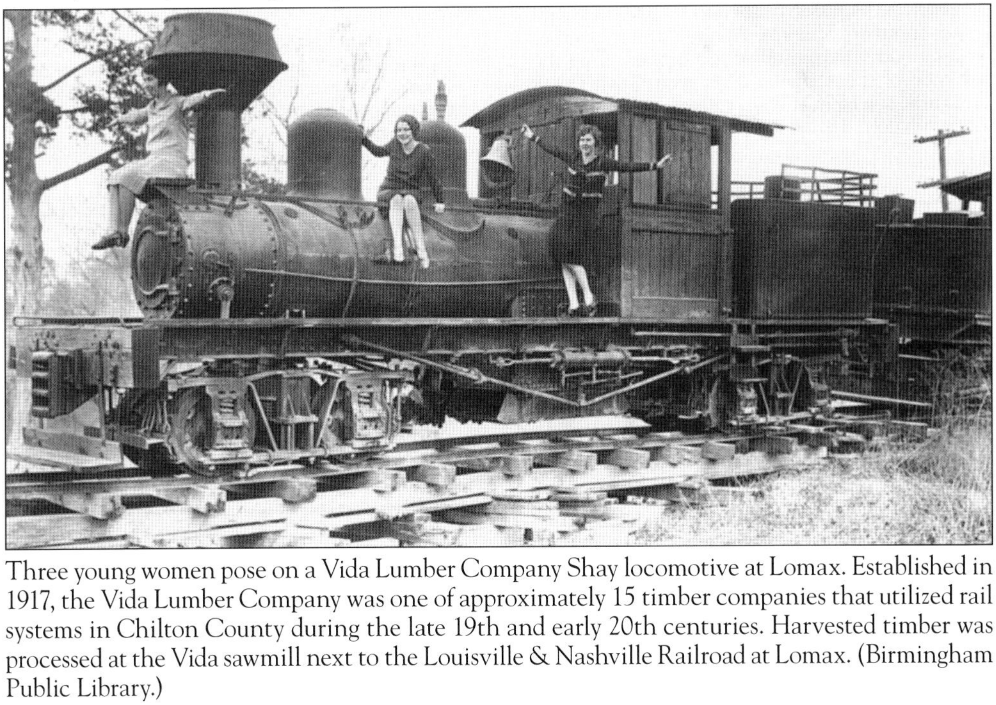

Three young women pose on a Vida Lumber Company Shay locomotive at Lomax. Established in 1917, the Vida Lumber Company was one of approximately 15 timber companies that utilized rail systems in Chilton County during the late 19th and early 20th centuries. Harvested timber was processed at the Vida sawmill next to the Louisville & Nashville Railroad at Lomax. (Birmingham Public Library.)

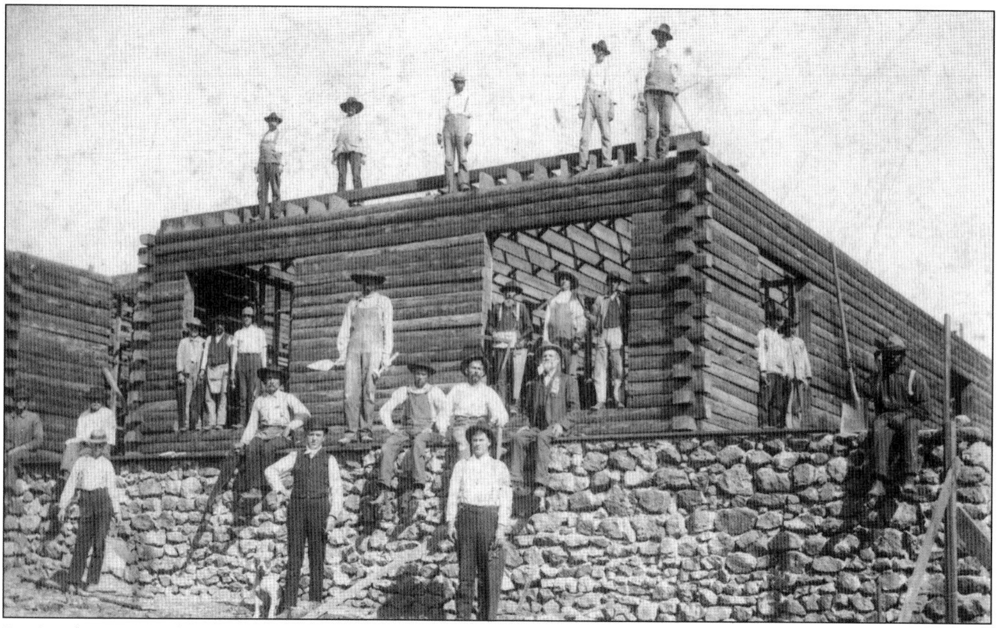

In April 1902, workers began construction of a facility at Mountain Creek in southeast Chilton County to house indigent or disabled Confederate veterans. Mountain Creek was considered an ideal site, because the combination of high elevation, fresh air, and abundant springs created a healthy environment for the veterans. The facility consisted of 22 buildings, including 10 cottages, an administration building, a hospital, a mess hall, and barns. (ADAH and Confederate Memorial Park.)

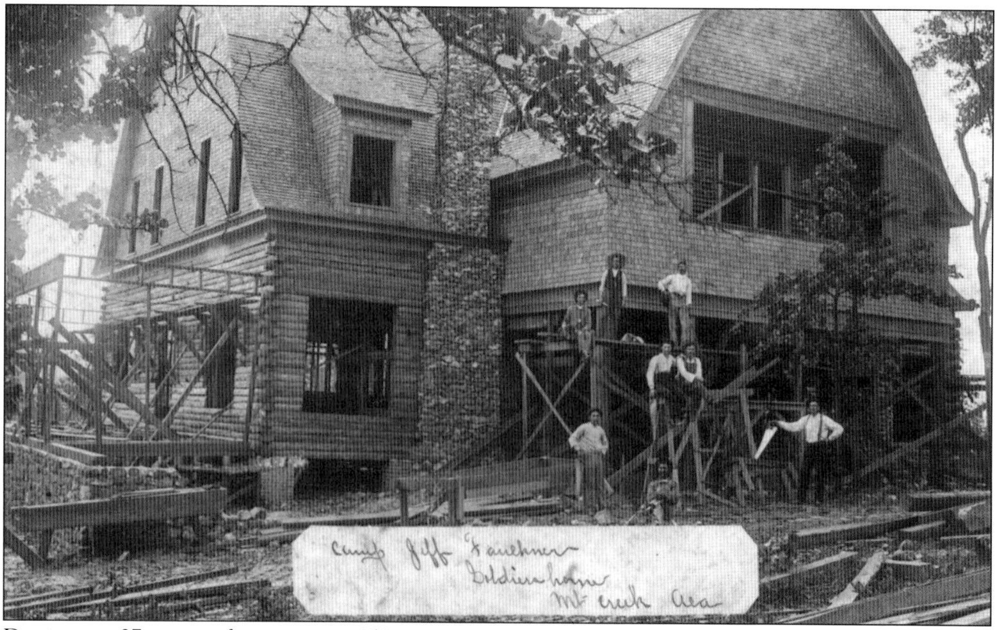

During its 37 years of operation, 650 to 800 veterans, their wives, and widows resided at the home. In June 1934, the last Confederate veteran residing at the home died. In October 1939, the facility was closed and the five remaining widows were transferred to the Alabama Department of Welfare. In 1964, the Alabama Legislature established Confederate Memorial Park to honor Alabama's citizens of the Confederacy. (ADAH and Confederate Memorial Park.)

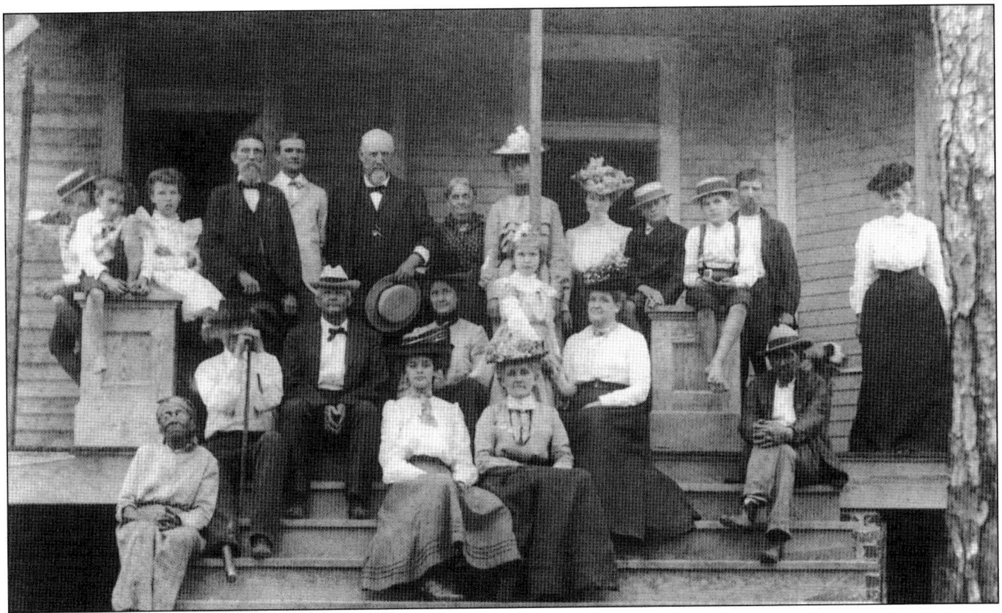

Jefferson Manley Faulkner (holding hat) served in the 8th Confederate Cavalry during the War between the States. A Montgomery attorney, Faulkner donated 102 acres of land near the community of Mountain Creek and organized public fund drives to finance construction of the soldiers' home. In 1903, the State of Alabama assumed ownership and administration of the facility. (ADAH and Confederate Memorial Park.)

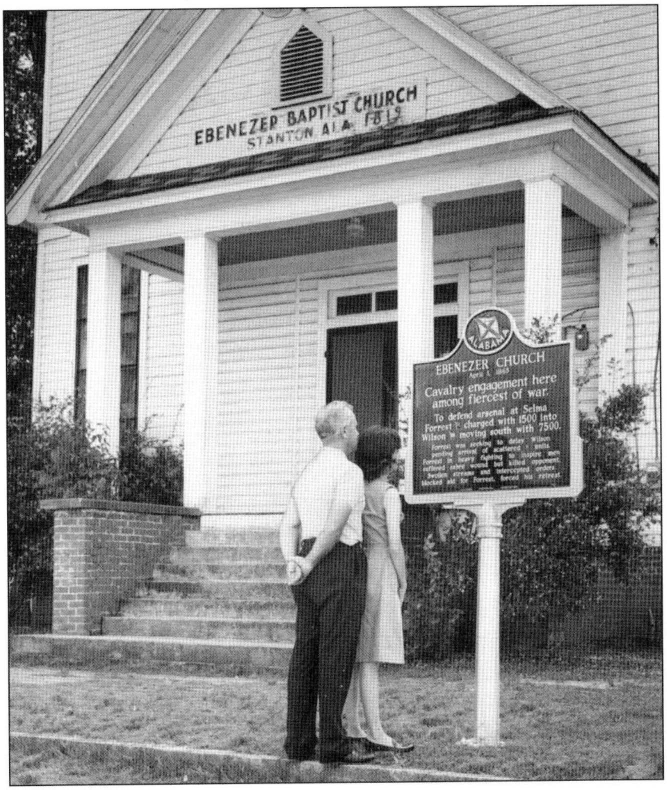

In July 1964, the Alabama Historic Commission erected a marker to commemorate the Battle of Ebenezer Church. On April 1, 1865, Confederate troops led by Gen. Nathan Bedford Forrest engaged the Union troops of Gen. James H. Wilson near the church in a heroic effort to protect the Confederate Ordnance and Naval Foundry at Selma. This historical marker was the first in Chilton County. (Author's collection.)

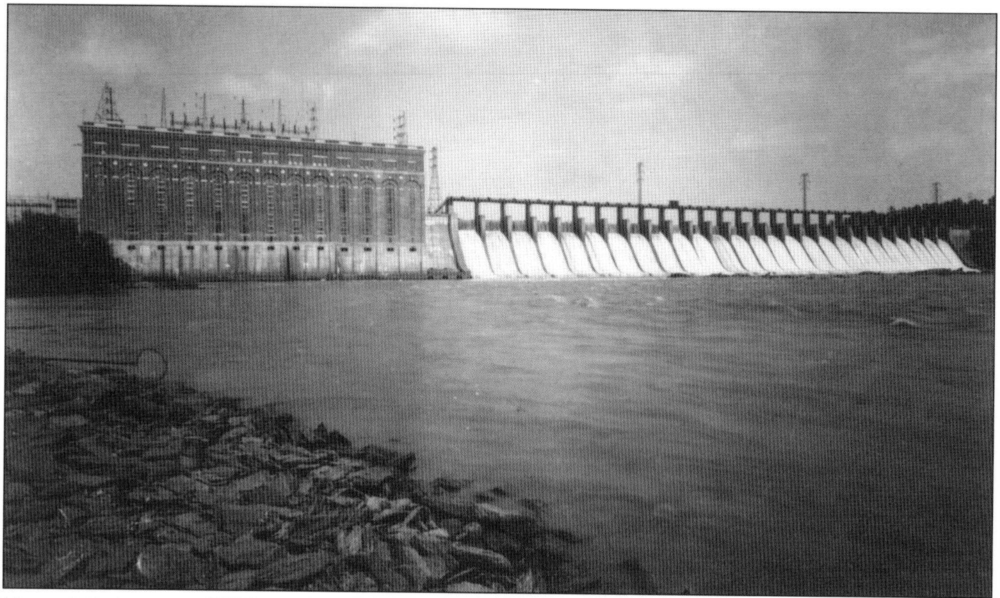

Named in honor of William Patrick Lay, a third-generation riverboat captain and founder of the Alabama Power Company, Lay Dam was begun in 1912 at the Lock 12 site on the Coosa River. The dam represented the first hydropower project of the Alabama Power Company. It was constructed by the MacArthur Brothers Company of New York. (APCA.)

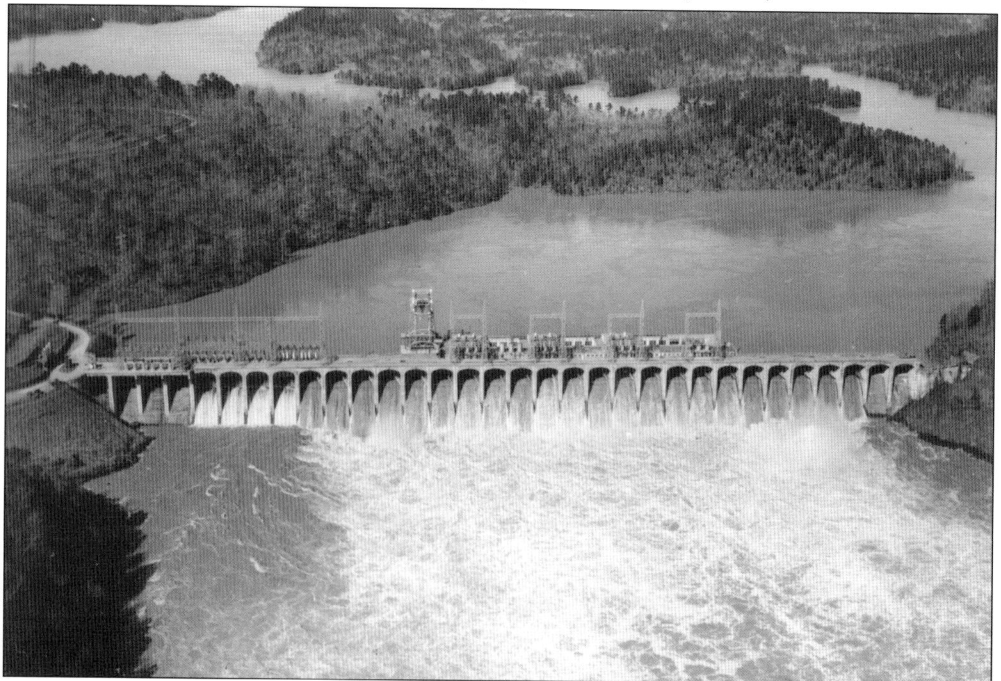

The second hydropower project in Chilton County was 14 miles downstream from Lay Dam at Duncan's Riffle. Completed in 1923, the structure is 1,277 feet in length and 106 feet in height. Lake Mitchell encompasses 5,850 acres and contains approximately 56 billion gallons of water at full pool. Mitchell Dam was named in honor of James Mitchell, who succeeded William Lay as president of the Alabama Power Company. (APCA.)

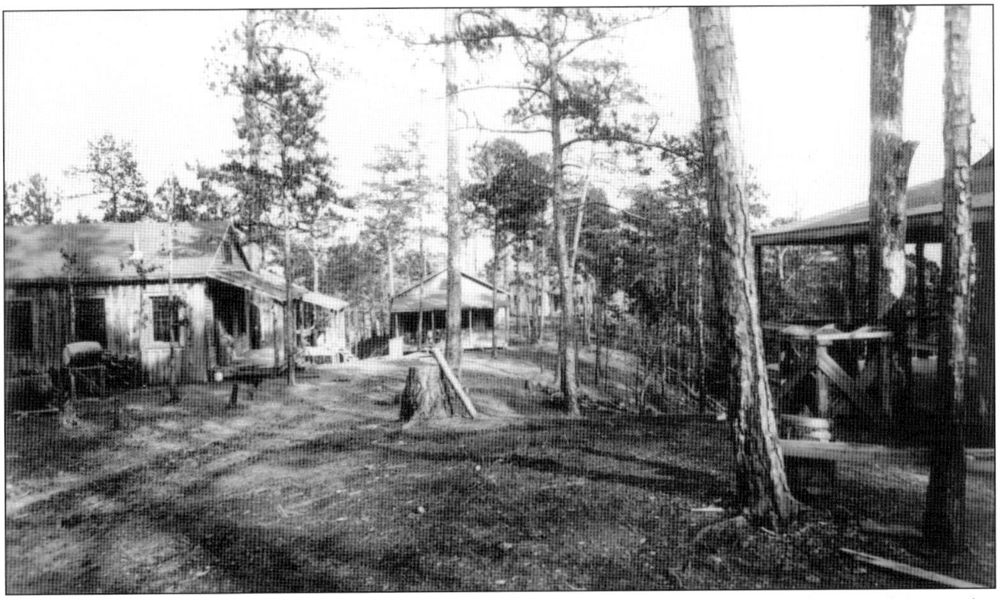

The isolated locations of the Lay and Mitchell Dams projects made travel to and from the construction sites difficult. Resident camps for workers and their families provided on-site accommodations and included a dining hall, commissary, living quarters, an infirmary, a church, and a school. After completion of construction, operators of the dams and their families continued to reside in the villages. (APCA.)

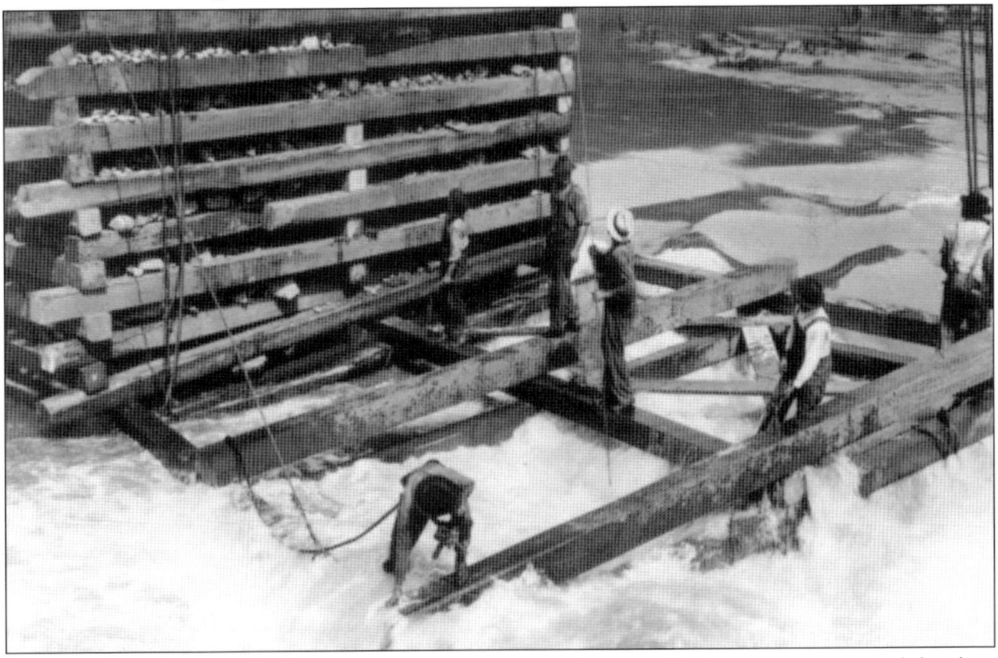

Workers construct a cofferdam to divert water from work areas. During construction of the dam at Lock 12, more than 6.6 million board feet of lumber was required. The completed dam was 2,260 feet in length and 115 feet in height. At full pool, the lake created by the dam encompasses 12,000 acres, has a maximum depth of 88 feet, and contains approximately 86 billion gallons of water. (APCA.)

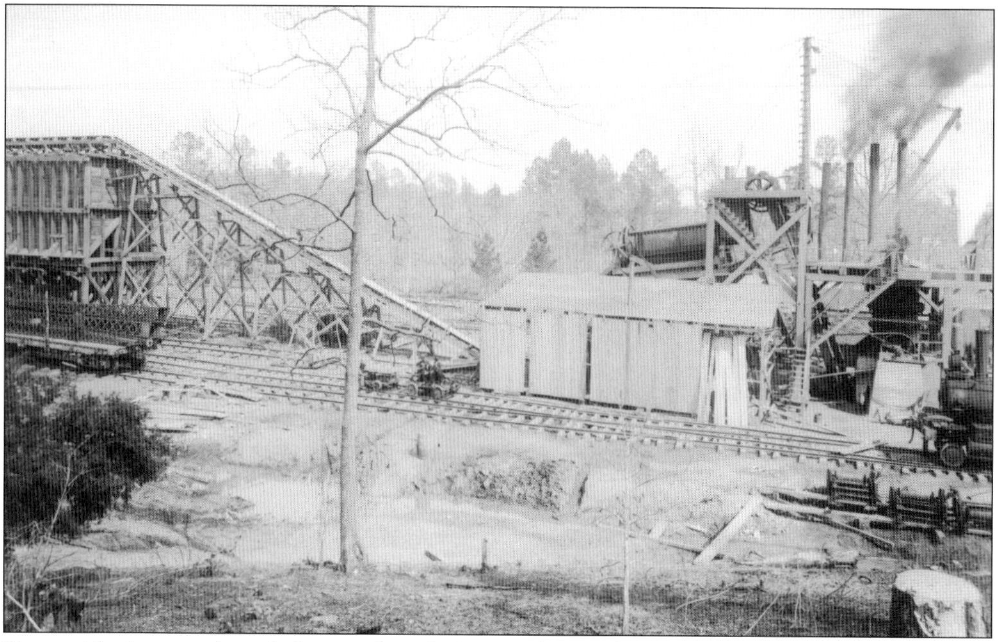

To provide the gravel needed to produce 340,000 cubic yards of concrete to construct Lay Dam, the Mount Zion and Ellison Quarries were established in proximity to the construction site. A rail system was created to transport blasted rock from the quarries to rock crushers and storage bins. The local rail system was also utilized to deliver coal for the steam engines that powered equipment at the quarry. (APCA.)

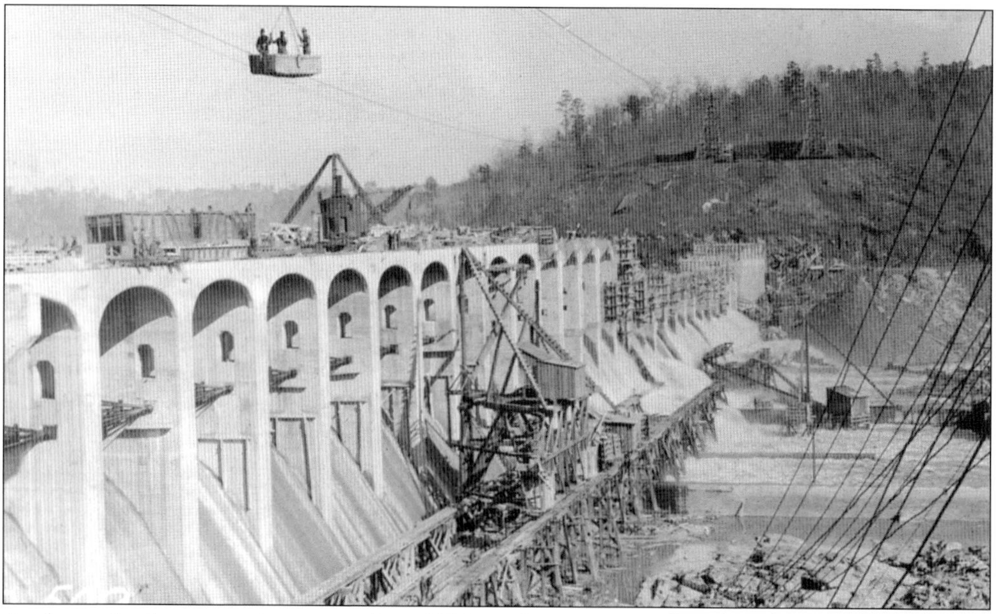

At the peak of construction, more than 1,500 workers were employed at the Lock 12 Dam site. The work force included Eastern European immigrants, Swedish and Italian craftsmen, African American workers from throughout the Southeast, and Chilton County residents. During construction, the work camp maintained a population greater than that of any community between Montgomery and Birmingham. (APCA.)

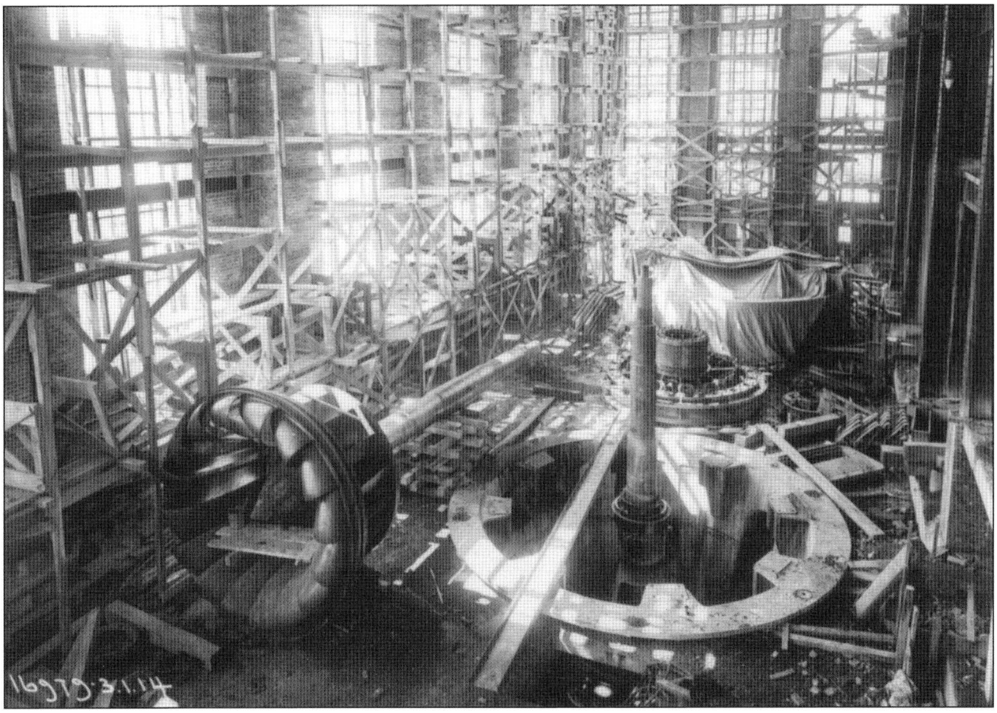

This March 1914 image shows the assembly of one of the waterwheels used to rotate the generator units in the powerhouse of Lay Dam. In April 1914, the first of six generator units began operation. The remaining units were brought on line over a period of three years. Today, each generator unit produces 29,500 kilowatts of electricity. (APCA.)

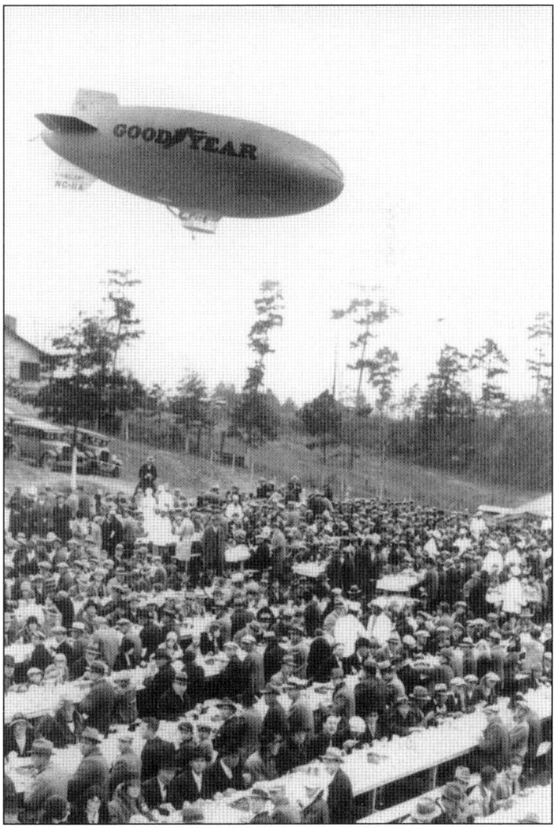

Construction of the Lock 12 Dam was completed in December 1913, and generators began producing electrical power in April of the following year. On November 29, 1929, dignitaries and guests gathered at the Lock 12 Dam site for the dedication ceremony in honor of William Patrick Lay, first president of the Alabama Power Company. The Goodyear blimp *Vigilant* orbited overhead as guests enjoyed a barbecue lunch. (APCA.)

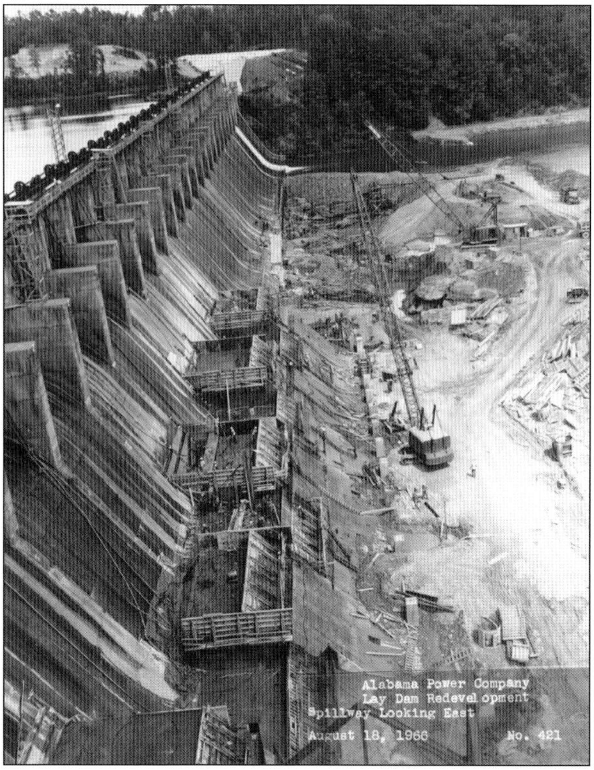

Renovated in 1966 under the Alabama Power Company Coosa River Development Program, the Lay Dam saw its height increased by 14 feet. During the renovation project, the powerhouse was also modified to increase production of electrical energy. (Author's collection.)

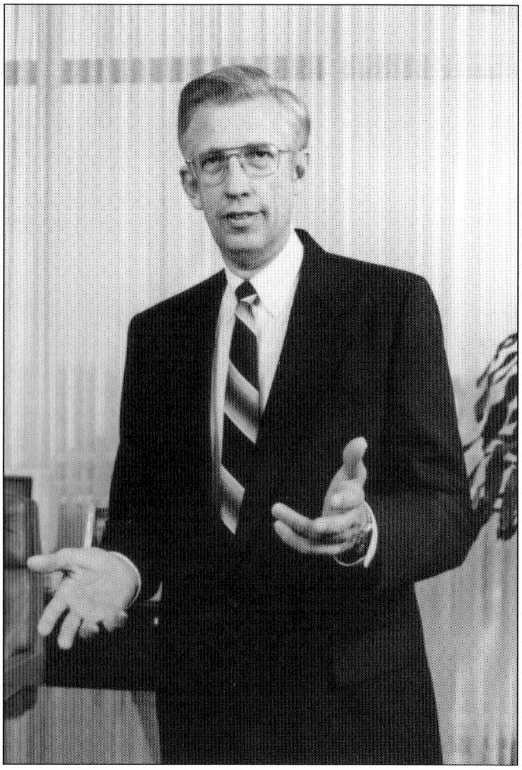

A native of Clanton, Elmer Harris began working with the Alabama Power Company in 1958 as a cooperative student while attending Auburn University. During his tenure at the Alabama Power Company, Harris served in number of management positions before being named president and chief executive officer. His term as president was noted for aggressive efforts at economic development throughout Alabama. (APCA.)

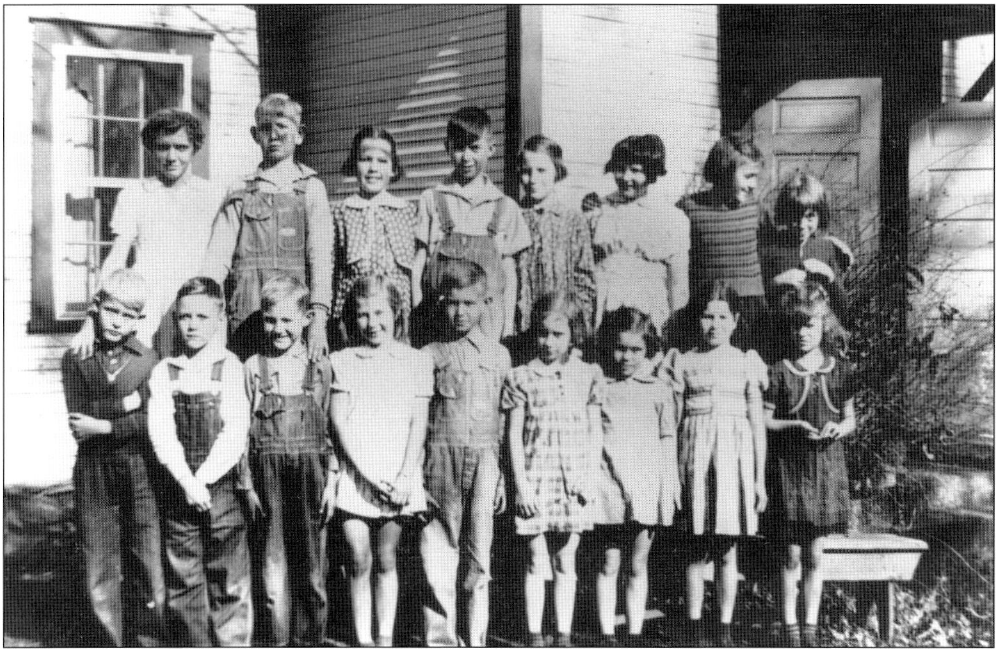

The teacher and students of the Mitchell Dam School pose for a 1938 photograph. The construction village of the Mitchell Dam project included a school for children of the workers. Once construction of the dam was complete, the village and school remained in operation for use by workers responsible for operation of the dam. The school was a one-room wood-frame building. (CCBE.)

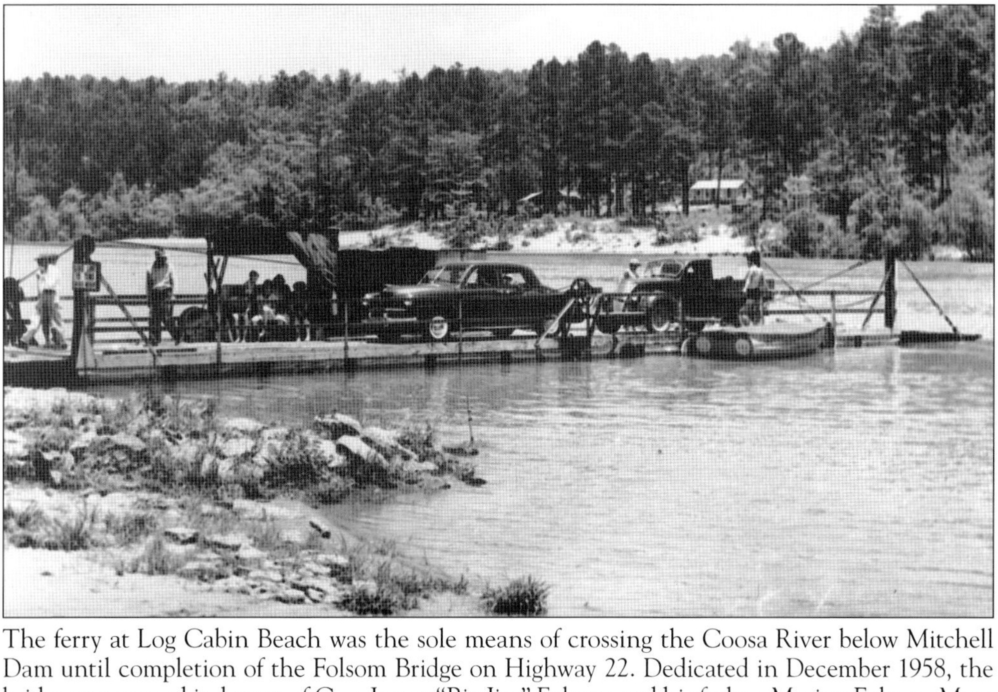

The ferry at Log Cabin Beach was the sole means of crossing the Coosa River below Mitchell Dam until completion of the Folsom Bridge on Highway 22. Dedicated in December 1958, the bridge was named in honor of Gov. James "Big Jim" Folsom and his father, Marion Folsom. More than 1,500 residents of Chilton County attended the ceremony, which included a barbecue and speeches by local dignitaries. (Chilton County.)

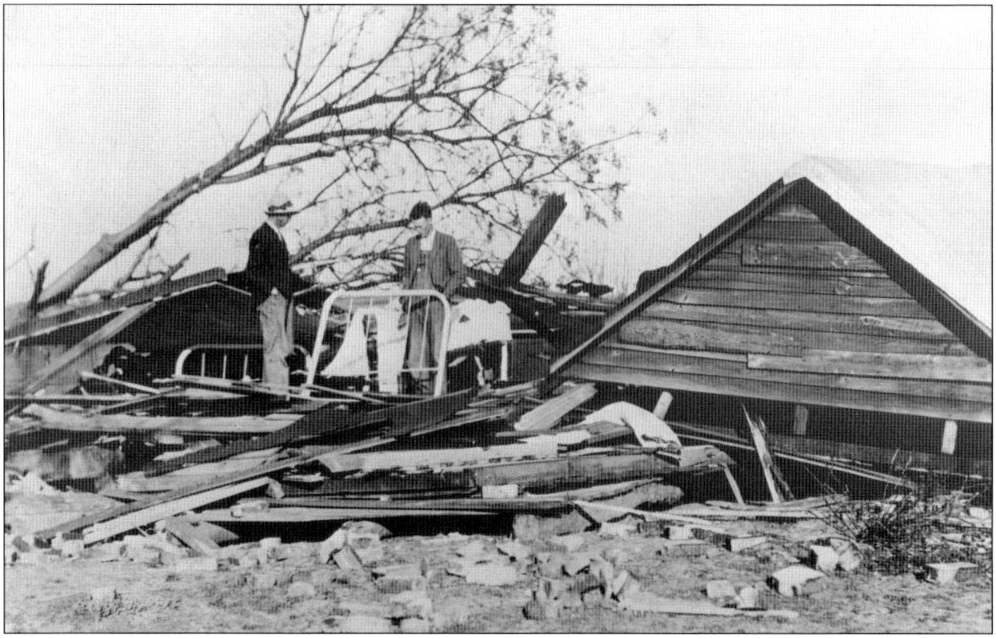

On Monday, March 21, 1932, two deadly tornadoes swept through Chilton County, killing more than 50 people and leaving more than 300 injured and homeless. Touching down one hour apart, these storms left widespread destruction and devastation of property. The event was described as the greatest calamity that has ever befallen the people of Chilton County. The tornadoes first struck near Plantersville in southwest Chilton County. (Author's collection.)

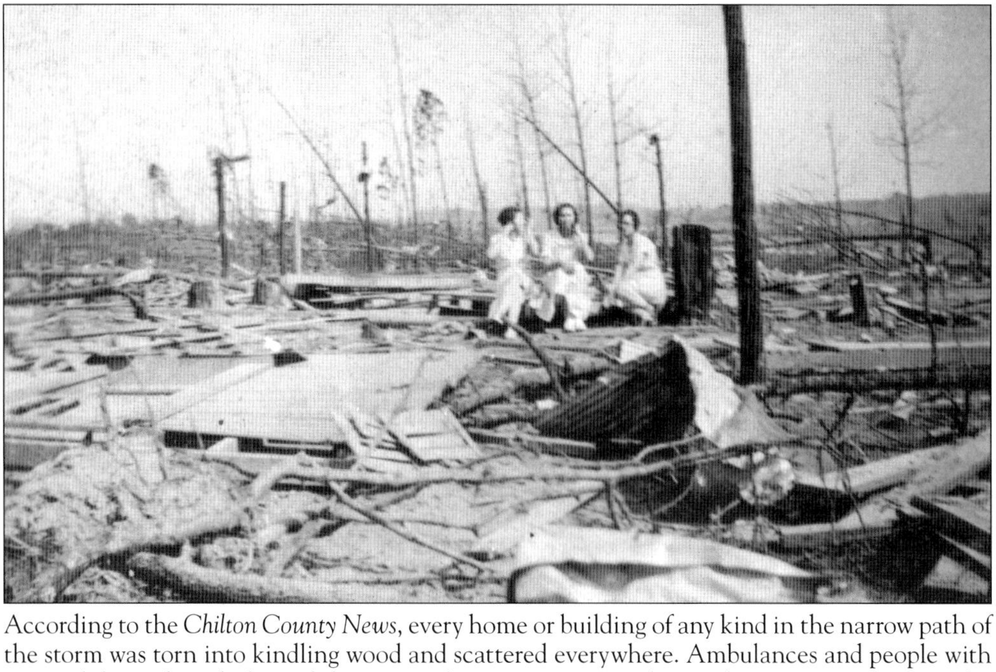

According to the *Chilton County News*, every home or building of any kind in the narrow path of the storm was torn into kindling wood and scattered everywhere. Ambulances and people with automobiles and trucks braved the raging elements to go into the stricken sections to rescue the victims. A strip of thickly settled country one mile wide from Thorsby to Union Grove suffered the heaviest damage. (Thorsby Historical Preservation Museum.)

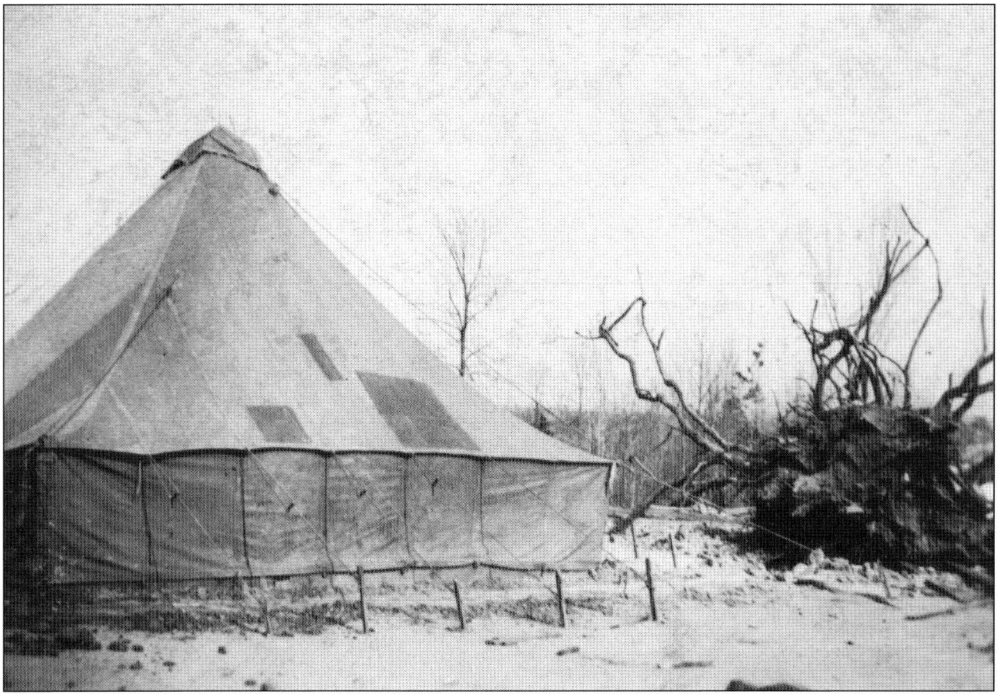

Within an hour of the storm, a steady stream of dead, dying, and injured began to arrive at the hospital at Clanton. Relief stations were established at doctors' offices in Clanton, Thorsby, and Jemison. The *Union Banner* newspaper reported the likelihood of widespread burials throughout Chilton County during the following week. Some churches conducted as many as five funeral services in one day. (Thorsby Historical Preservation Museum.)

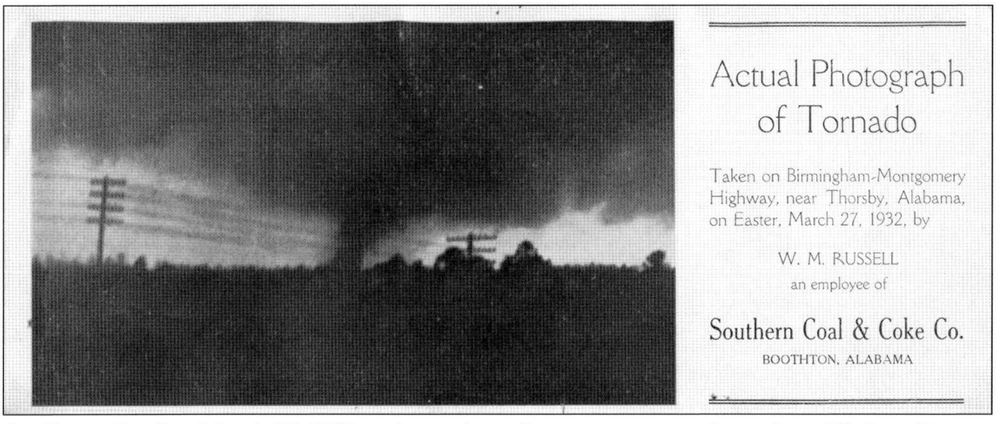

On Easter Sunday, March 27, 1932, only six days after communities throughout Chilton County were devastated by tornadoes, the Lawley community was struck by a second storm that fatally injured six people. Tents that had been erected for victims of the first storm were ripped apart and destroyed by the second storm. This image was captured by W.M. Russell of the Southern Coal and Coke Company of Boothton. (Thorsby Historical Preservation Museum.)

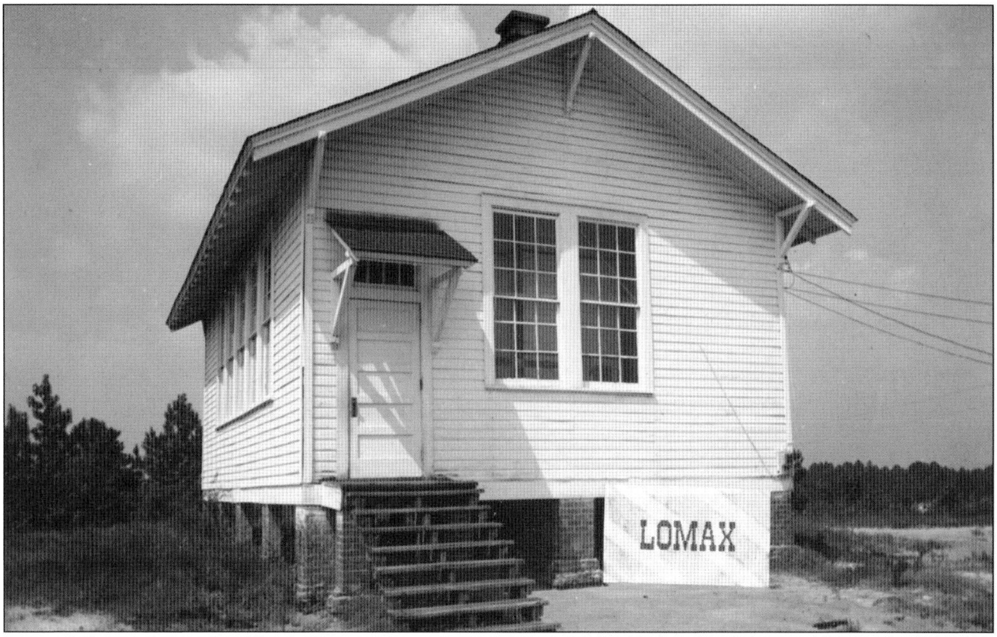

Early in the 20th century, one-teacher schools were common throughout Chilton County. These schools were typically located outside of municipalities in settlements and small communities. The one-teacher school was a wood-frame building with a single large classroom to accommodate students of all ages. One-teacher public schools did exist in some larger communities as segregated schools for small African American populations. (CCBE.)

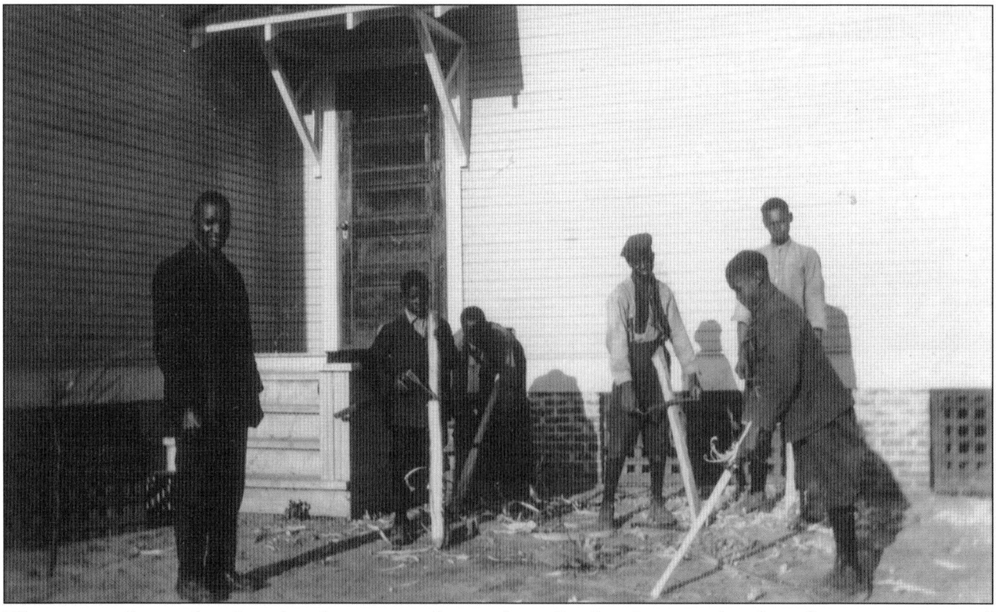

The curriculum of early schools was not limited to the fundamentals of reading, writing, and arithmetic. Often, students received training to develop skills useful in everyday life. In Lomax, African American students were taught to fabricate handles for axes and other tools. The one-teacher schools provided only a basic level of academic instruction, as economic necessity required young people to enter the workforce at an early age. (ADAH.)

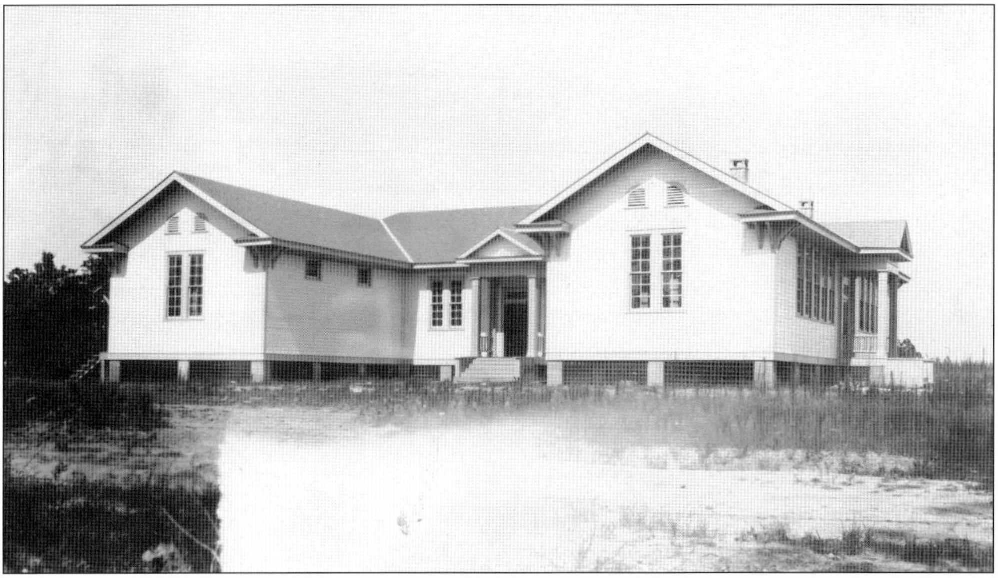

The Chilton County Training School (above) and the Clanton School (below) were created to provide secondary education for African American students in Chilton County. Land for the schools was donated by local residents, while funding for construction was obtained through the Julius Rosenwald Fund. In 1924, the Chilton County Training School began serving students from Clanton, New Convert, Verbena, Jemison, and other communities in Chilton County. Initially, a single school bus was used to transport students from their homes in outlying communities. In December 1949, the main building was destroyed by fire. A new brick building was constructed in 1951 and remained in service until 1969, when desegregation of the school system was mandated by the federal Civil Rights Act of 1964. In 2007, the school was listed in the Alabama Register of Landmarks and History. (Both, Fisk University.)

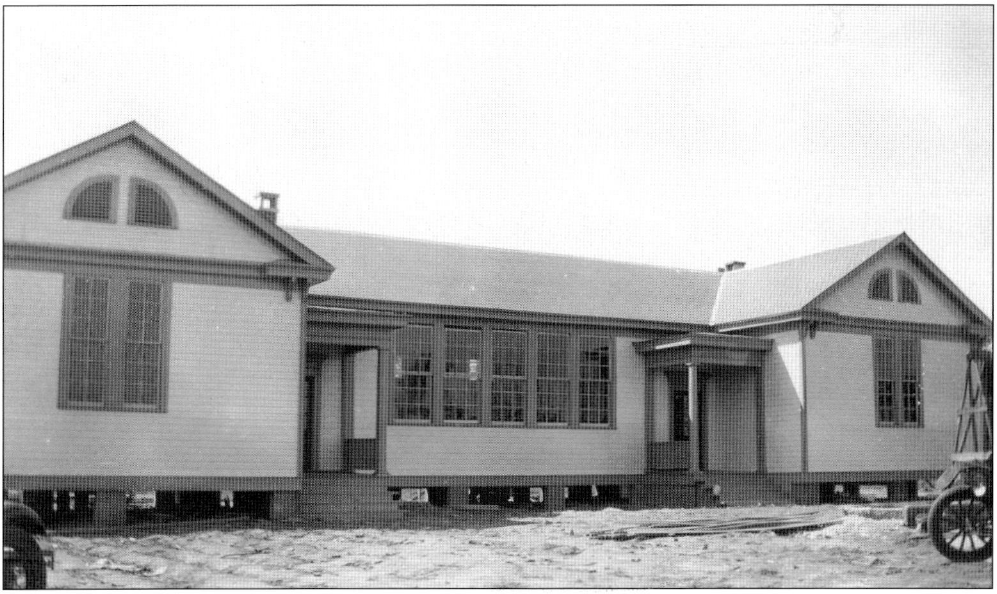

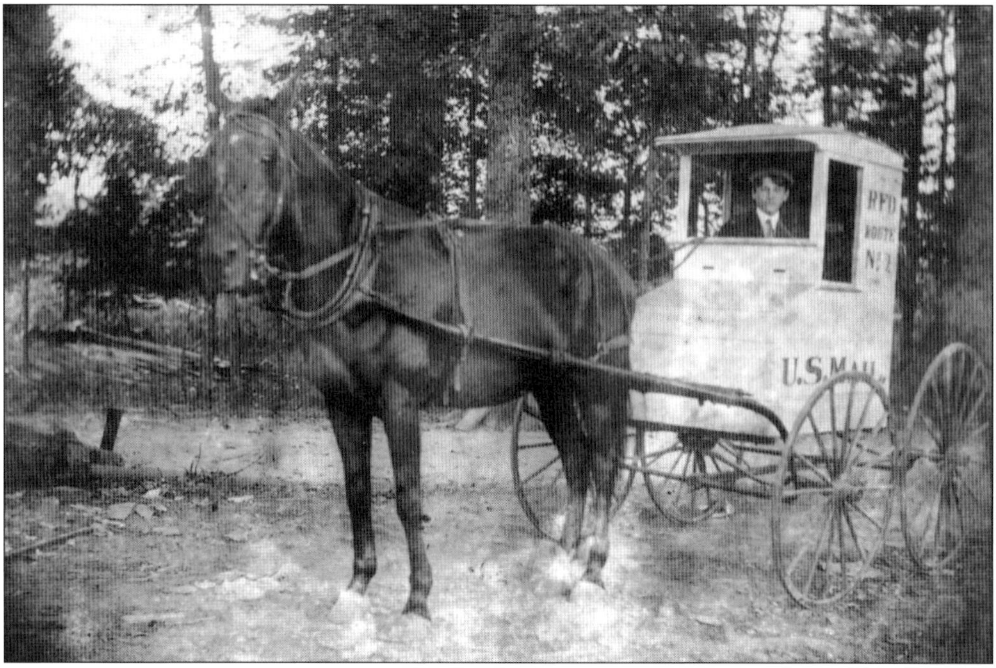

In 1890, sixty-five percent of the population of the United States lived in rural areas. Although mail delivery was provided to the homes of city dwellers, rural families often had to travel great distances or hire private carriers to collect their mail from a distant post office. To alleviate this hardship, Postmaster General John Wanamaker instituted the Rural Free Delivery system to deliver mail directly to rural farm families. (Maplesville Historical Society.)

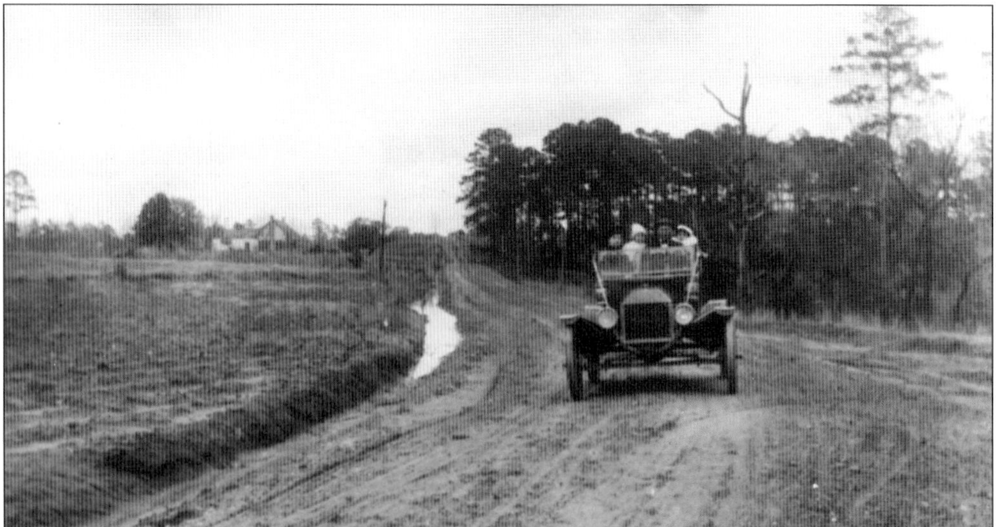

The arrival of the railroad initiated the decline and demise of travel by stagecoach. The arrival of the automobile would ultimately have the same effect on rail travel in Chilton County. Before completion of the Montgomery-to-Birmingham Road, an automobile trip between the cities required two full days of travel, excluding delays caused by mechanical breakdowns and muddy road conditions. (ADAH.)

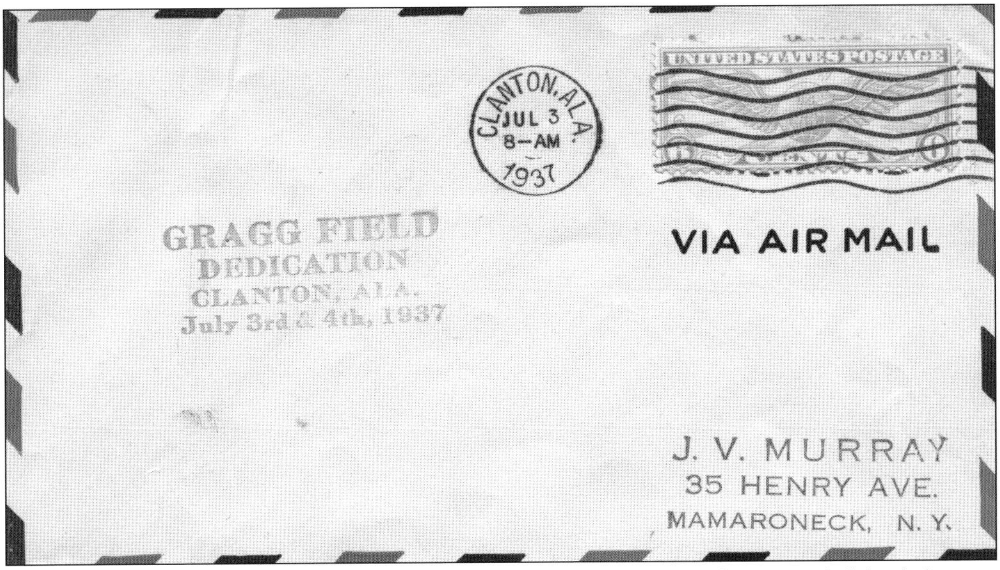

During the 1937 Fourth of July weekend, hundreds of Chilton County residents attended the dedication of the new Chilton County Airport. Events included aircraft aerobatic exhibitions, parachute jumps, a model airplane contest, formation flying by the 106th Observation Squadron from Birmingham, and a street dance in downtown Clanton. On Sunday, all activities ceased from 11:00 a.m. until 2:00 p.m. out of respect and observance of the church hour. (Author's collection.)

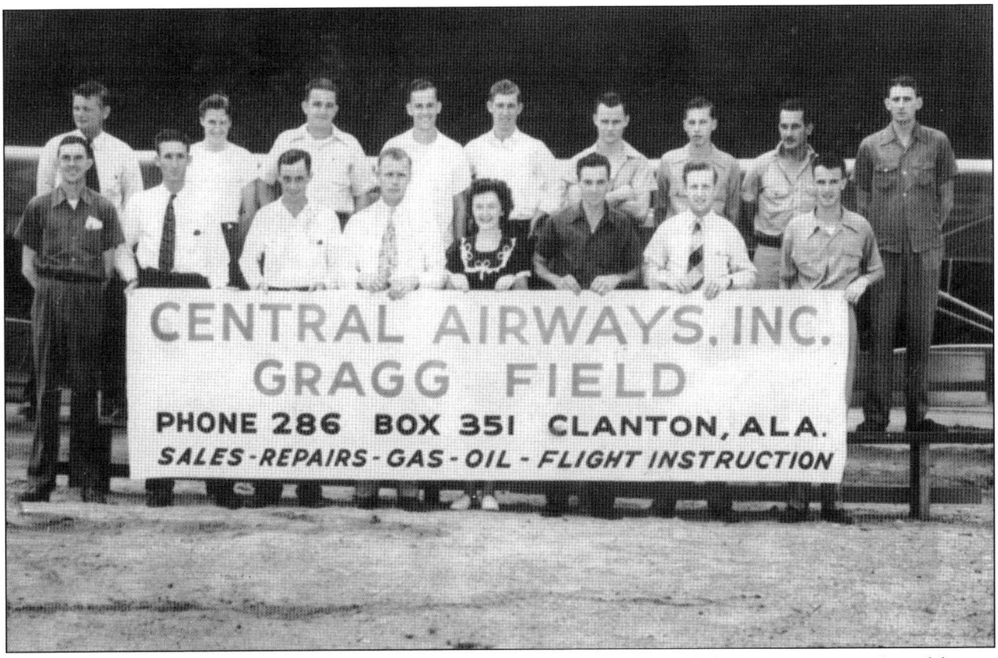

The Chilton County Airport has always been an integral part of the community. In addition to serving the aviation needs of the citizens, the airport hangars have been used for concerts, barbecues, gospel singings, and pageants, and as an assembly point for parades and local gatherings. Following the Second World War, veterans took advantage of their military service benefits by learning to fly at Gragg Field. (Preston Little.)

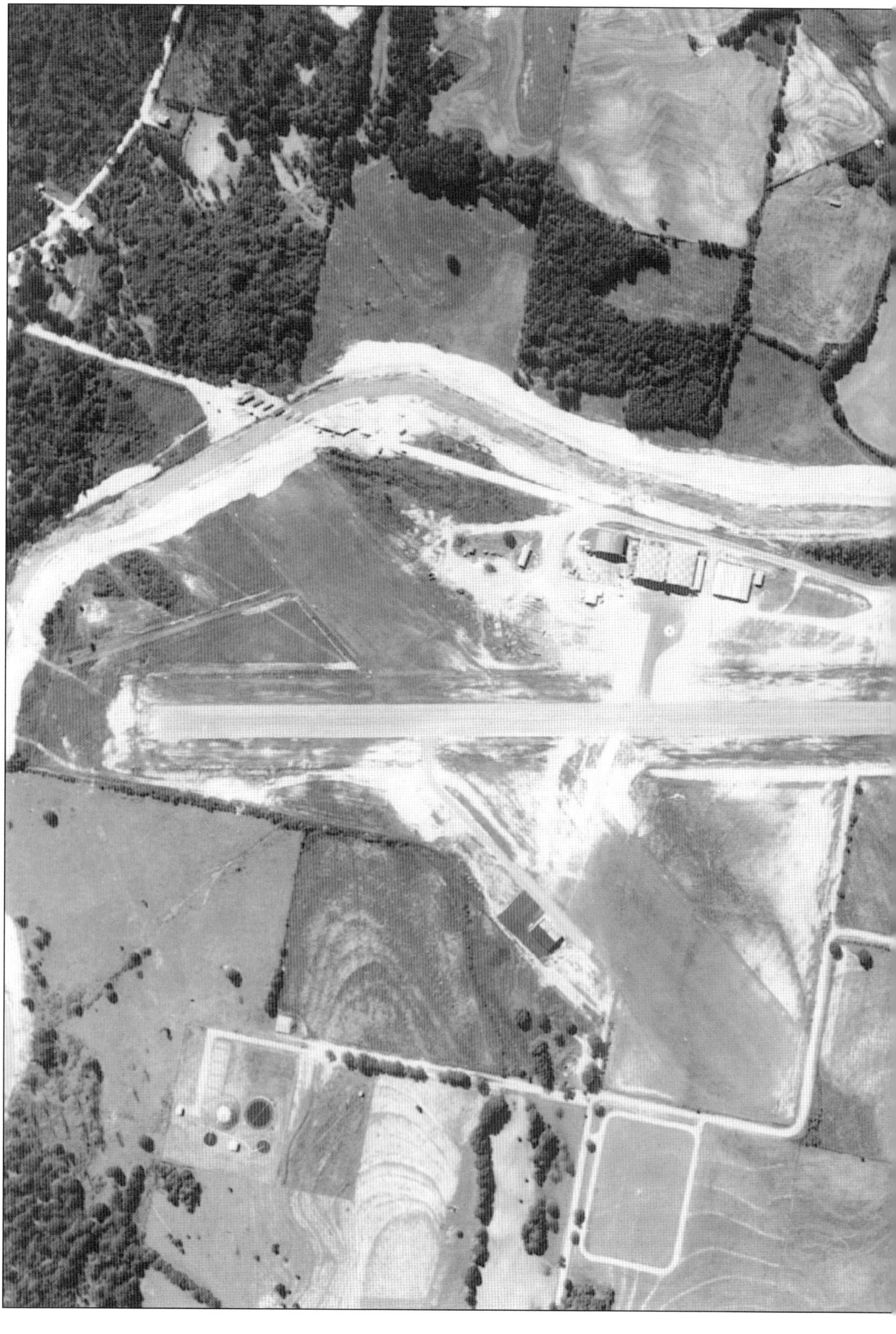

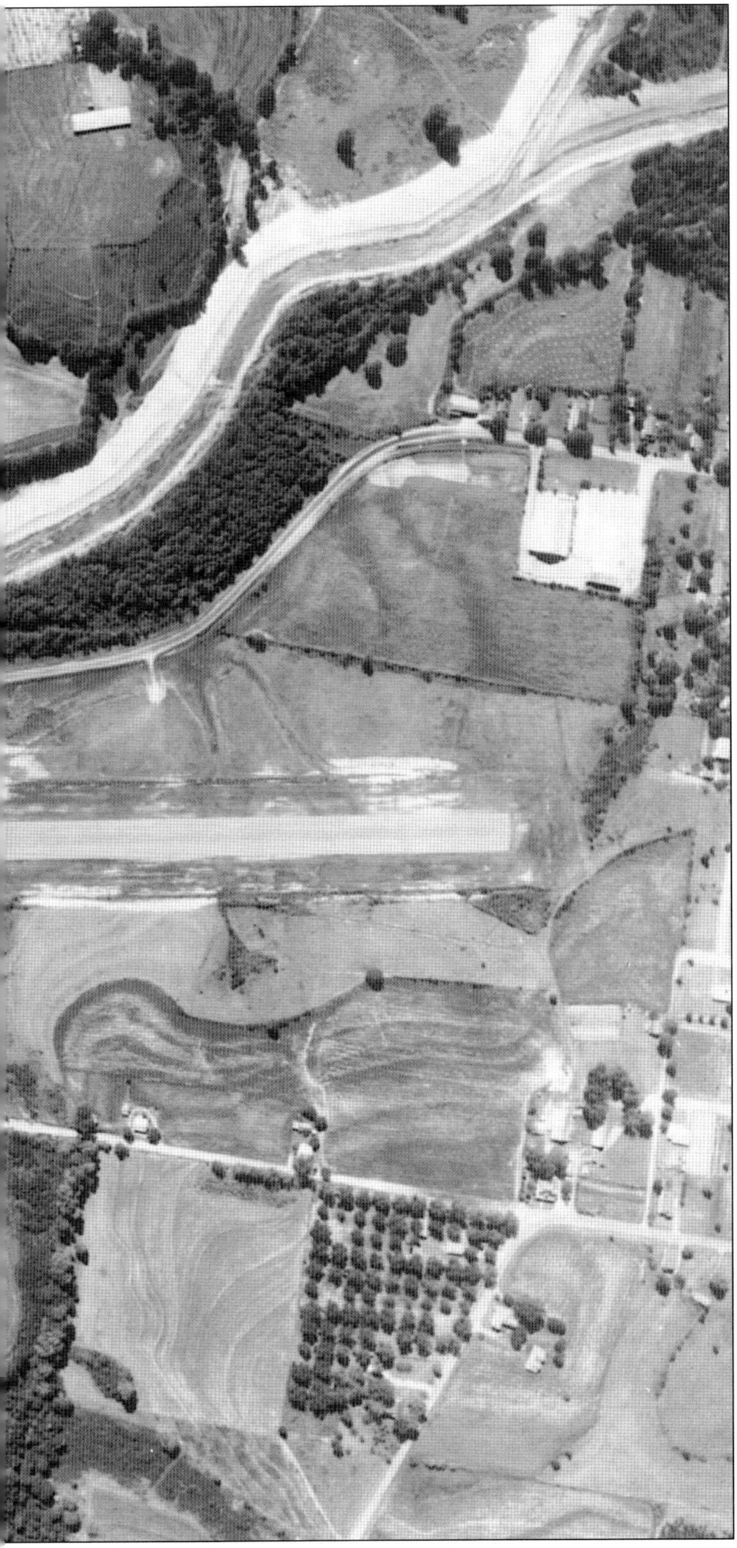

Construction of the Chilton County Airport began in 1934 under the provisions of the Depression-era Civil Works Administration and subsequent Works Progress Administration. Completed in 1937, the original facility included two sod runways and a brick hangar for storage of aircraft. The field was named in honor of Dr. V.J. Gragg, a local physician, civic leader, and aviation enthusiast. The name was later expanded to Gragg-Wade Field in honor of local aviation pioneer Charles Wade. In 1940, the airport was designated Site 27, an emergency landing field on the Memphis-to-Tampa airway. In 1948, a surplus metal hangar was obtained from the Tuskegee Army Air Field, transported to Chilton County, and reassembled on the airport. The Chilton County Airport is one of the oldest continuously operating airports in Alabama. (ADAH.)

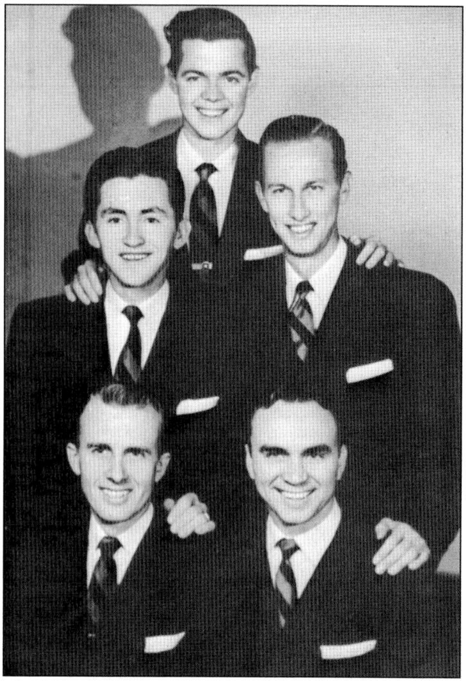

The Blackwood Brothers Gospel Quartet was scheduled to perform at the Chilton County Airport as the concluding event of the 1954 Peach Festival. Members of the group are, from left to right, (bottom row) lead singer James Blackwood and baritone R. W. Blackwood; (middle row) tenor Bill Shaw and bass Bill Lyles; and pianist Jackie Marshall. The quartet won the Arthur Godfrey Talent Scouts competition on national television. (Author's collection.)

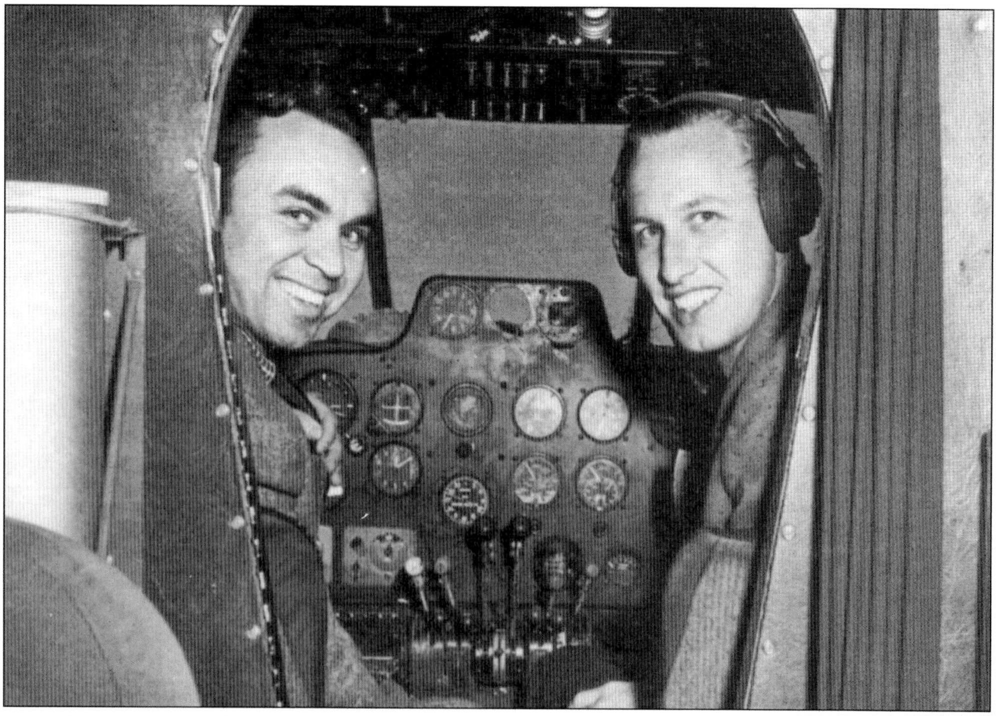

Forty-five minutes before the concert was to begin, pilot R.W. Blackwood (left) and copilot Bill Lyles took off in the group's twin-engine Beechcraft Model 18 for a brief test flight. At the last minute, Blackwood and Lyles were joined on the flight by local resident Johnny Ogburn. During a second attempt at landing, the aircraft stalled and impacted the ground. The three occupants perished in the crash. (Author's collection.)

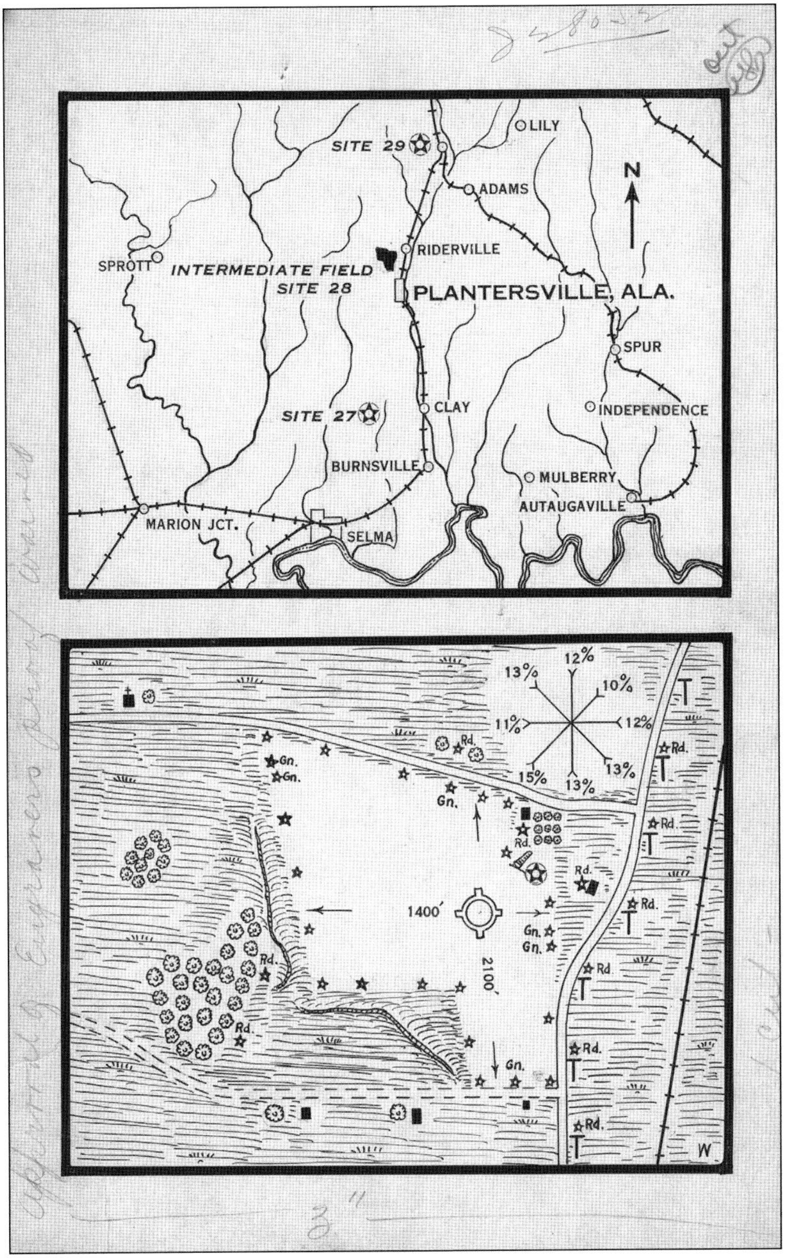

The Chilton County Airport was not the first airfield to serve Chilton County. With the inauguration of airmail service from Mobile to Atlanta on May 1, 1928, emergency landing fields were constructed at intervals of 30 miles along the route to provide suitable facilities should inclement weather or mechanical problems require an unscheduled landing. Designated Site 27 on Commercial Air Mail Route 23, an emergency landing field was located one mile north of Plantersville. The landing area was lighted and included an airway beacon to guide pilots flying at night or in reduced visibility. Property owners were paid to maintain the field and operate the gasoline generators that powered the lighted beacon, a financial incentive especially beneficial during the onset of the Great Depression. The field was closed in 1932, when Commercial Airmail Route 23 was rerouted through Montgomery. (ADAH.)

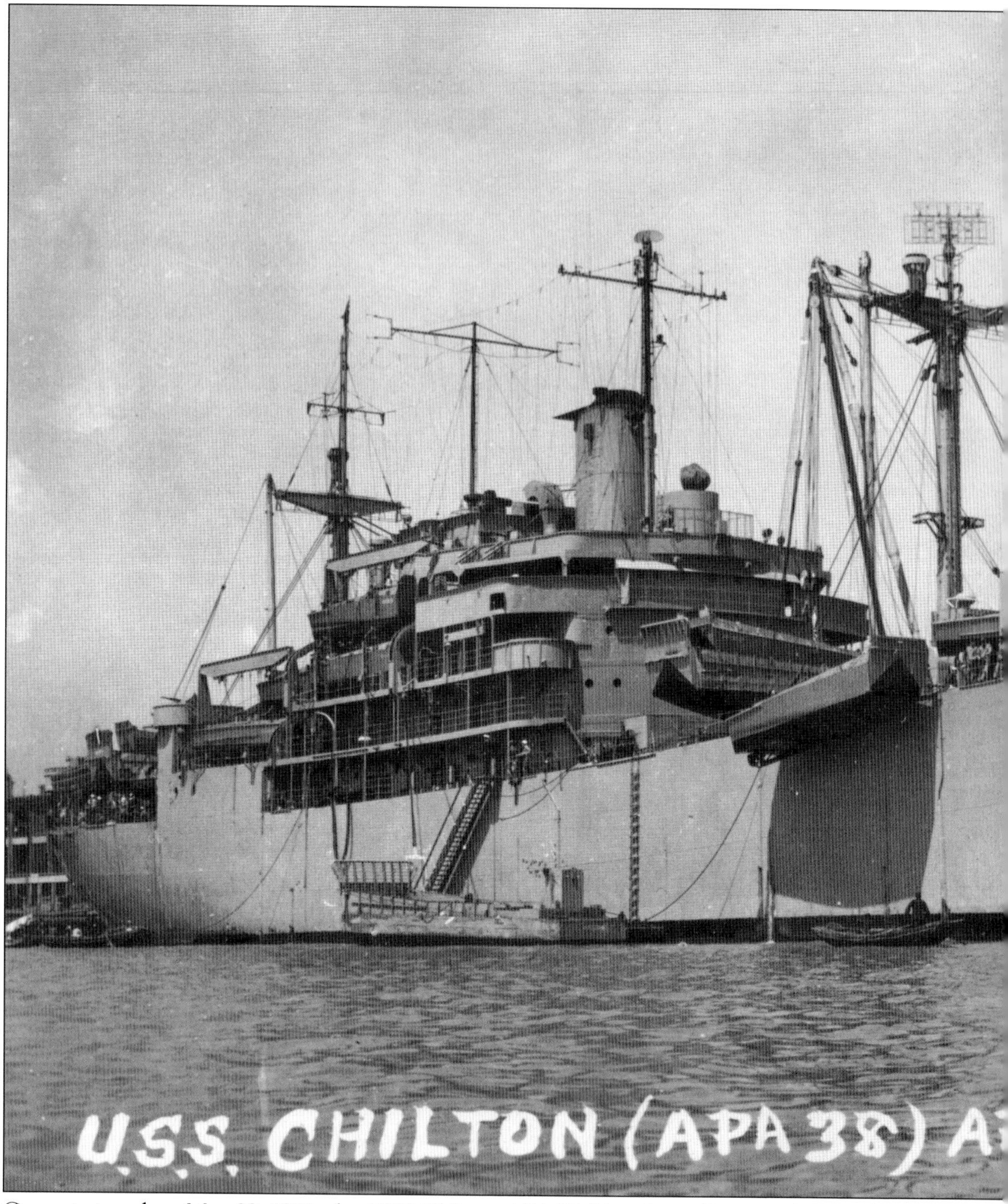

Commissioned on May 29, 1943, the USS *Chilton*, APA-38 (Auxiliary, Personnel, Attack), was named in recognition of the people of Chilton County for their support of the war effort through purchases of war savings bonds. During the Second World War, the ship and crew served with distinction in the Pacific theater of operations. For almost 30 years, the USS *Chilton* supported military operations around the world, including Korea, the Cuban Missile Crisis, and Southeast

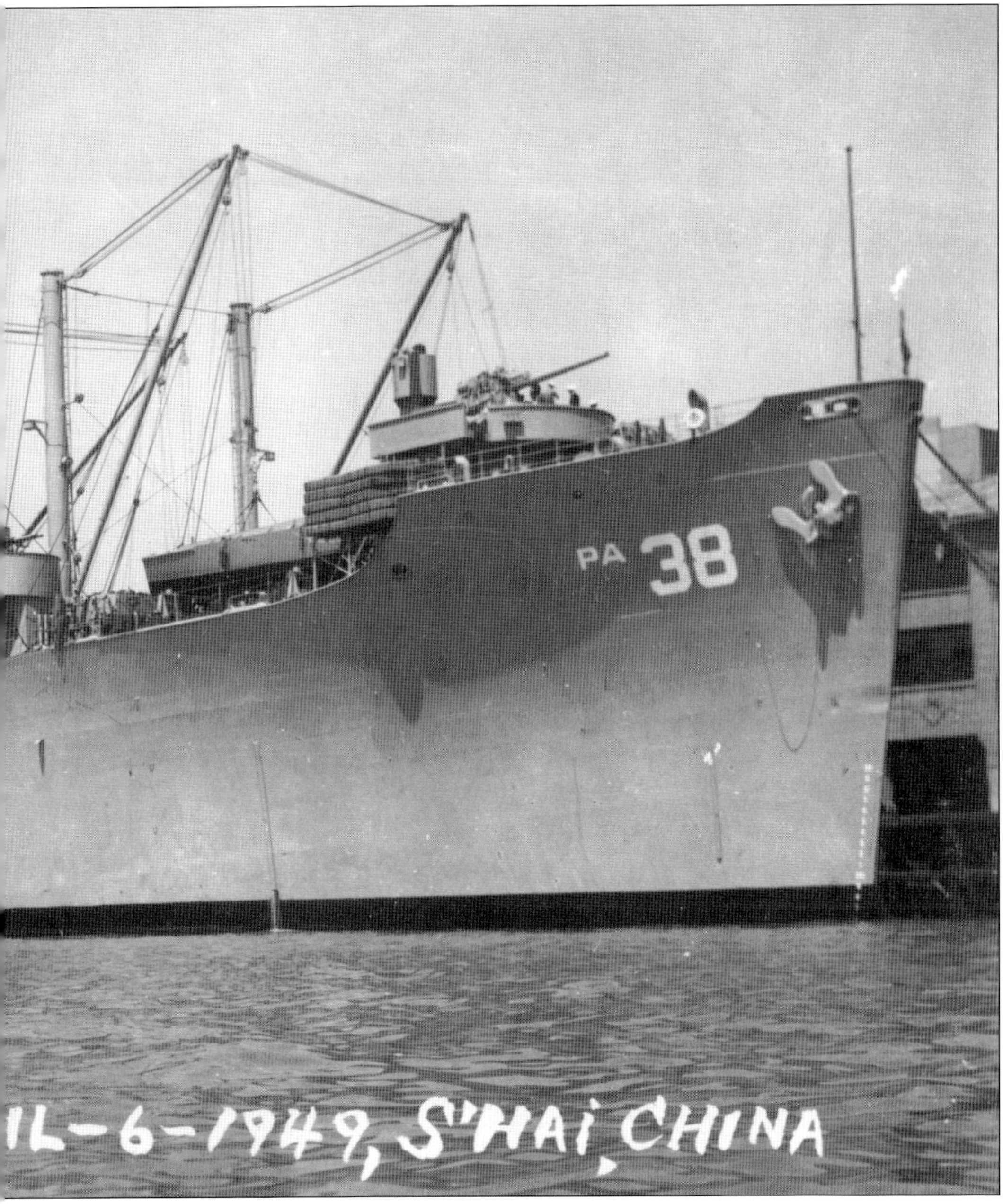

Asia. The USS *Chilton* also participated in numerous humanitarian missions, evacuating refugees from areas impacted by natural and man-made disasters. The USS *Chilton* was decommissioned in July 1972, bringing to an end the career of a ship that served with honor and distinction for three decades. (Author's collection.)

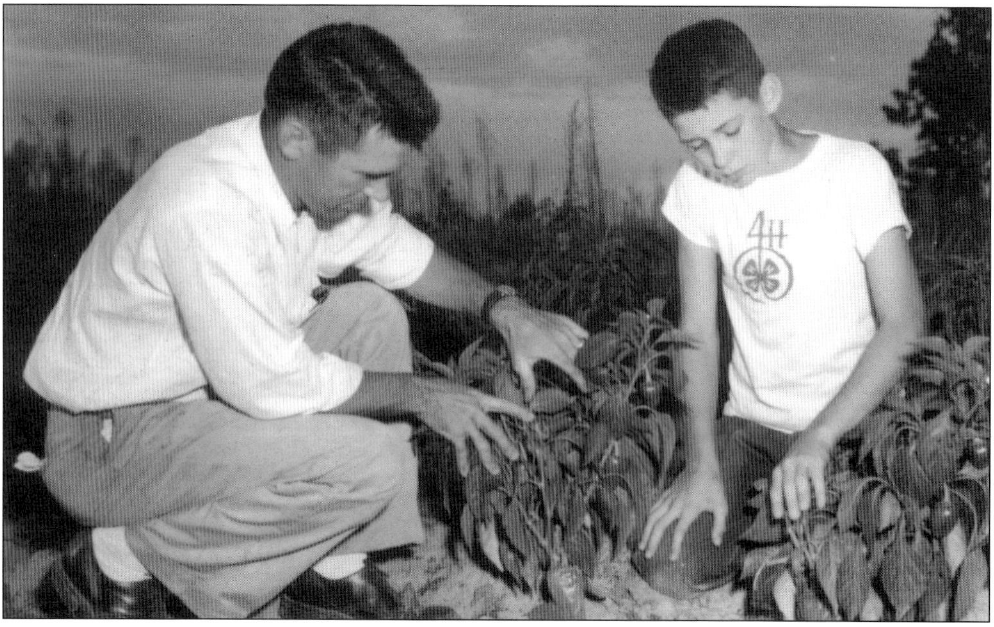

For more than 100 years, the 4-H clubs of Chilton County have promoted the concept of practical and hands-on learning experiences for young people. Today, 4-H clubs make up the largest youth development organization in the nation. The cloverleaf emblem of the 4-H club represents the four areas of personal development—Head, Heart, Hands, and Health. "To Make the Best Better" is the 4-H club motto. (Chilton County Extension Service.)

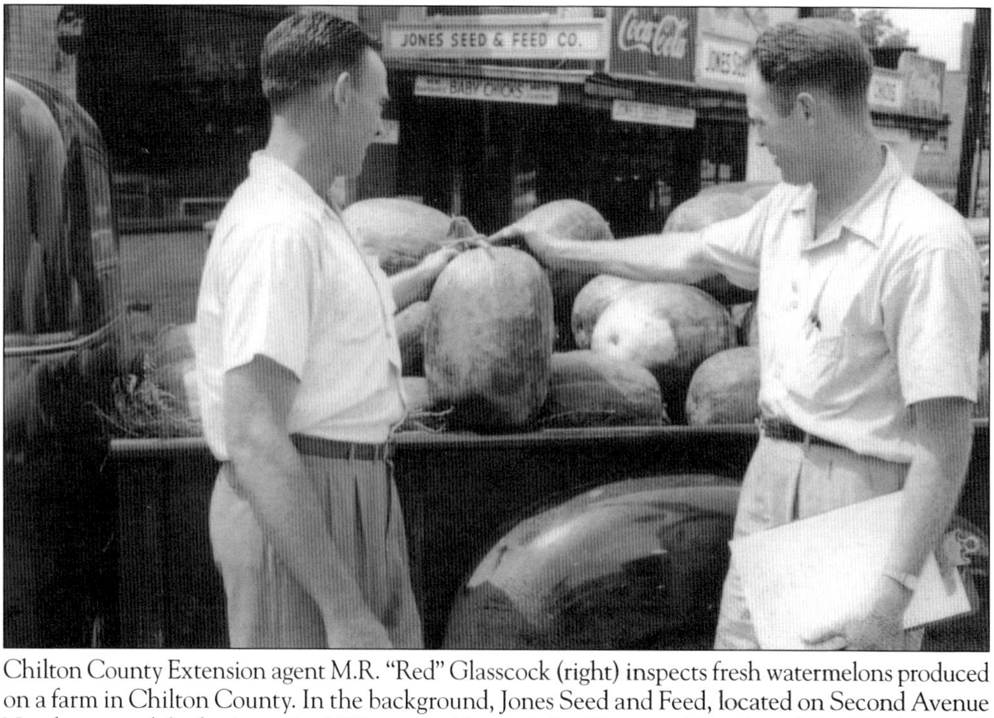

Chilton County Extension agent M.R. "Red" Glasscock (right) inspects fresh watermelons produced on a farm in Chilton County. In the background, Jones Seed and Feed, located on Second Avenue North, opened for business in 1935 to provide seed, fertilizer, and Jazz brand feed for livestock belonging to Chilton County farmers. (Chilton County Extension Service.)

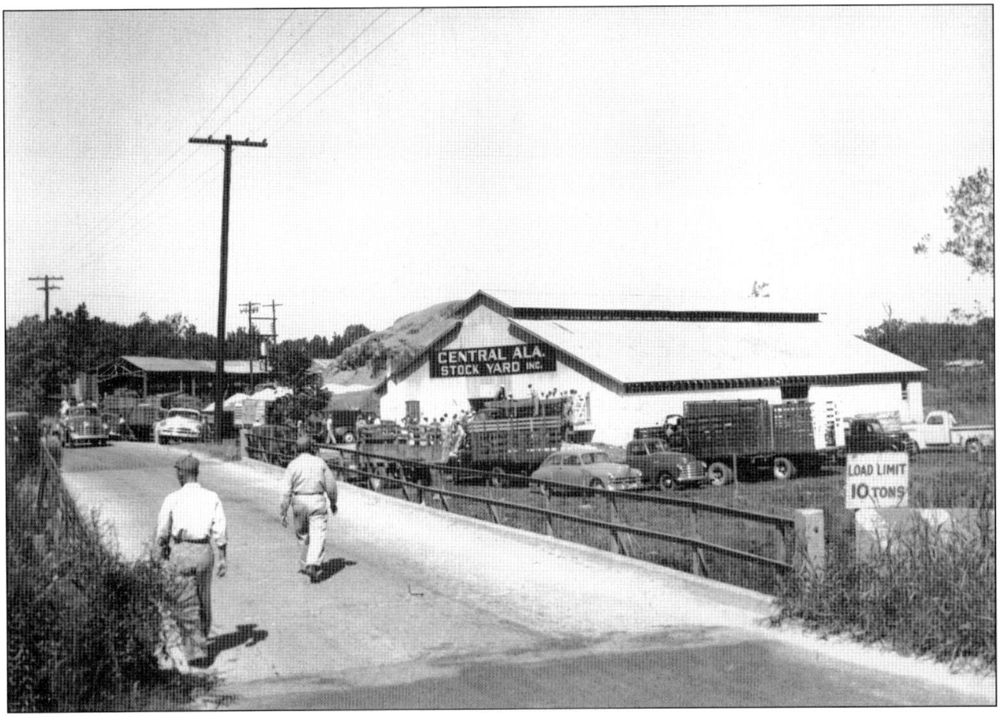

In addition to the agriculture and timber industries, livestock has remained an important component of the economy of Chilton County. Opened in October 1951, the Central Alabama Stock Yard was located on Sixth Street, approximately two blocks south of downtown Clanton. During weekly sales, livestock would be presented for auction to the highest bidder. This bridge spans Poley Bridge Creek. (City of Clanton.)

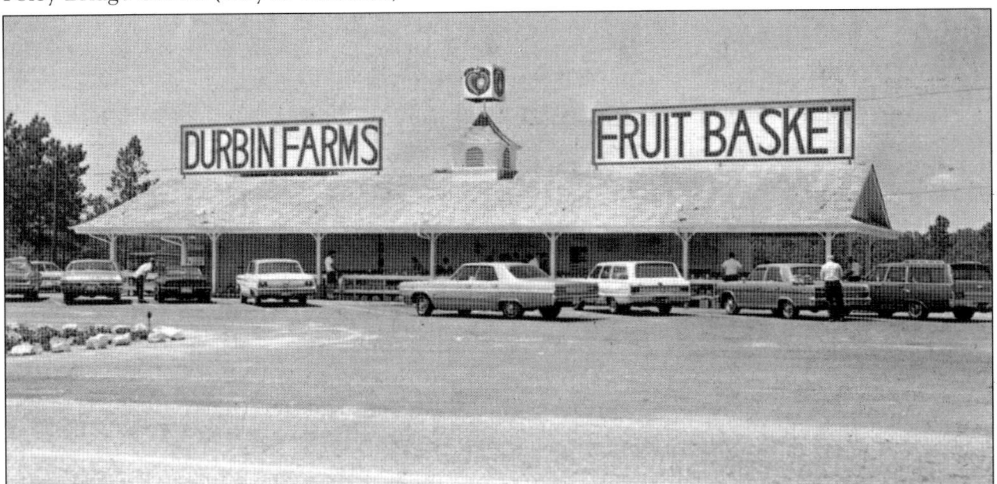

Durbin Farms—"Where Life Is a Peach!"—is located on Highway 31 adjacent to Interstate 65. Durbin Farms has been providing customers with Chilton County peaches, peach ice cream, peach pie, and other peach specialties for more than 50 years. The convenient location makes Durbin Farms a must stop for summer tourists traveling to the beach. Note the iconic peach emblem adorning the building. (Author's collection.)

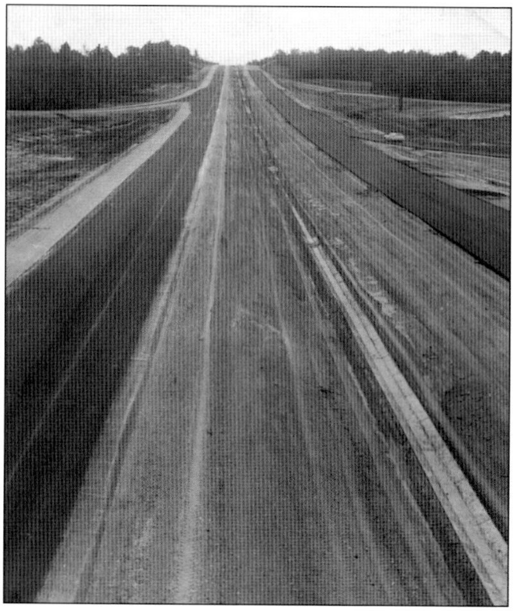

Construction of the new interstate highway through Chilton County was not without controversy. Many residents believed the route of the new highway would have a negative impact on the communities of Verbena, Clanton, Jemison, and Thorsby. However, the interstate became the largest and most progressive highway program in the history of the state, and Interstate 65 would evolve into the most heavily traveled highway in Alabama. (Author's collection.)

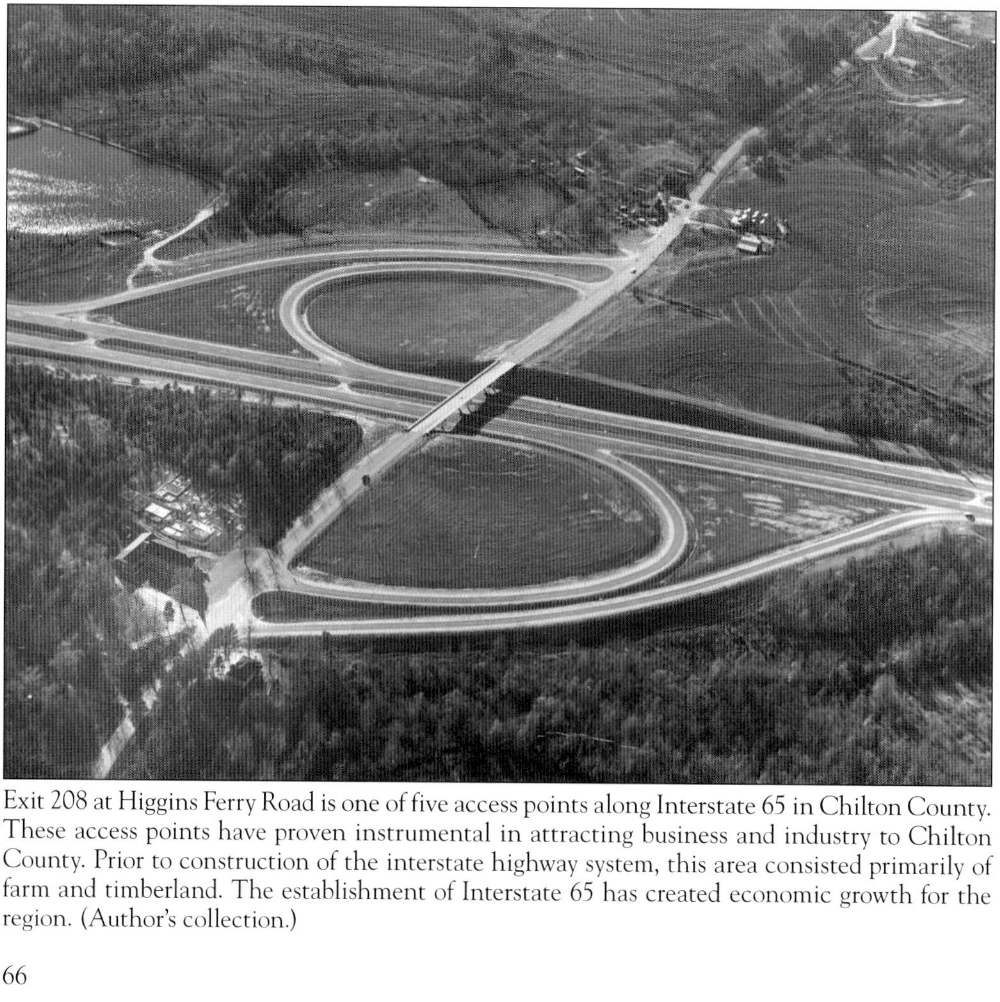

Exit 208 at Higgins Ferry Road is one of five access points along Interstate 65 in Chilton County. These access points have proven instrumental in attracting business and industry to Chilton County. Prior to construction of the interstate highway system, this area consisted primarily of farm and timberland. The establishment of Interstate 65 has created economic growth for the region. (Author's collection.)

Three

Clanton

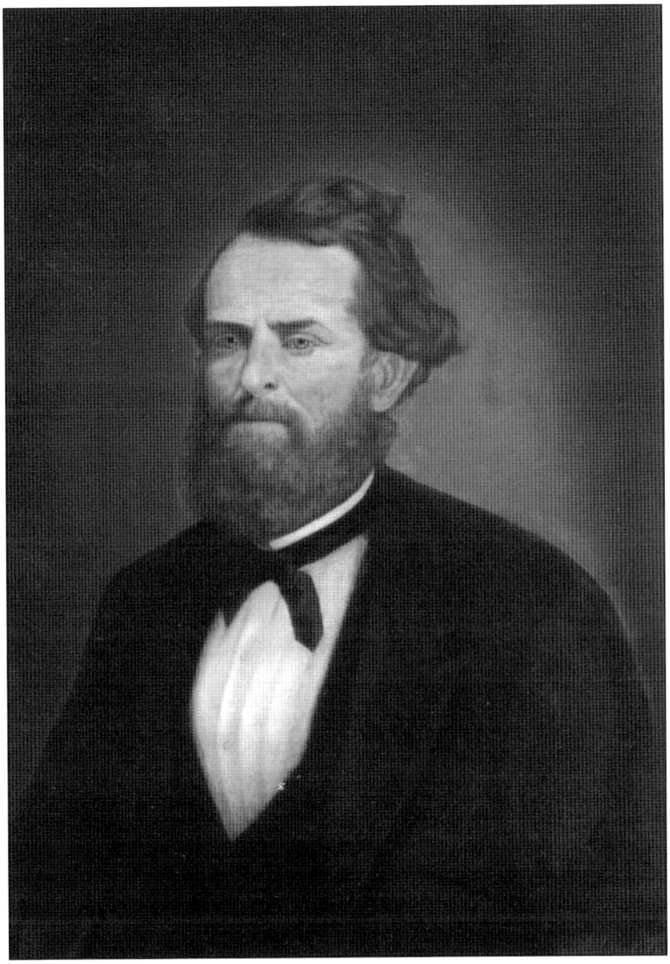

Born in Columbia County, Georgia, James Holt Clanton (1827–1871) attended the law school of William Parish Chilton. Clanton served in the state legislature before joining the 1st Alabama Cavalry during the War between the States. As a brigadier general, Clanton served with distinction until March 1865, when he was seriously wounded and captured at Bluff Springs, Florida. In 1870, the settlement of Goose Pond was renamed in his honor. (ADAH.)

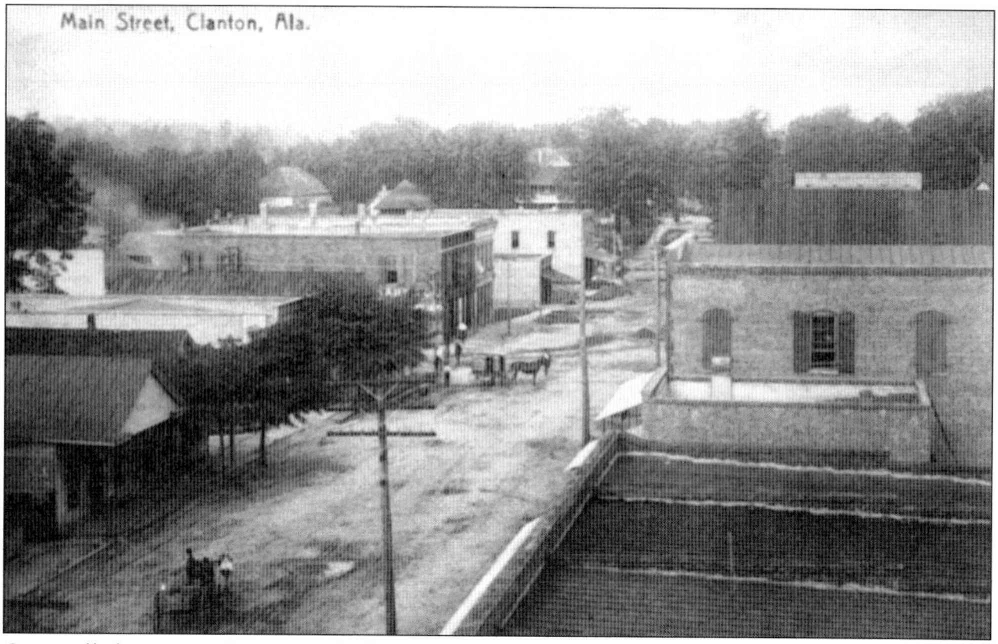

Originally known as Goose Pond, the town that would become Clanton was conceived by early settler and landowner Alfred Baker. Surveyed in 1872, the town was established along the South & North Alabama Railroad. This early view from the tower of the 1896 courthouse shows the businesses along Second Avenue North. Prior to the construction of Highway 31, Second Avenue North was the main street in Clanton. (Author's collection.)

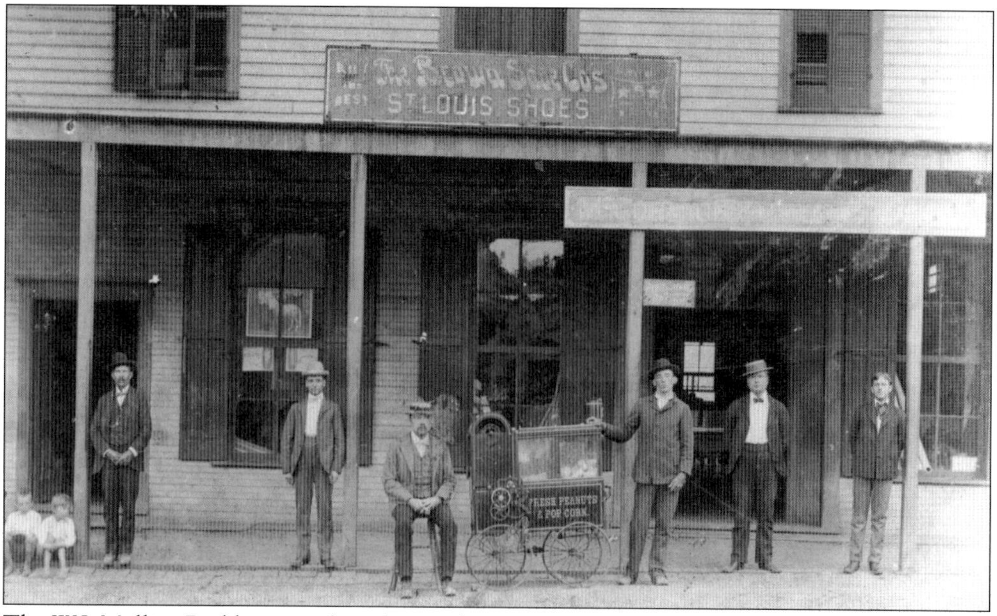

The W.I. Mullins Building stood on the northeast corner of Seventh Street and Second Avenue North for more than 40 years. Originally constructed in 1889 to house the Earhman General Mercantile Company, the building was later purchased by W.I. Mullins (seated) and became the center of business activity in Clanton. The building was demolished in 1935, during a modernization of the downtown area. (Richard Moore.)

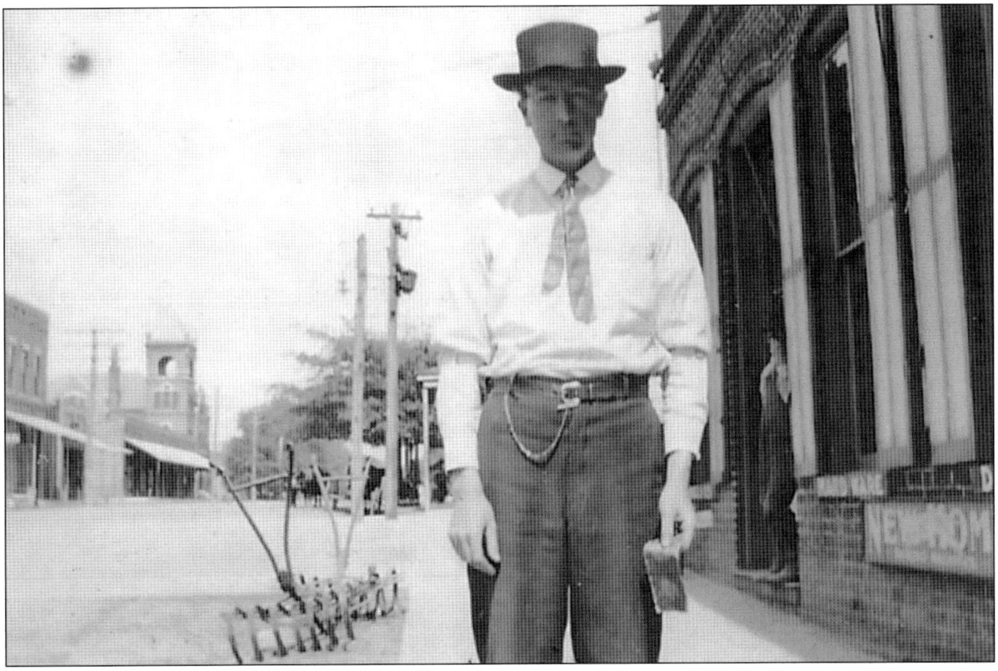

This image of resident John Morgan standing along Second Avenue North illustrates the contrasts of life in Clanton during the early 20th century. The farm implements on display along the street were pulled by horse or mule. In the background, horse-drawn carriages are parked along the dirt street, while a utility pole of Clanton Power & Light Company provides electricity to select homes and businesses in the area. (Kim Gillespie.)

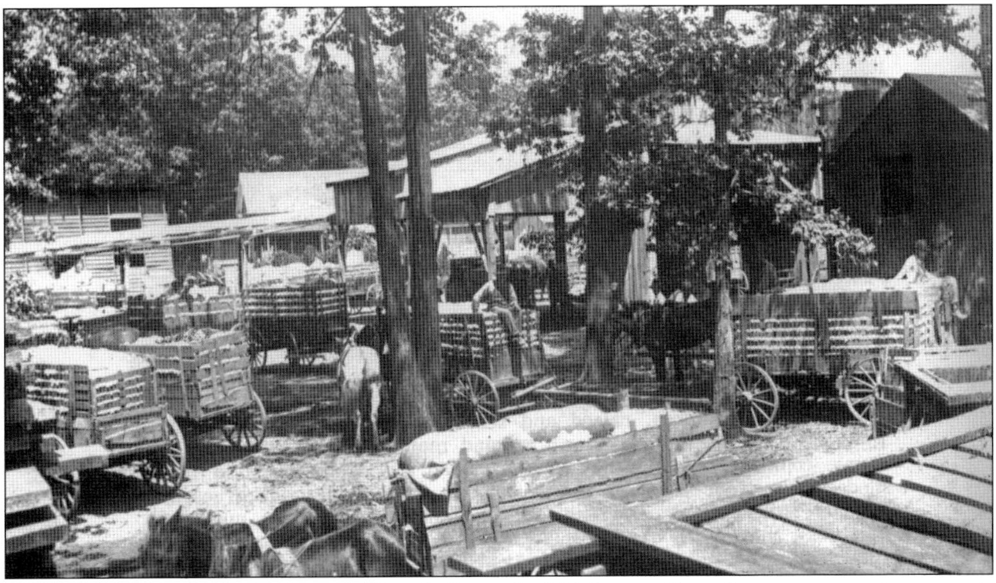

Before Chilton County became the Peach Capital of Alabama, King Cotton was a primary cash crop for local farmers. Each fall, cotton on farms throughout the county would be picked by hand before being loaded on wagons for transport to the local cotton gin. Often, the wait to unload the cotton at the gin provided time for farmers to visit and exchange family and community news. (Thomas Wyatt.)

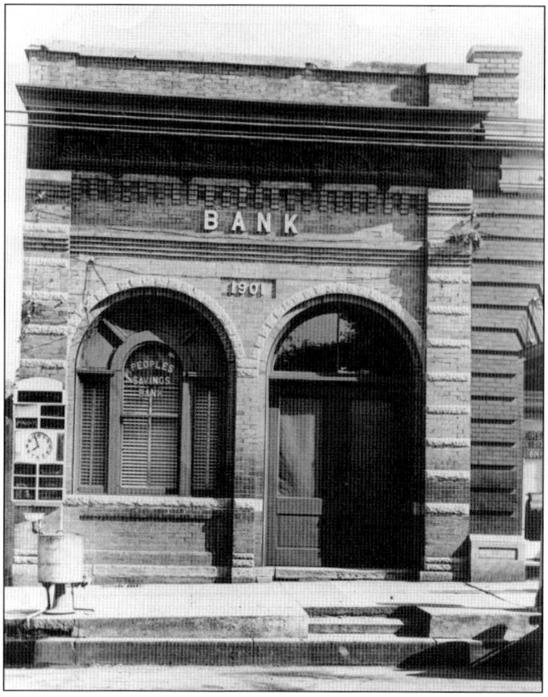

Founded in 1901, the Peoples Savings Bank was one of the first banks to be organized in Chilton County. When the bank was opened, Clanton had no paved roads, electrical lights, or automobiles. The bank was founded by W.T. Holloway of Montgomery. W.T. Callen of Clanton served as cashier. The bank was located on Second Avenue North next to the W.I. Mullins Building. (Richard Moore.)

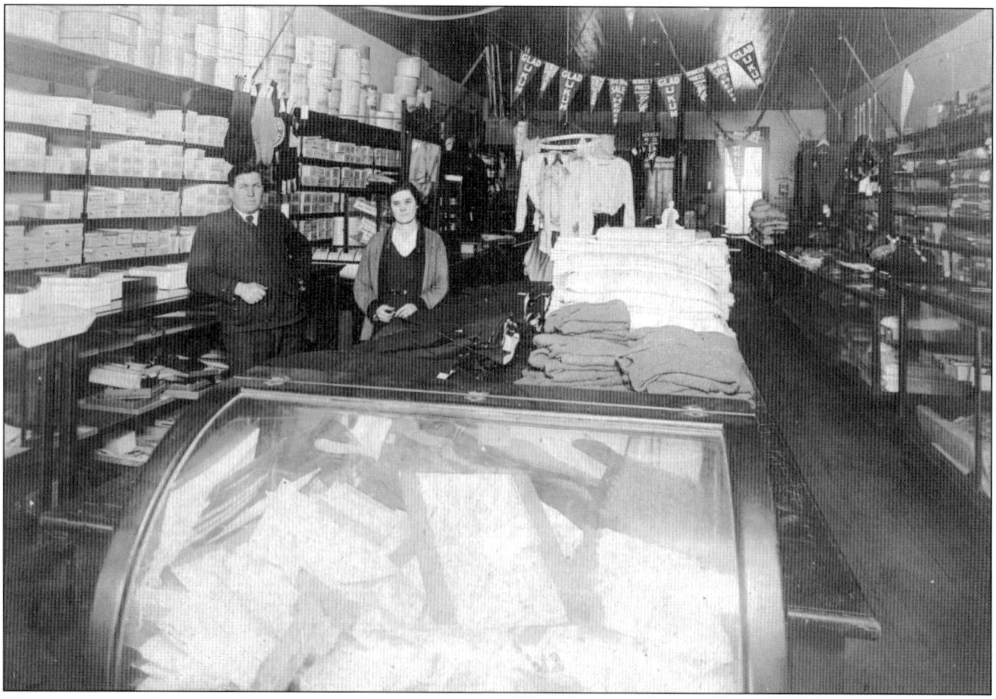

The interior of the W.T. Bean Dry Goods store illustrates the wide variety of products offered for sale. Overhead banners proclaim "The Big Sale Is Here" as display cases and cabinets are filled to capacity with shoes, sweaters, trousers, and dresses. The volume of merchandise available for purchase was so great that the brooms being sold had to be hung from the ceiling to the left of the banners. (City of Clanton.)

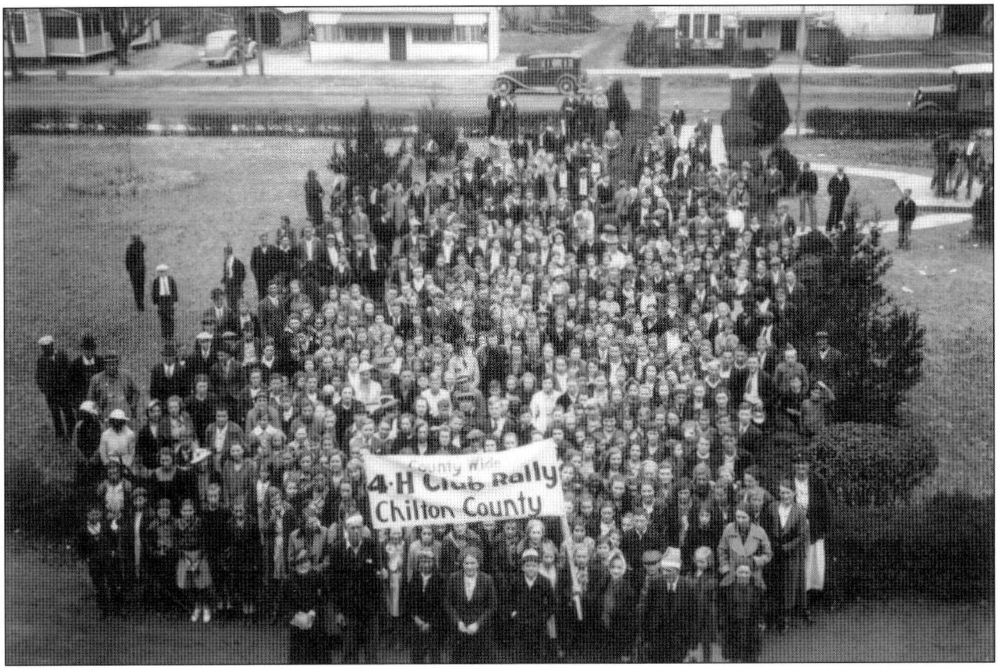

The Annual 4-H Club Rally attracted members from throughout Chilton County. Hundreds of young men and women enjoyed a day of programs and activities designed to build better citizenship. Sponsored by the Clanton Kiwanis Club, the event included judging of the most original and worthwhile projects of the various clubs. The winner received a $5 shrubbery award for his or her local school. (Kim Gillespie.)

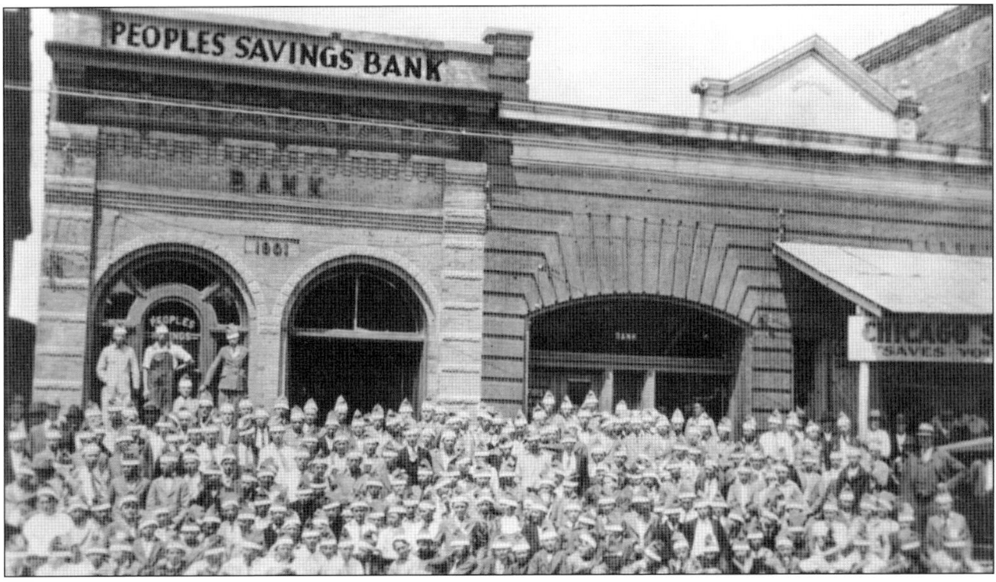

In April 1928, three hundred members of Chilton County 4-H clubs attended a rally in Clanton. Gathering at the high school, the group listened to inspirational talks given by leading citizens. Marching to downtown in parade fashion, members were treated to free ice cream and a movie. The group then assembled in front of the Peoples Savings Bank and adjoining First National Bank buildings for a photograph. (Chilton County Extension Office.)

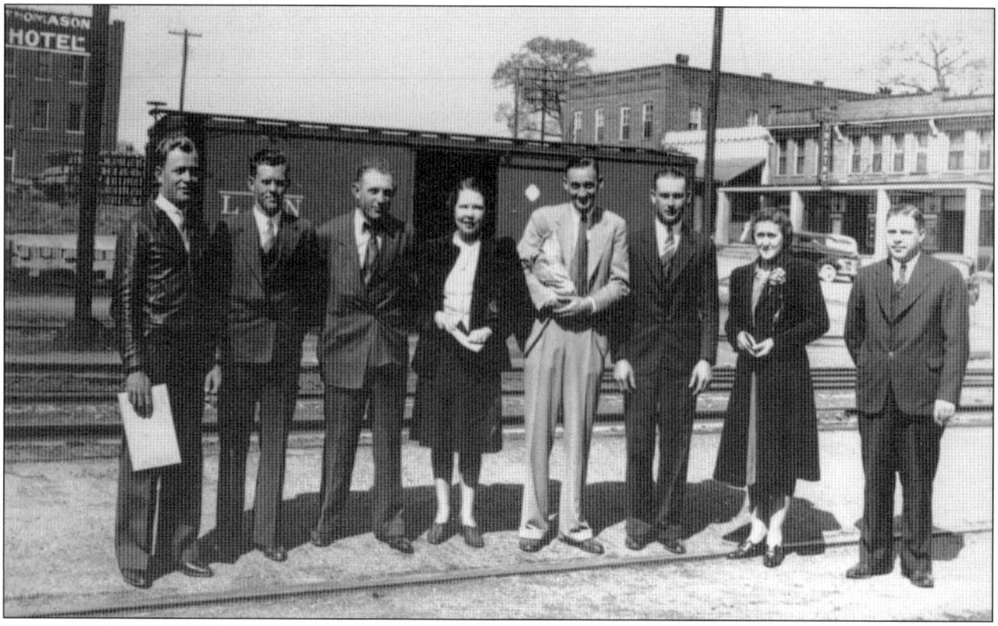

Prior to the Second World War, the Louisville & Nashville Railroad Depot served as the transportation hub for residents of Clanton traveling in and beyond Chilton County. Overnight service to the cities of Chicago, Cincinnati, and New Orleans was available using Pullman sleeping and dining cars. This 1941 image was taken from the platform of the depot. (City of Clanton.)

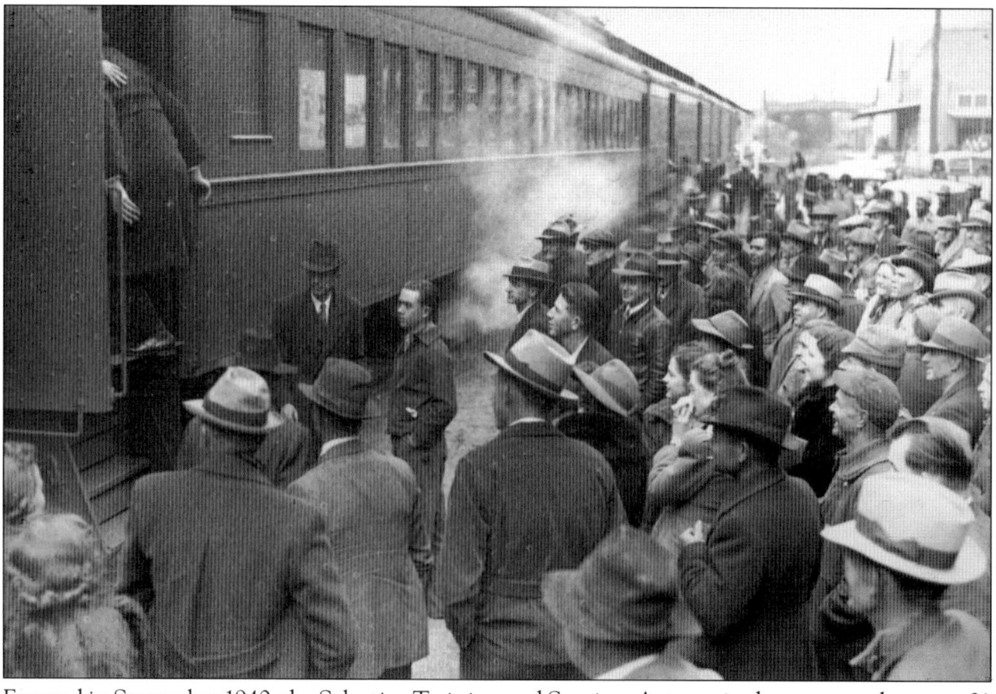

Enacted in September 1940, the Selective Training and Services Act required young men between 21 and 35 years of age to register for the first peacetime conscription in US history. Friends and family gathered at the Louisville & Nashville Railroad Depot in Clanton in April 1941 to say goodbye as young draftees departed home for service in the nation's armed forces. (City of Clanton.)

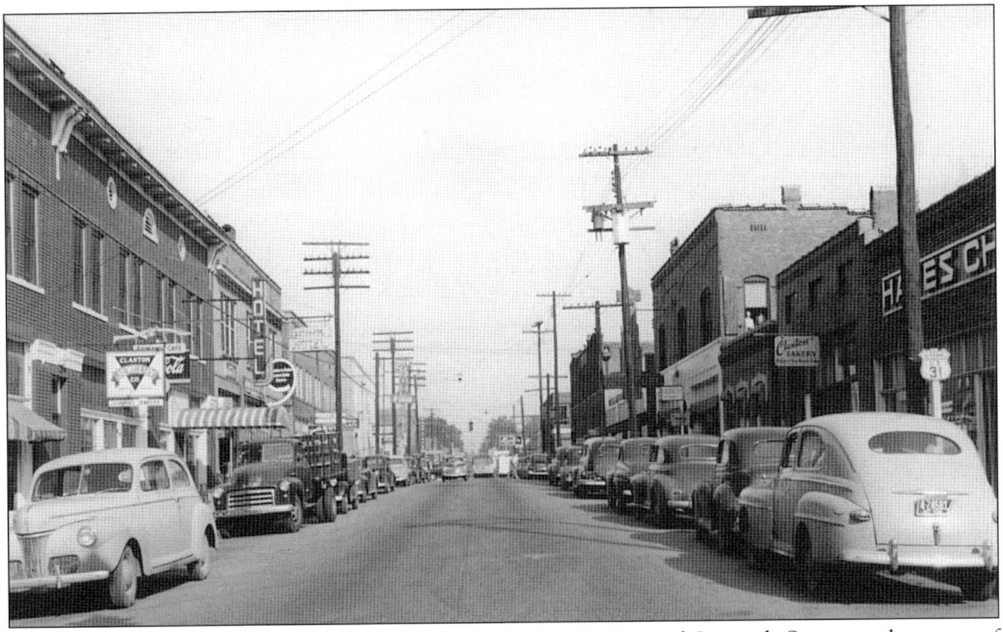

In February 1925, the Alabama Highway Commission designated Seventh Street as the route of the new state highway through Clanton. In subsequent years, Highway 31 would replace Second Avenue North as the main thoroughfare in Clanton. In 1947, advertising along Seventh Street enticed travelers to stop at the Exchange Hotel and Café, Hotel Willingham, or Clanton Bakery to enjoy a delicious meal or comfortable lodging. (Kim Gillespie.)

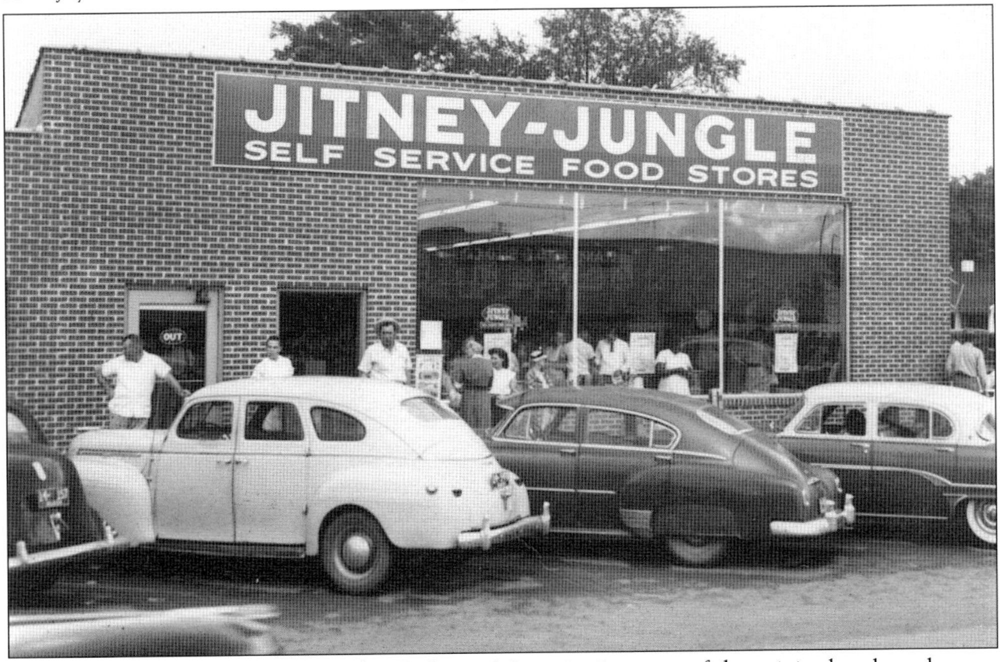

The Jitney Jungle chain originated in Jackson, Mississippi, as one of the original cash-and-carry, self-serve food markets. The name was derived from the concept that the customer could save a jitney (a nickel) for every 25¢ spent on a jungle of bargains. The Jitney Jungle that served Clanton was near the intersection of Sixth Street and Third Avenue North. (City of Clanton.)

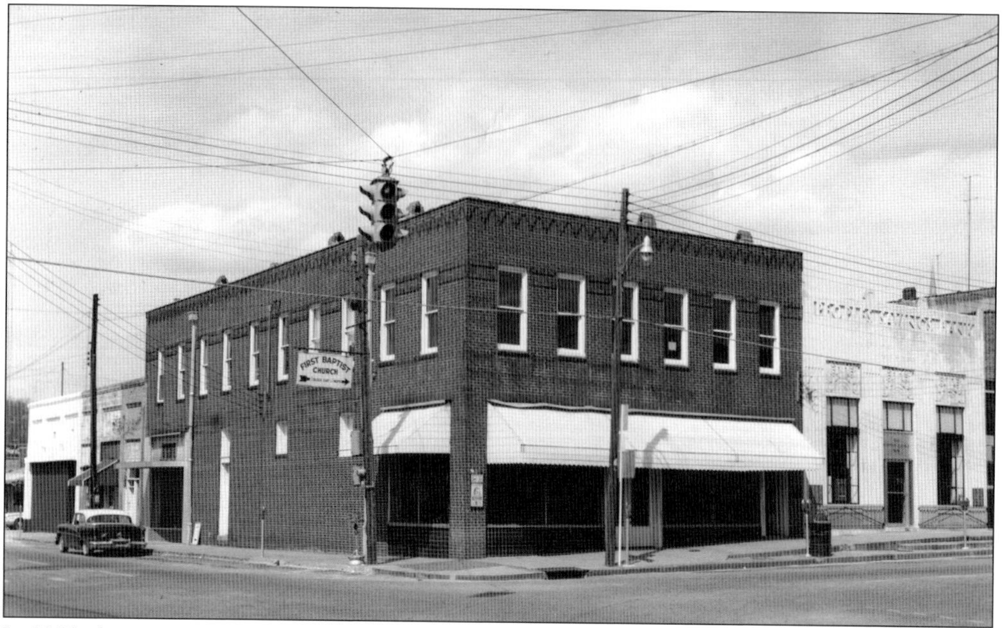

In 1935, the new Moore Building was constructed on the former site of the W.I. Mullins Building. The lower floor of the new all-brick building was leased to the Great Atlantic & Pacific Tea Company (A&P) grocery store. In the upstairs section, the Modern Beauty Shoppe and Modern Beauty School offered the latest innovations in beauty culture, including the Royal Patricia permanent waving machine. (Richard Moore.)

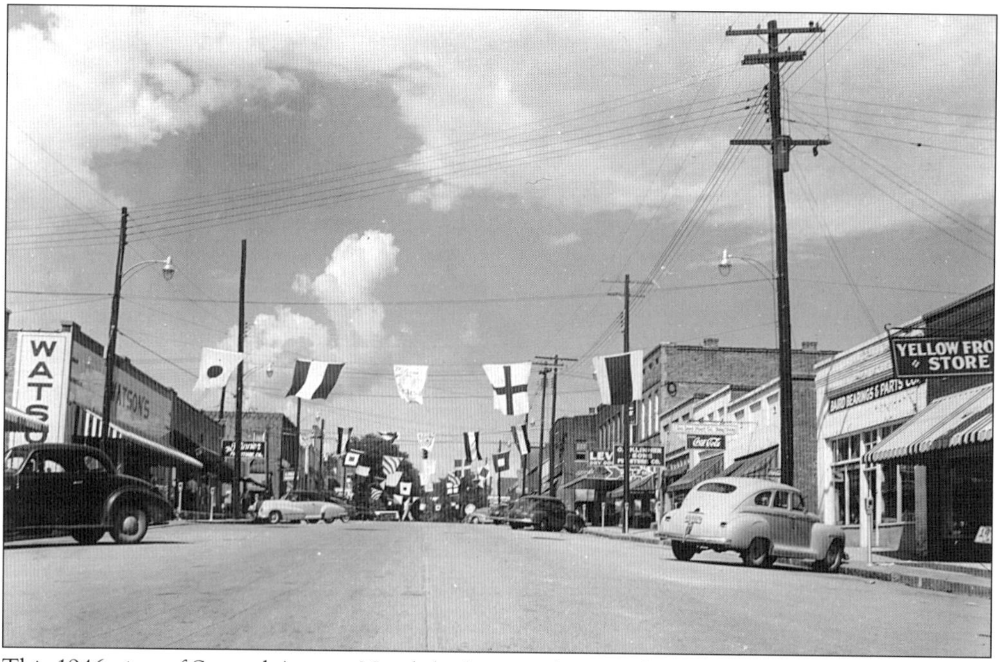

This 1946 view of Second Avenue North looking to the east shows the Yellow Front Store, part of a chain operated by the Sumter Farm and Stock Company that specialized in groceries and general merchandise. The chain was known for its Live and Let Live pricing. The O. P. Klinner and Sons Furniture Store and Levin's Dry Goods are also visible. (City of Clanton.)

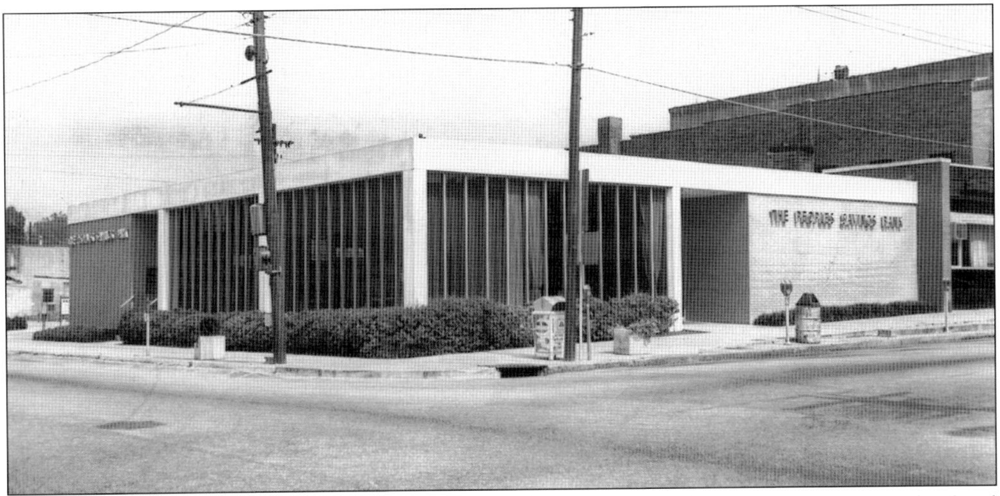

In April 1964, the corner of Second Avenue North and Seventh Street again became the focal point of progress in downtown Clanton. The Moore Building was demolished to create space for an expansion of the Peoples Savings Bank. In 1985, a second floor was added. The Peoples Savings Bank, later renamed Peoples Southern Bank, has served the residents of Chilton County for more than 115 years. (Richard Moore.)

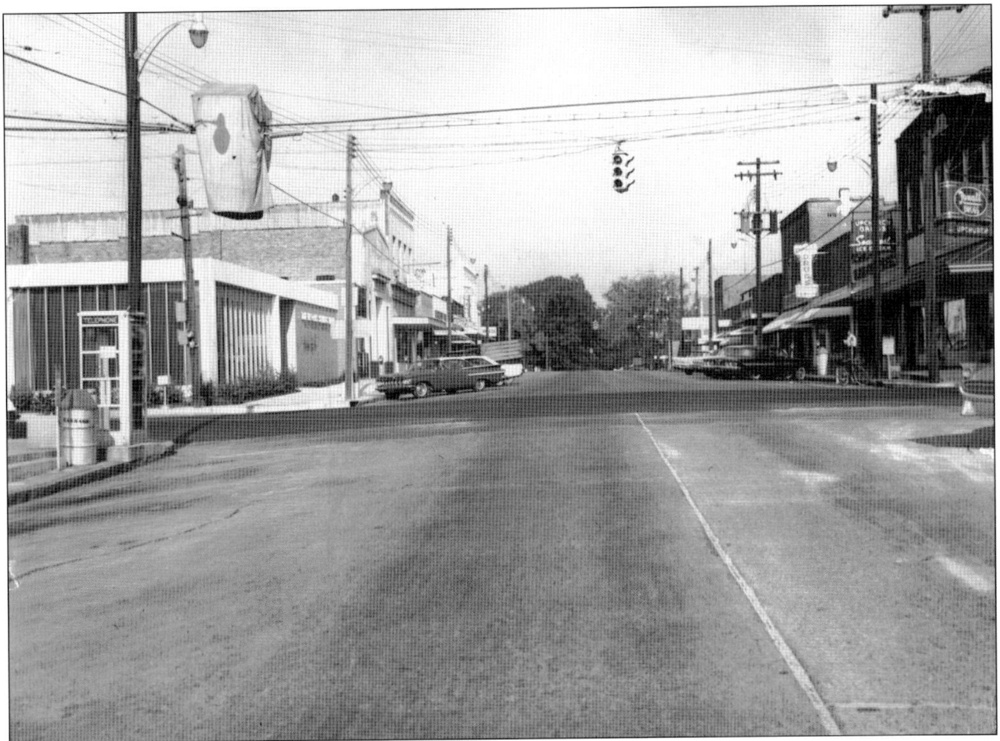

This view of the intersection of Second Avenue North and Seventh Street shows the new single-story Peoples Savings Bank (left) and Upchurch Drug Company on the opposite corner. Located next to the Upchurch Drug Company are the V.J. Elmore Store, Alred Drugs, and the Thrifty Store. The telephone booth visible in the image is now a rapidly disappearing aspect of modern culture. (City of Clanton.)

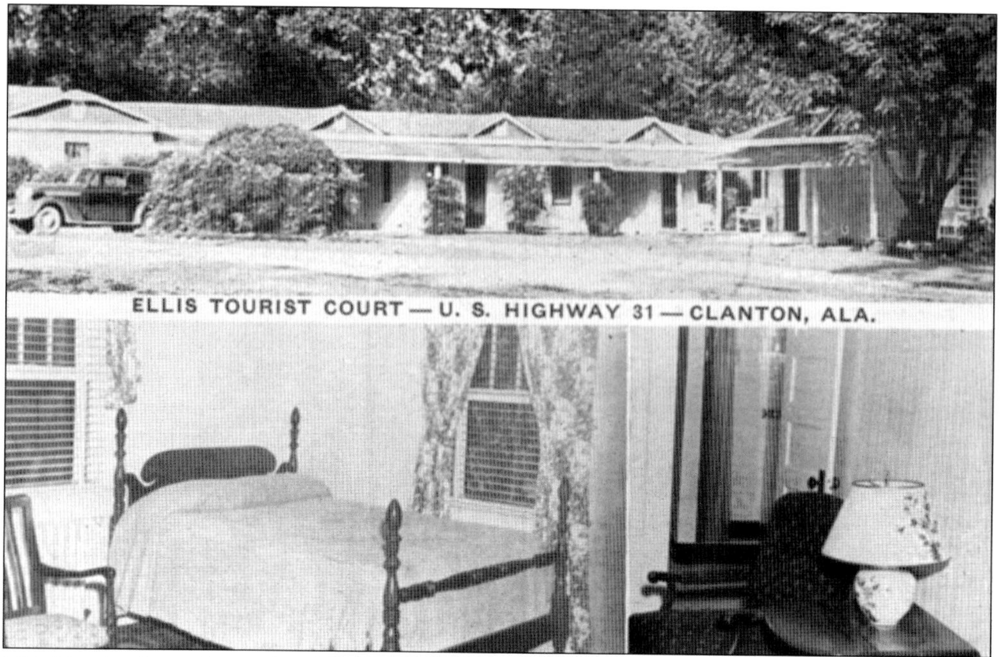

Ellis Tourist Court, located on Highway 31 in Clanton, was advertised as the "Best Stop between Key West and the North Pole!" Every cottage included a private bath. Travelers could make a reservation at the Ellis Tourist Court by asking the operator to dial Clanton 571 to reach the front desk. For guests who preferred a fireproof, fully carpeted, air-cooled room with tile baths and modern Panelray heat, the Cloverleaf Motel was conveniently located on Highway 31 one mile south of Clanton. Prior to the completion of the interstate, Highway 31 was the main thoroughfare through Chilton County, with hotels, motels, restaurants, and service stations located along the route in Verbena, Clanton, Lomax, Thorsby, and Jemison. These businesses supported the economies of their local communities. (Both, author's collection.)

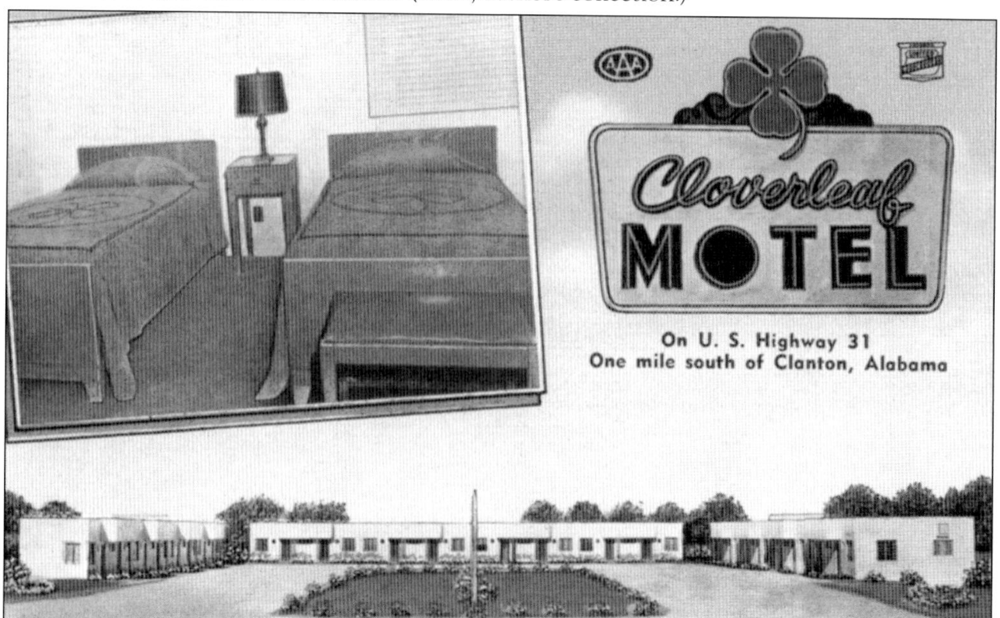

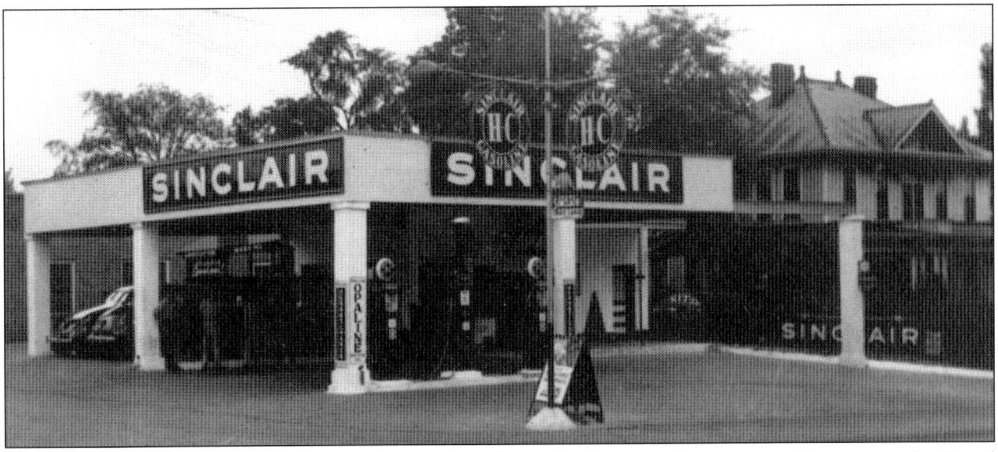

The Sinclair full-service station was located on Seventh Street in downtown Clanton and offered a complete line of automobile services for the traveling public. Sinclair Houston Concentrate (HC) was the original high-octane premium gasoline for motorcars. Opaline brand motor oil ensured long engine life and low oil consumption. The company trademark, Dino the dinosaur, adorns the Sinclair sign near the center of the photograph. (City of Clanton.)

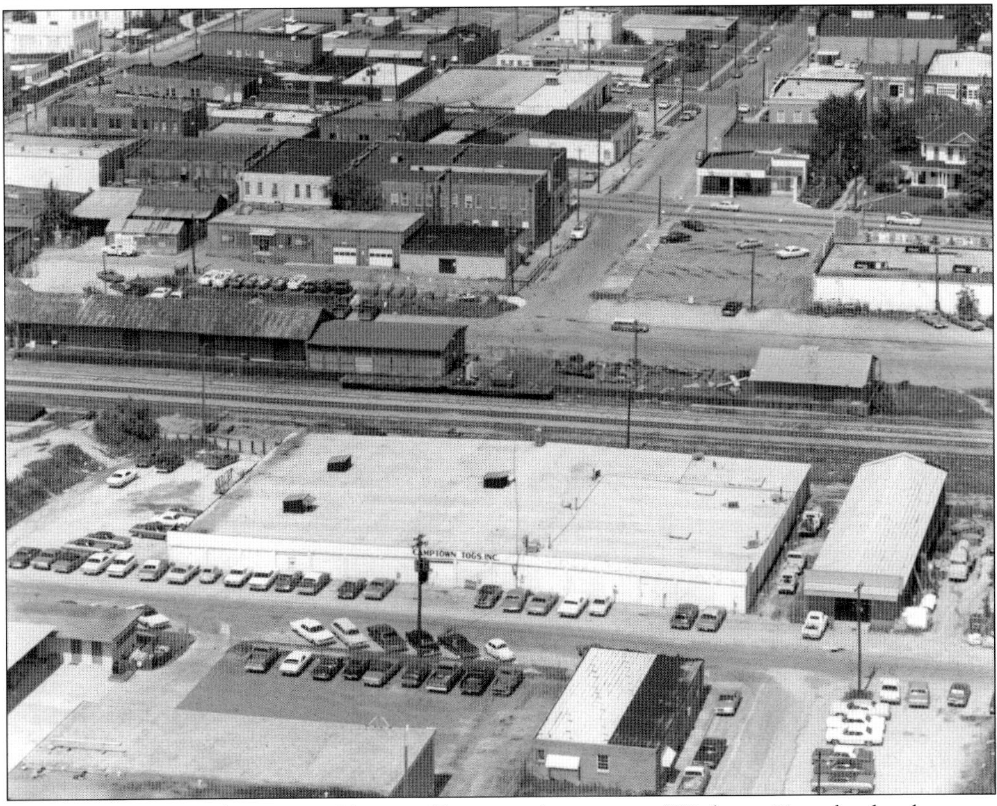

This aerial image of downtown Clanton illustrates the impact of Highway 31on the development of the city. By 1967, passenger service on the Louisville & Nashville Railroad had ended, even though the depot was still being utilized for shipments of freight. Older homes along Seventh Street had been replaced by businesses created to provide services to travelers on Highway 31. (Chilton County Chamber of Commerce.)

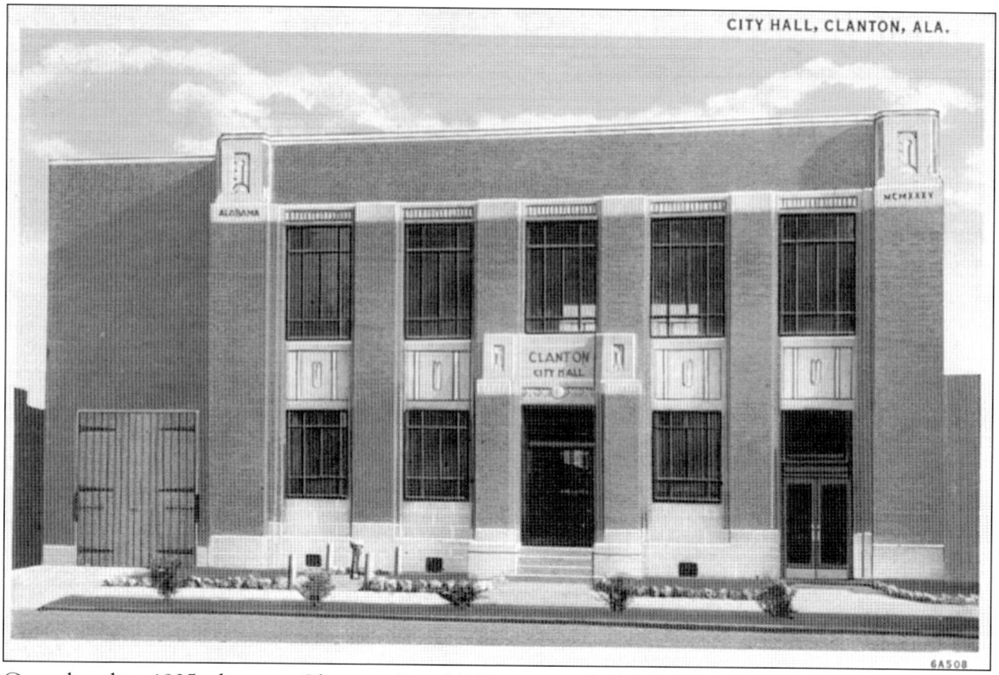

Completed in 1935, the new Clanton City Hall consisted of adequate space for the offices of all city officials, a jail, a library, a courtroom, and a public auditorium. Funding for the new structure was obtained through the Works Progress Administration (WPA), a public works program of the federal government. (ADAH.)

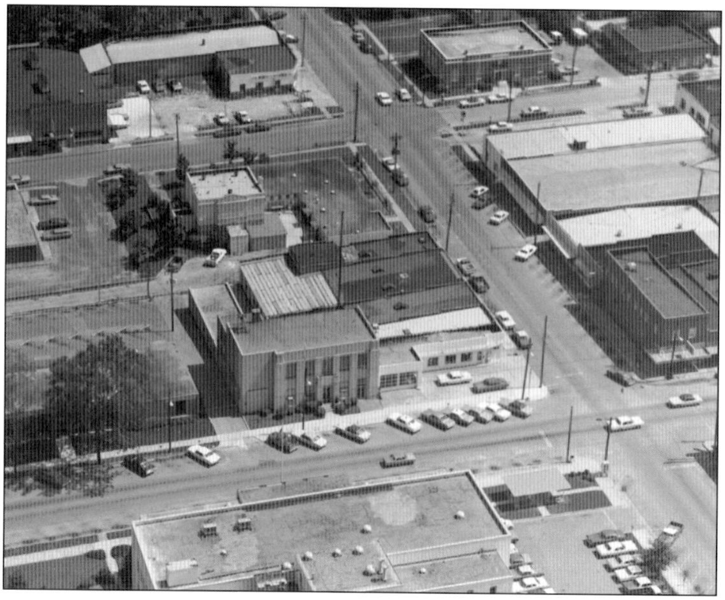

This aerial view shows the recently constructed Clanton City Hall. To the immediate right of the structure is the Woco Pep automobile service station, at the corner of Second Avenue North and Sixth Street. An expansion of the city hall building, completed in March 1975, occupies the former site of the Woco Pep station. The new county jail is visible behind the city hall building. (Chilton County Chamber of Commerce.)

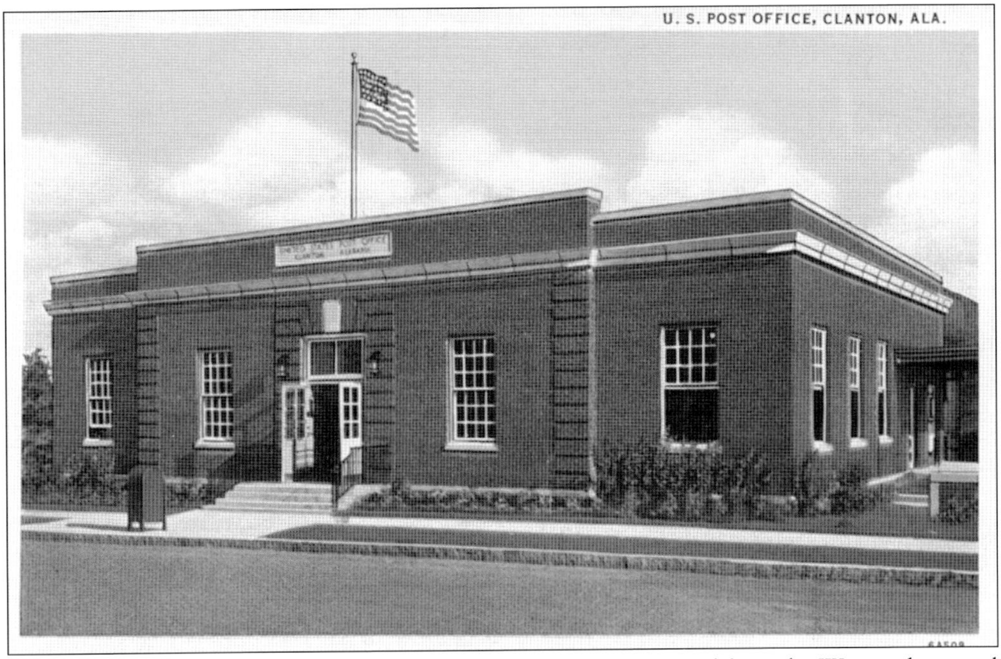

Established in May 1871, the first post office in Clanton received mail from the Wetumpka postal route on a weekly basis. The new post office building, completed in 1935, included five service windows for the distribution of stamps, money orders, parcel post, and registered mail. The limestone and brick structure was described by the *Union Banner* newspaper as one of the most attractive federal buildings located between Birmingham and Montgomery. (Author's collection.)

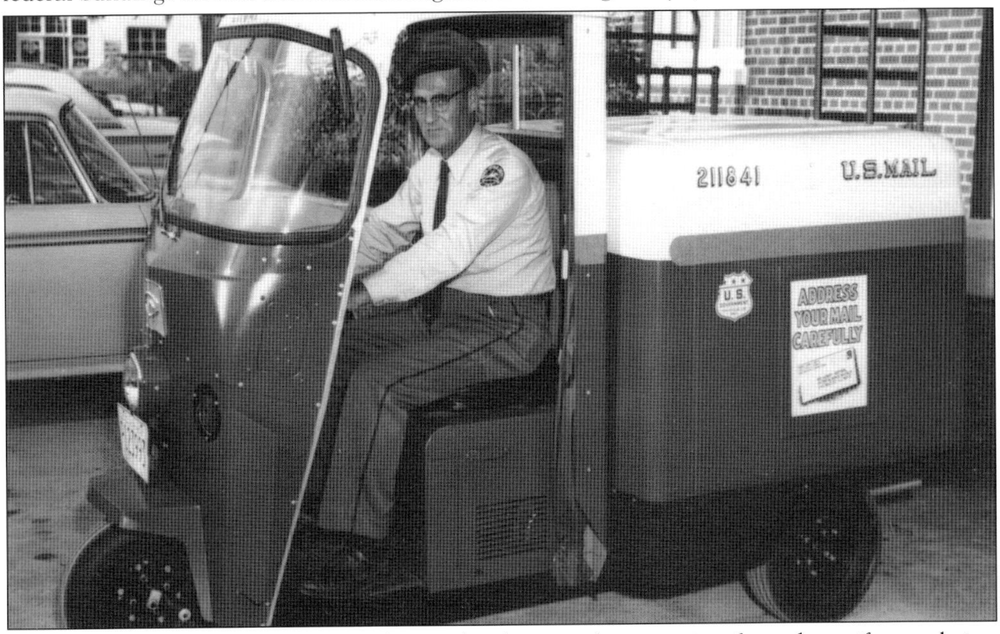

Neither snow nor rain nor heat nor gloom of night stays these couriers from the swift completion of their appointed rounds. Increasing volumes of mail and the growth of suburban areas created the need for motorized vehicles for mail delivery. The three-wheeled Mailster was utilized for more than 10 years in Clanton to deliver mail in a cost-efficient and timely manner. (City of Clanton.)

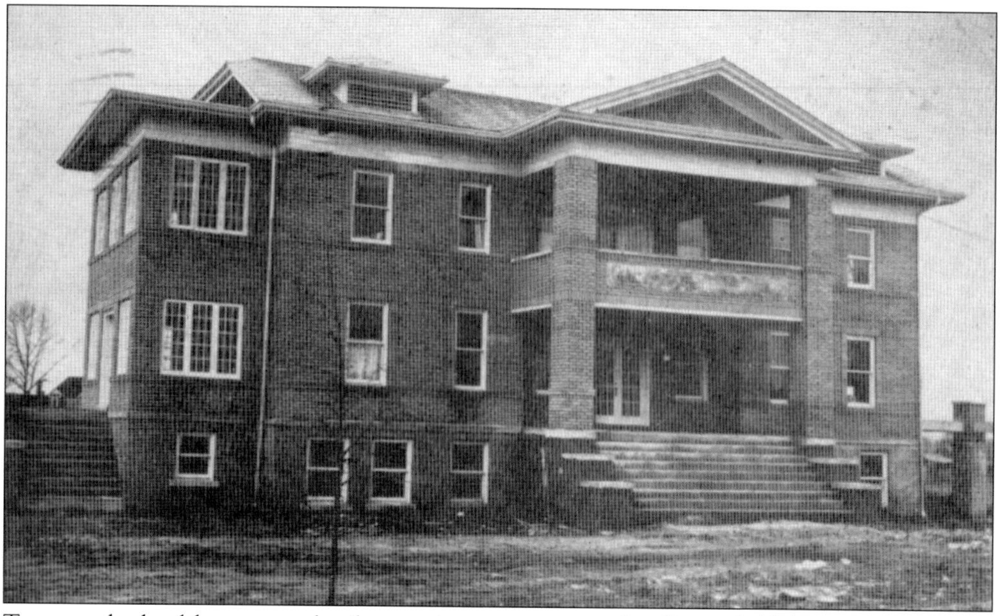

To meet the health-care needs of a growing community, the Central Alabama Hospital was incorporated in 1921 by Dr. V.J. Gragg and a group of local investors. Dr. Gragg served as president of the hospital for the first 25 years of operation. The hospital was located on a spacious and attractive parcel of property on Fifth Avenue. The facility closed as construction of the new hospital was completed. (Kim Gillespie.)

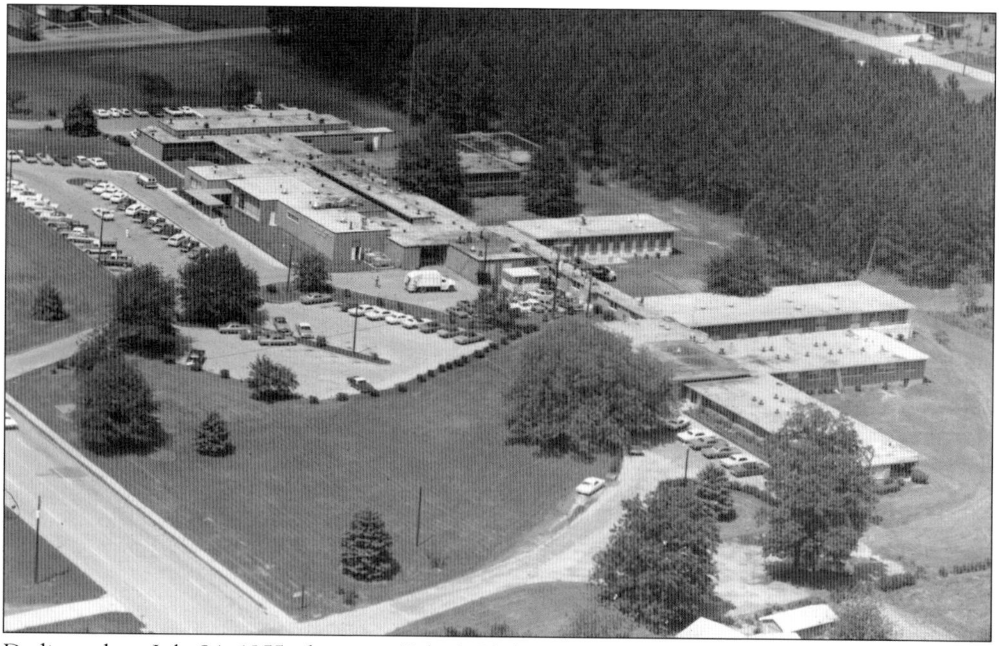

Dedicated on July 24, 1955, the new 40-bed Chilton County Hospital was constructed under provisions of the Hill-Burton Act to increase the availability of health care throughout the United States. Two years later, a 30-bed nursing home facility was added to care for elderly patients. In February 1960, the hospital was expanded to accommodate 10 additional beds. This hospital facility served the community for 56 years. (Chilton County Chamber of Commerce.)

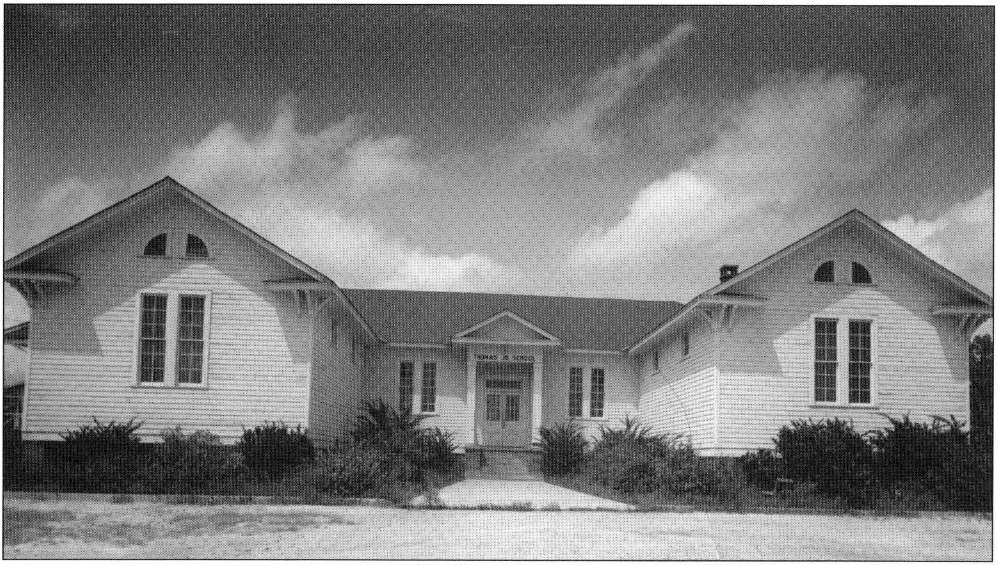

Like other community schools in Chilton County, the Thomas Junior High School was a frame building with four classrooms. Folding doors that separated the classrooms could be opened to allow the space to be used as an auditorium. The school was constructed in 1927 on land donated by Will Thomas. Located four miles south of Clanton, the Thomas school replaced older schools at Bethel, Maple Springs, and Popular Springs. (CCBE.)

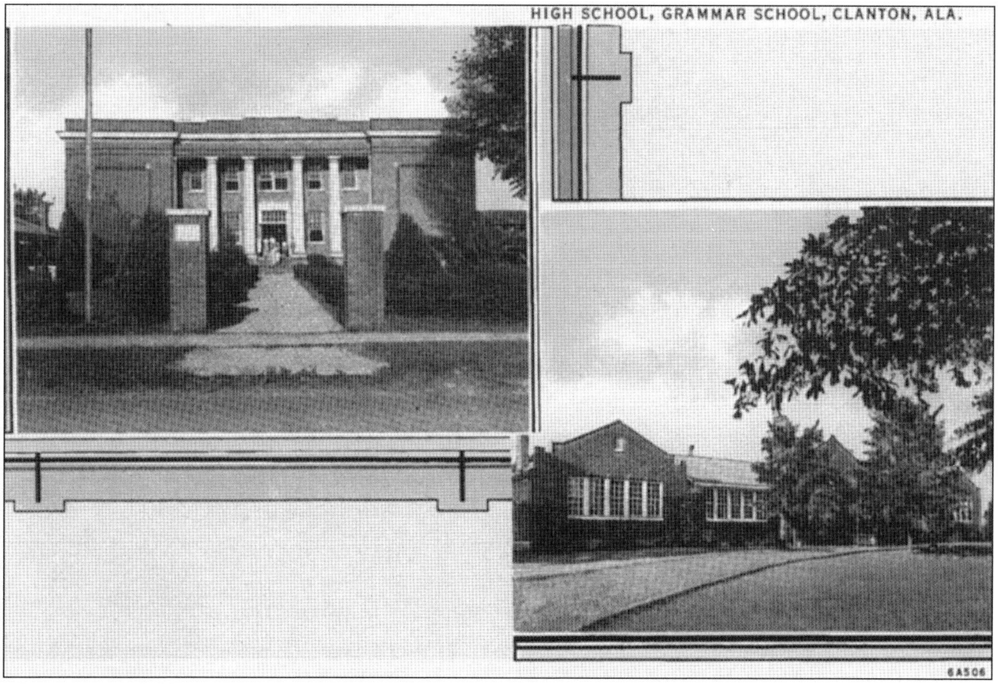

This postcard illustrates the new all-brick grammar and high school buildings in Clanton. The Chilton County High School was constructed in 1914 following a decision by the Alabama High School Commission to locate the facility in Clanton as opposed to Jemison. The high school was constructed on the former Gowan site, east of town between the Clanton Cemetery and Higgins Ferry Road. (ADAH.)

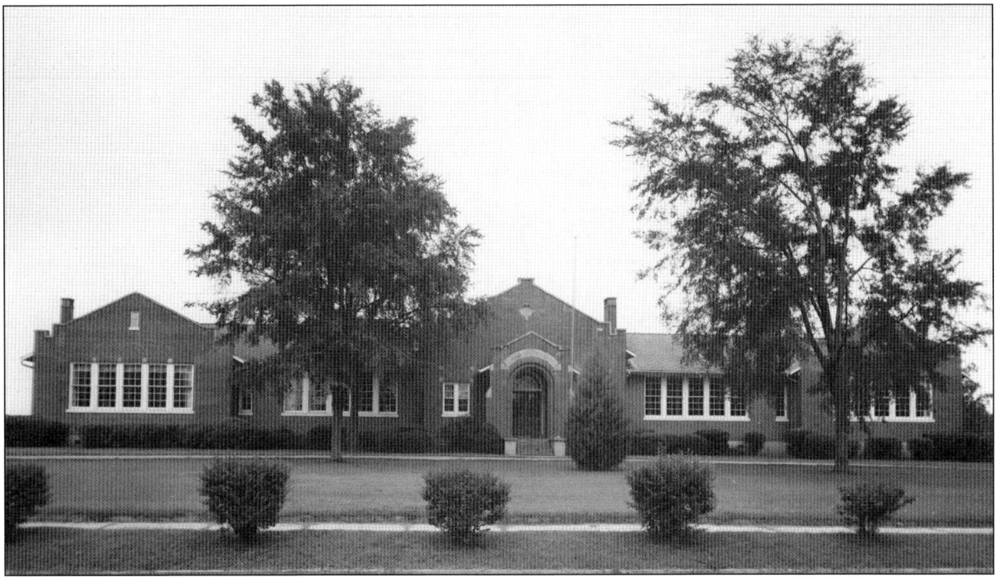

The Clanton Grammar School was constructed in 1928 on Fifth Avenue North. The structure replaced the original frame building on the same site. The school was permanently closed in 1973 and was later utilized as an emergency assistance center as well as a meeting place for senior citizens. In August 1999, the structure was destroyed by fire. (CCBE.)

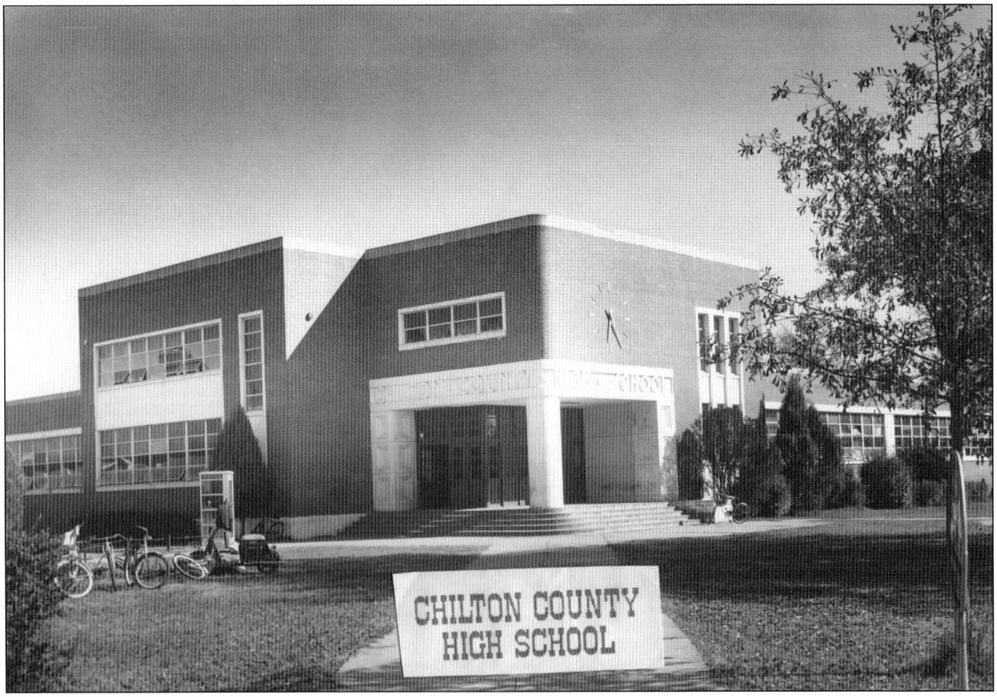

In November 1938, the main building of the Chilton County High School was destroyed by fire. A new, modern structure was opened in September 1940. The school served the city of Clanton until 1962, when a new high school was completed. The buildings of the former high school were utilized as the Henry M. Adair Junior High School and, subsequently, a middle school before being demolished. (CCBE.)

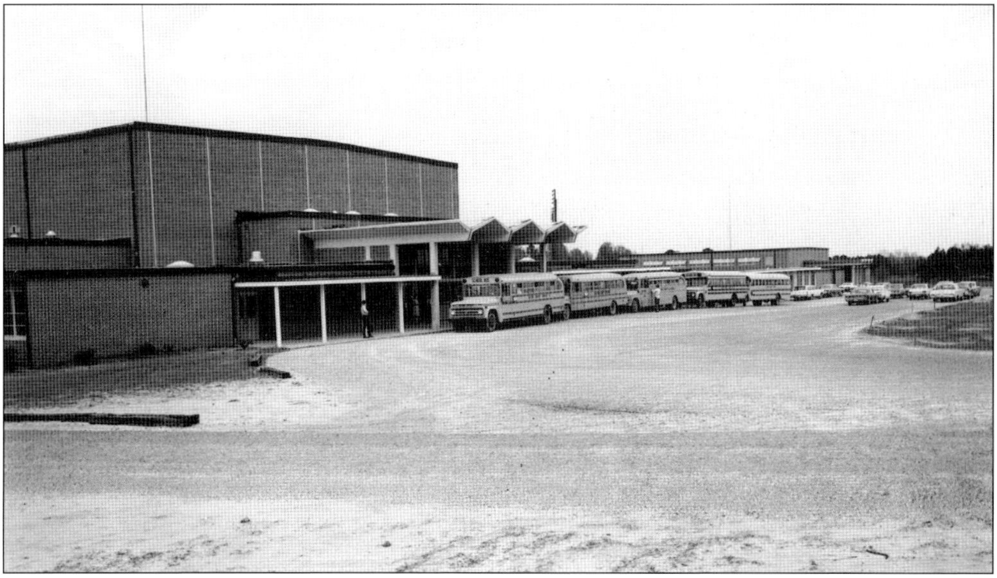

The new Chilton County High School was constructed in 1962 adjacent to Highway 31 to the south of Clanton. The facility was first opened to students at the beginning of the 1962–1963 school year. In 1967, a new gymnasium was added to the school. In subsequent years, the Clanton Elementary and Middle Schools were relocated in proximity to the high school. (City of Clanton.)

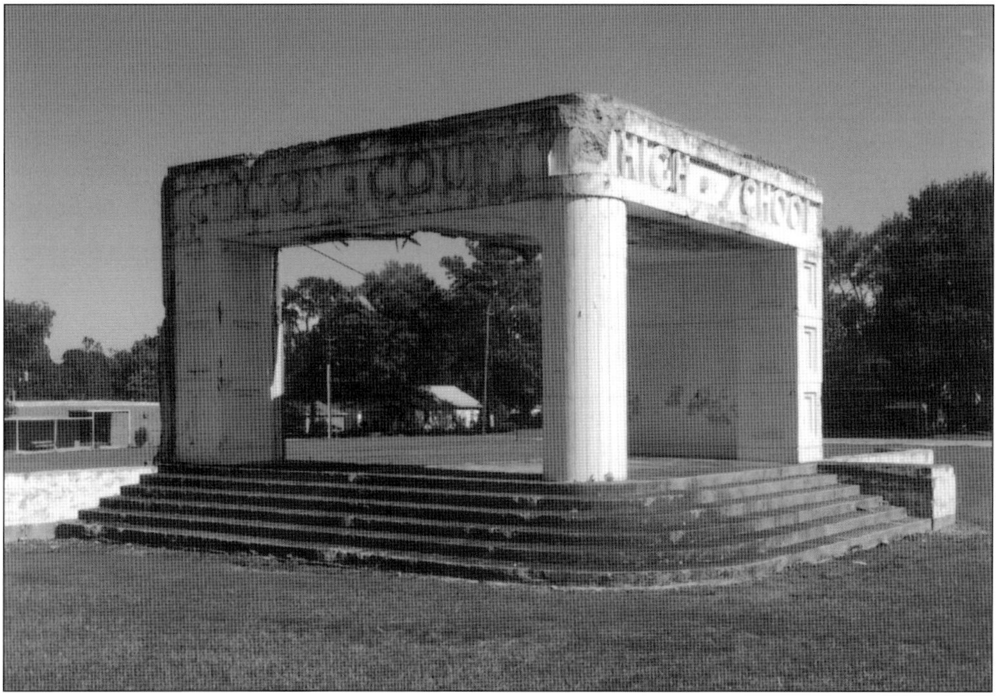

In March 2006, the buildings of the former high school were demolished after serving the educational needs of the community for more than six decades. For the first time in more than 90 years, the parcel of property at the corner of First Street and Higgins Ferry Road was bare. The columns were left standing as a tribute to the former students and faculty of the school. (Author's collection.)

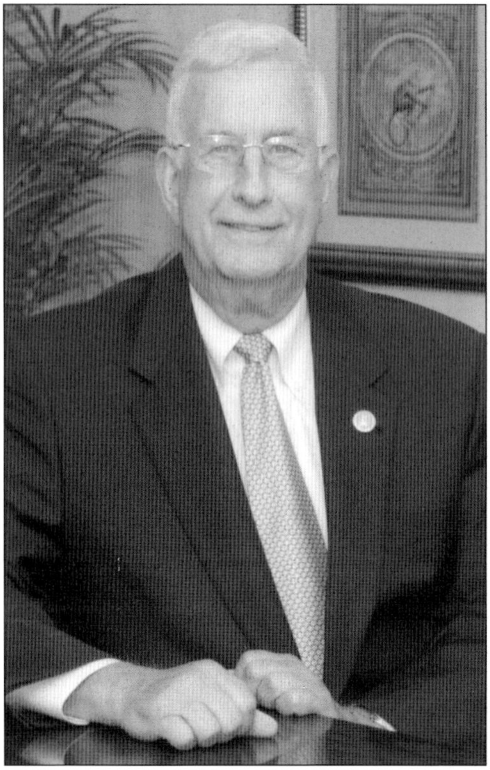

In May 2011, *Business Alabama Magazine* named Billy Joe Driver one of Alabama's Favorite Mayors. Elected in 1984, Driver has served eight terms and more than 30 years as mayor of Clanton. First elected to the city council in 1972, Driver has never been defeated in a local election. A city employee since 1953, he has served the residents of Clanton for more than 60 years. (Becky Tucker.)

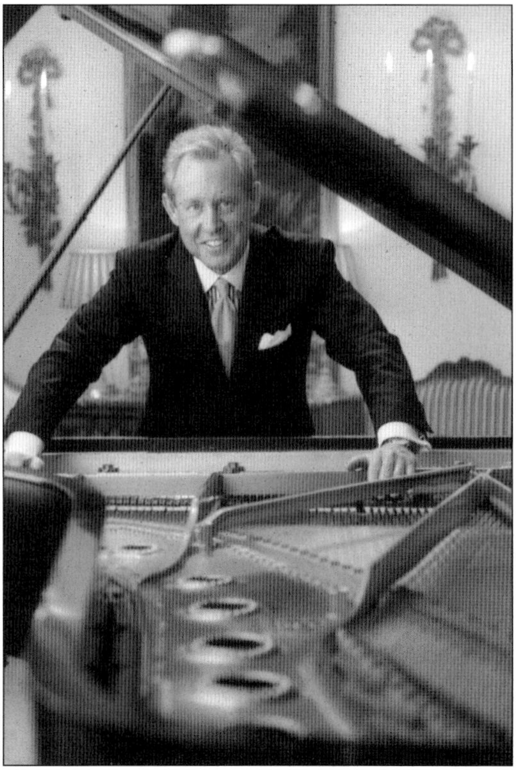

Randall Atcheson began piano lessons at six years of age. Enrolled at Samford University at age 12, Atcheson was later accepted at the Julliard School, becoming the first student allowed to pursue and receive simultaneous degrees in piano and organ performance. He made his debut at Carnegie Hall in 1991 and performed in that venue 12 times. Atcheson has performed on five continents and recorded 16 albums. (Randall Atcheson.)

Minter Carney "Jackie" Hayes was born July 19, 1906, in Clanton. A graduate of Chilton County High School, Hayes played second base for the University of Alabama before making his professional baseball debut in August 1925 with the Washington Senators. In 1932, Hayes joined the Chicago White Sox, where he became known as the best double-play second baseman in baseball. After prematurely losing his eyesight to the effects of glaucoma, Hayes retired from baseball. He returned to Chilton County and was elected to the office of tax collector, a position he held for more than a decade. In August 1946, Hayes was honored with Jackie Hayes Day at Comiskey Park, home of the Chicago White Sox. In 1976, he became the first resident of Chilton County to be inducted into the Alabama Sports Hall of Fame. (Both, author's collection.)

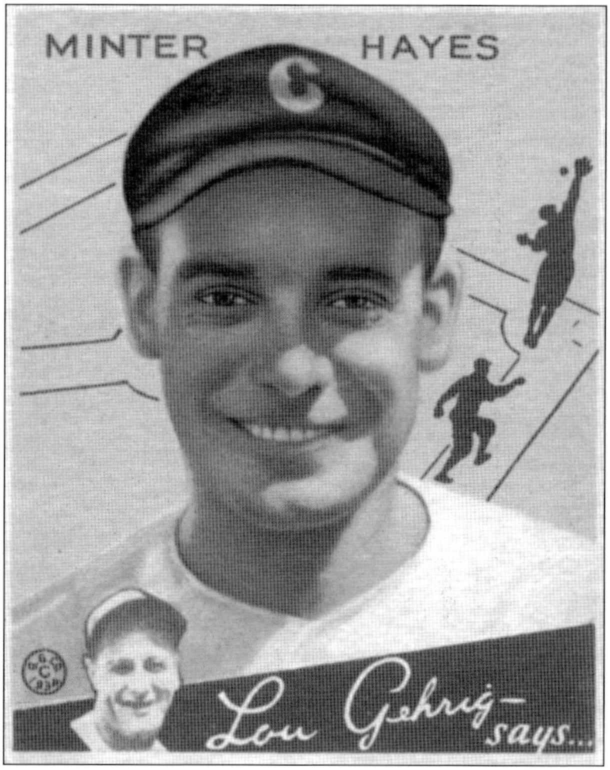

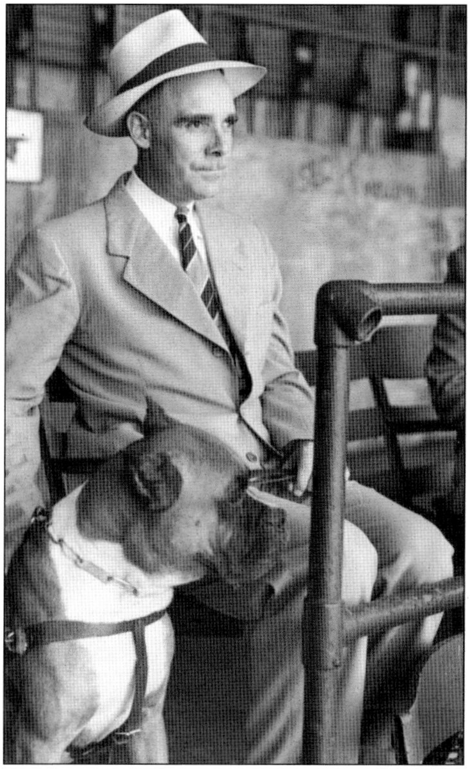

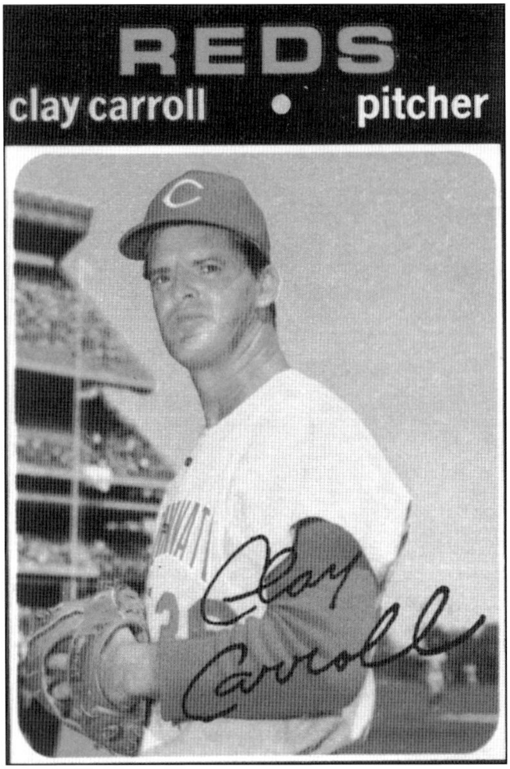

Clay Palmer Carroll was born on May 2, 1941, in Clanton. The son of a cotton mill worker, Carroll made his professional baseball debut with the Milwaukee Brewers. Considered one of the best relief pitchers in professional baseball, Carroll appeared in three World Series games and was the winning pitcher for the Cincinnati Reds in Game 7 of the 1975 World Series. A two-time National League All-Star, Carroll set the record for 37 games won as a closing pitcher, a mark that stood for 12 years. Before retirement in 1979, Carroll played for the Chicago White Sox and the Pittsburgh Pirates. In 1980, Clay Carroll was inducted into the Cincinnati Reds Hall of Fame. In 1992, Carroll joined Jackie Hayes as an inductee into the Alabama Sports Hall of Fame. (Both, author's collection.)

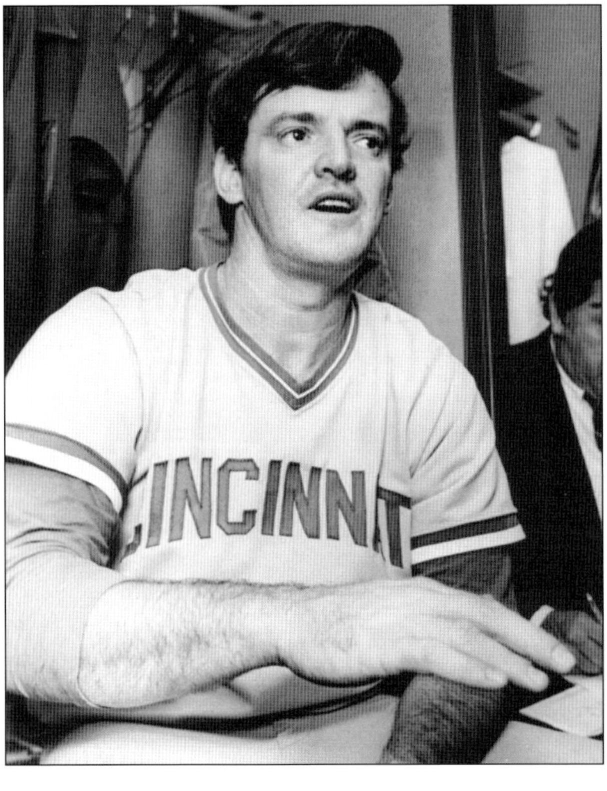

Four

Jemison

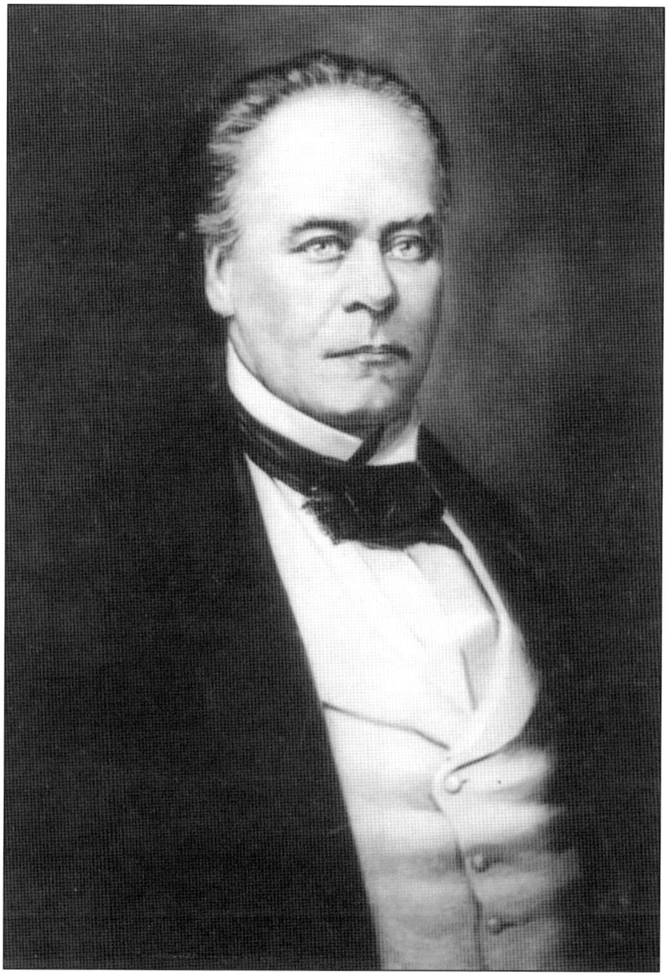

Born in Lincoln County, Georgia, Robert Jemison Jr. (1802–1871) co-owned and operated the Jemison, Powell, Ficklen & Company Stage Line. A pioneer industrialist and entrepreneur, Jemison was instrumental in the development of the city of Birmingham and the mineral district of Alabama. Jemison served as a member of the Alabama Senate and Confederate Congress. Originally incorporated in 1907, the town of Jemison is named in his honor. (ADAH.)

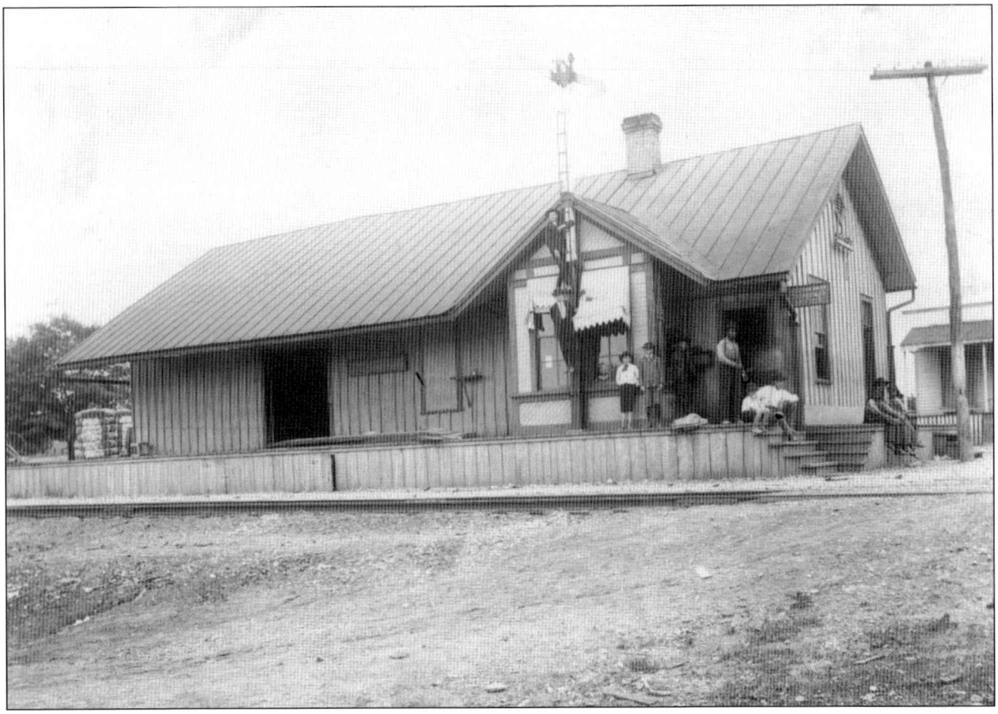

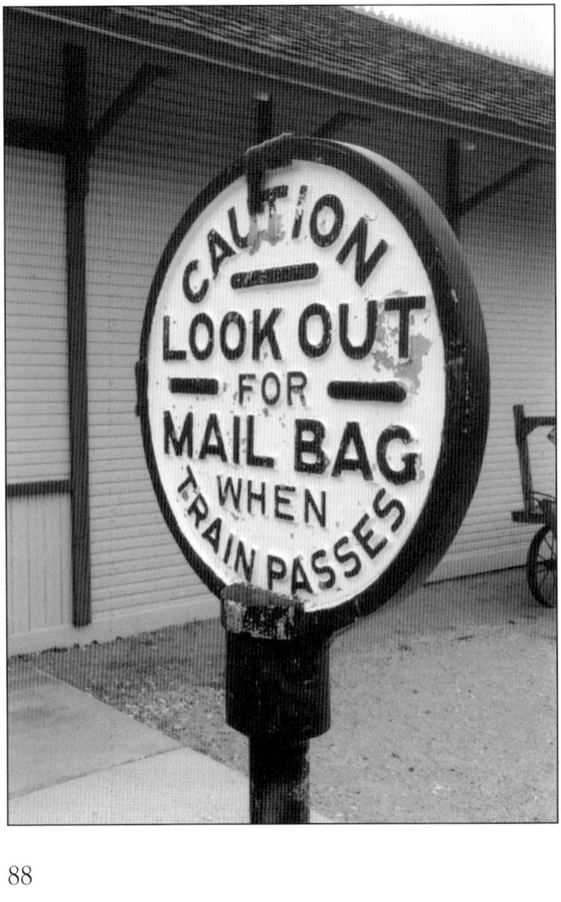

Originally known as Langston Station, the town of Jemison was established adjacent to the rail line of the South & North Alabama Railroad. In 1872, a railroad depot was constructed to accommodate passenger, freight, and mail service. The establishment of the railroad was the catalyst that attracted growth to the town, including a hotel, a post office, a sawmill, and numerous merchants. (ADAH.)

Through trains did not always slow down when delivering mail at a scheduled drop point. It was not an uncommon practice for the conductor to throw the mailbag to the waiting station agent or postmaster as the train passed the depot. To prevent injury to bystanders, warning signs were posted at these depots to alert passengers of the danger of mailbags being thrown from moving trains. (Author's collection.)

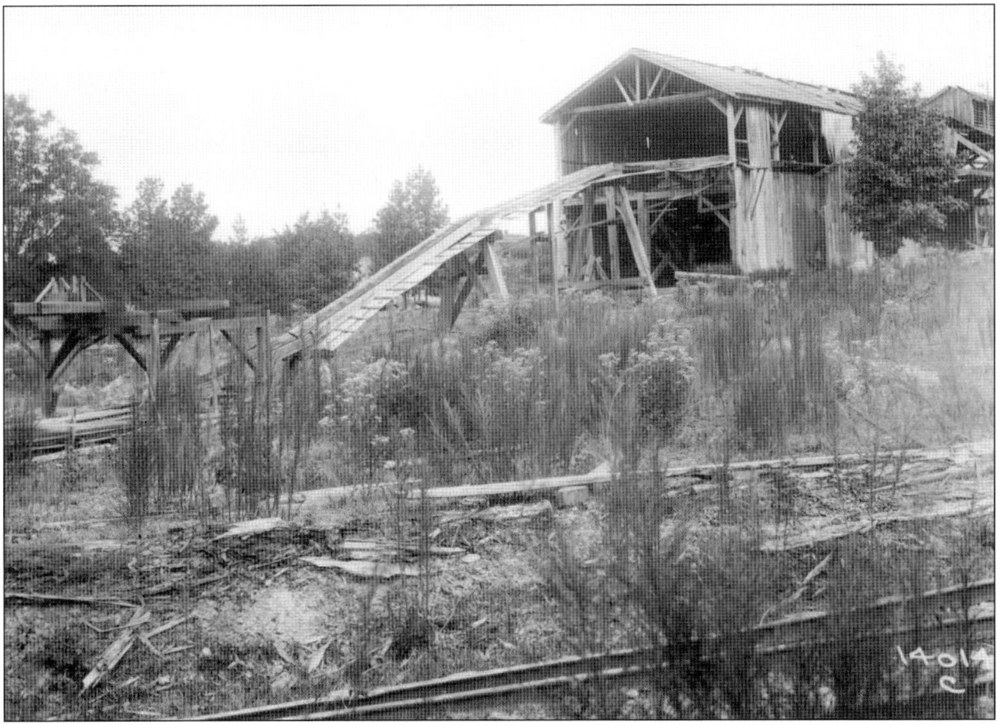

In 1902, the Clear Creek Lumber Company constructed a sawmill at Ocampo, a small settlement located on the Louisville & Nashville rail line five miles north of Jemison. The Clear Creek Lumber Company utilized three locomotives and 23 railcars to harvest timber along 14 miles of track between Ocampo and the Coosa River. The company ceased logging operations in June 1909 and abandoned the mill. (APCA.)

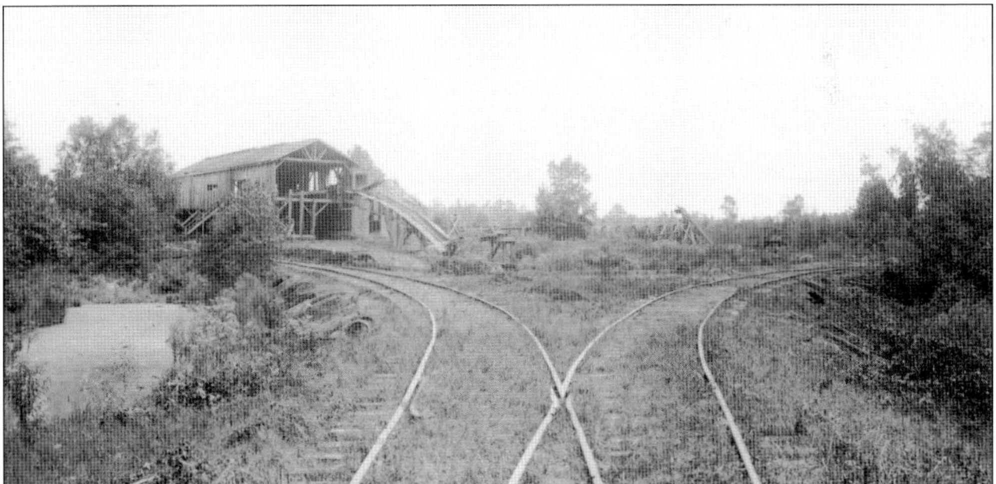

To supply materials for the construction of the first hydroelectric power project in the state, the Alabama Power Company obtained the rights to the former Clear Creek rail line from Ocampo to the Coosa River. Railcars of construction materials arriving at Ocampo on the Louisville & Nashville Railroad were transferred to the rail spur leading to the Lock 12 (Lay Dam) construction site. (APCA.)

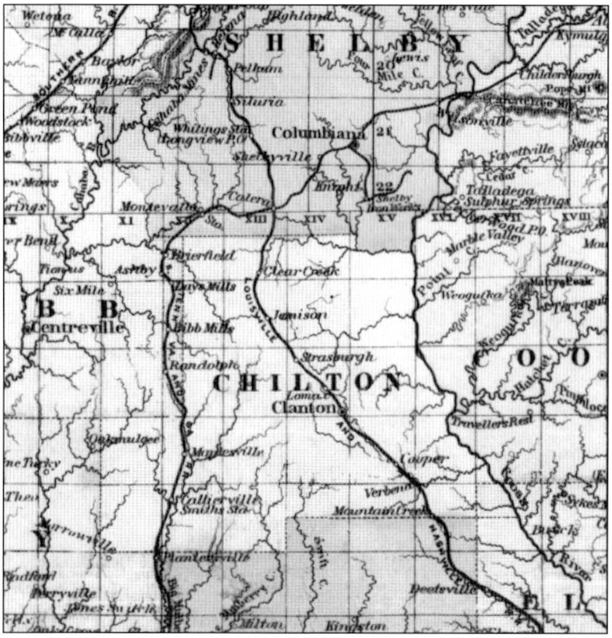

This 1881 map produced by O.W. Gray and Son depicts the town of Jamison on the Louisville & Nashville Railroad between the depots at Strasburgh and Clear Creek in Chilton County. From 1871 until 1890, Jemison was predominantly shown on railroad and other maps as Jamison. Beginning in 1891, the current spelling of the town name was used exclusively. (ADAH.)

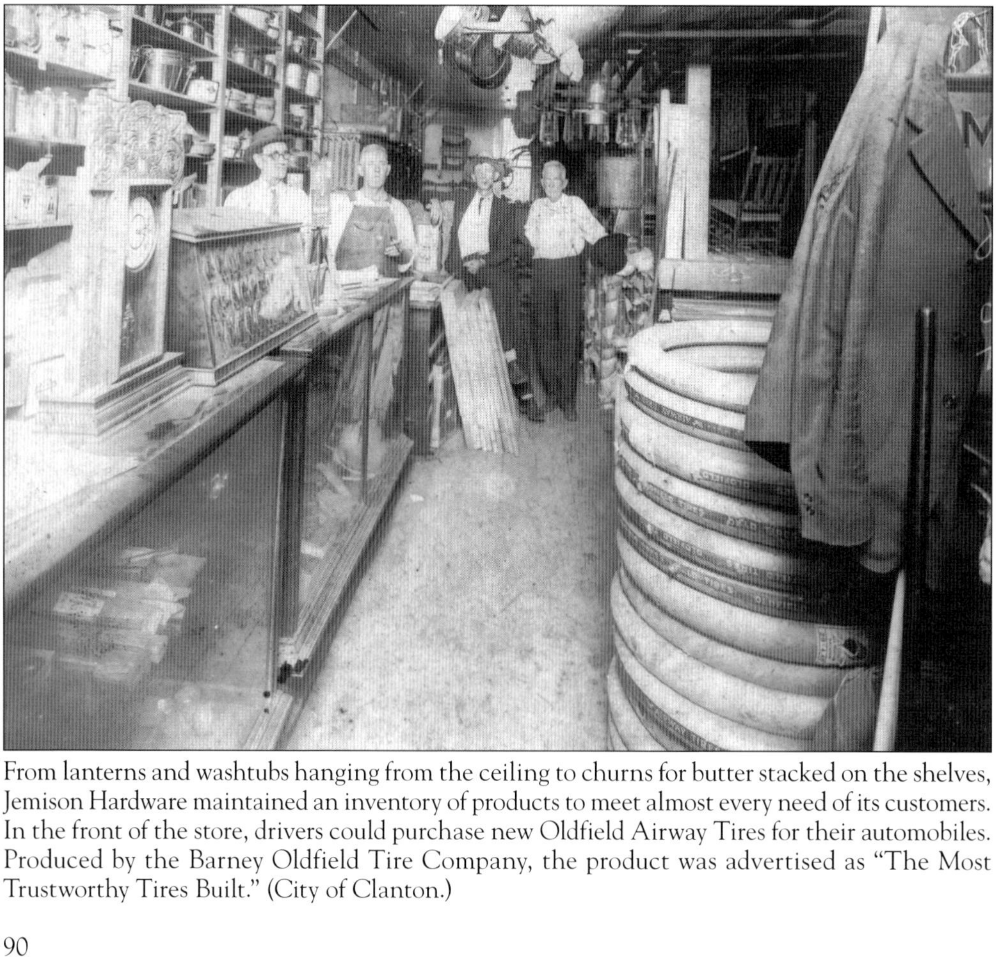

From lanterns and washtubs hanging from the ceiling to churns for butter stacked on the shelves, Jemison Hardware maintained an inventory of products to meet almost every need of its customers. In the front of the store, drivers could purchase new Oldfield Airway Tires for their automobiles. Produced by the Barney Oldfield Tire Company, the product was advertised as "The Most Trustworthy Tires Built." (City of Clanton.)

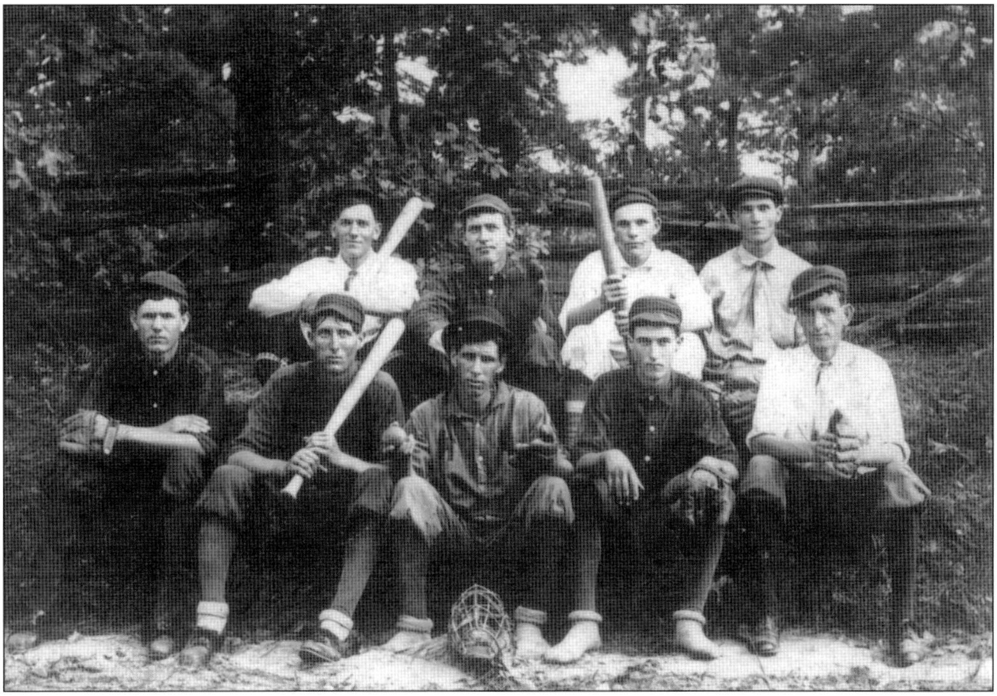

Before the convenience of radio and television brought sporting venues into every home, residents often spent their weekend afternoons in the spring of the year attending baseball games between independent teams from communities throughout Chilton County. Mars Hill and other teams in Chilton County often traveled by wagon, railroad, or on foot to compete in tournaments and games with other communities. (ADAH.)

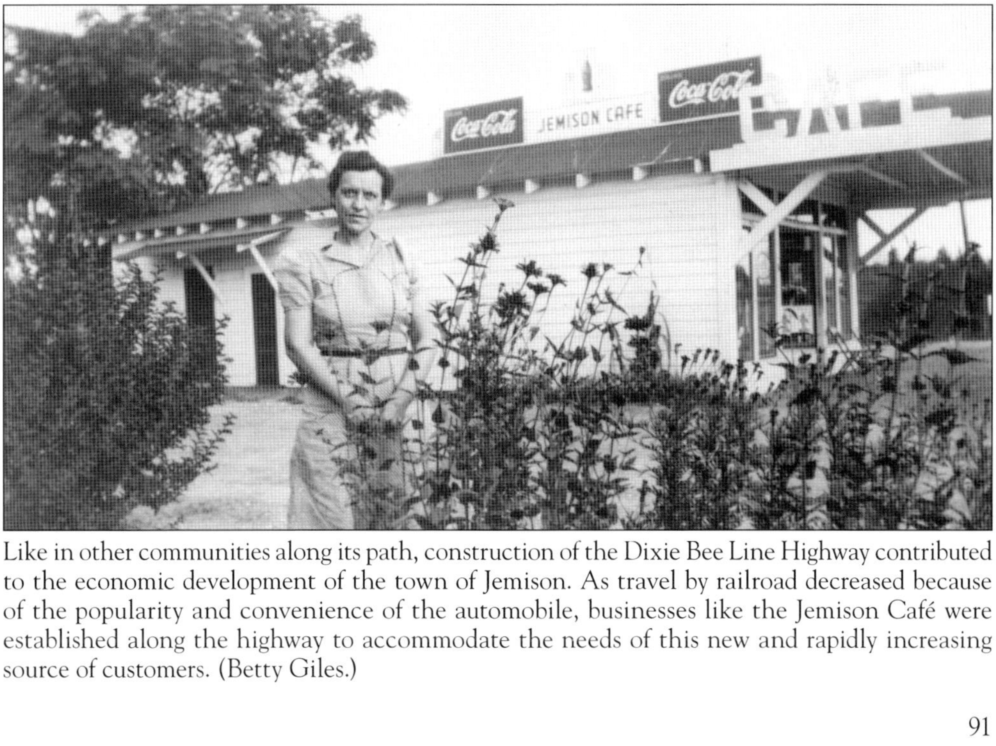

Like in other communities along its path, construction of the Dixie Bee Line Highway contributed to the economic development of the town of Jemison. As travel by railroad decreased because of the popularity and convenience of the automobile, businesses like the Jemison Café were established along the highway to accommodate the needs of this new and rapidly increasing source of customers. (Betty Giles.)

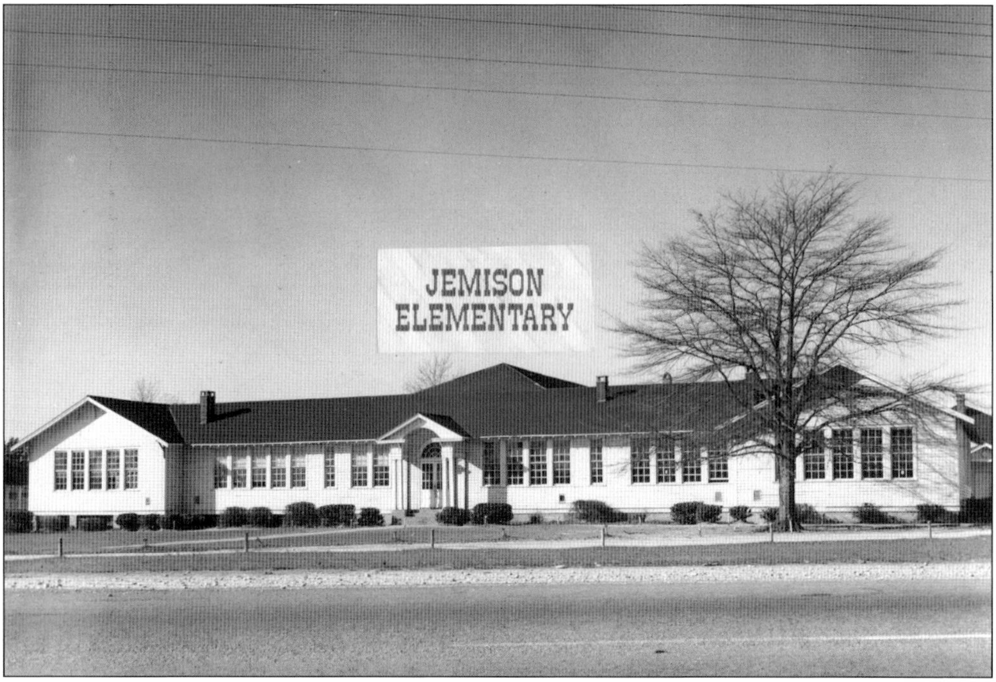

Constructed in 1925, the Jemison Elementary and High Schools were considered among the best in Chilton County. Because of a lack of funding for education, teachers were initially paid in scrip, much like employees of local timber companies. The lack of available funds also limited the school year to a maximum term of five and a half months. (CCBE.)

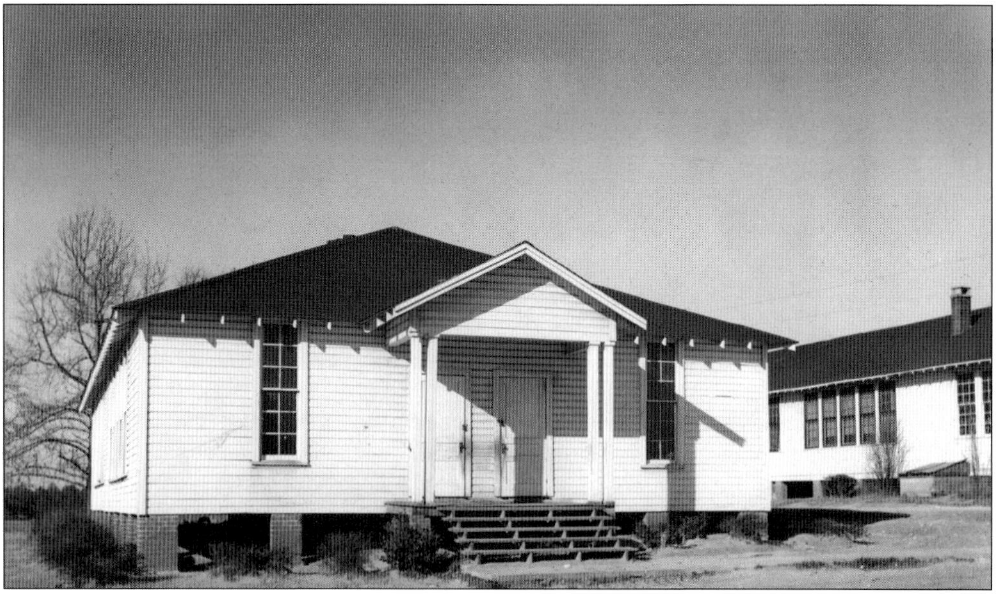

By 1935, increased enrollment in the Jemison Elementary School required additional classrooms. A frame building consisting of four classrooms was constructed to accommodate students of the first and second grades. Classrooms were heated by woodstoves in the winter and cooled through open windows in the spring. To raise funds for the purchase of classroom supplies, residents of Jemison hosted oyster suppers during the school year. (CCBE.)

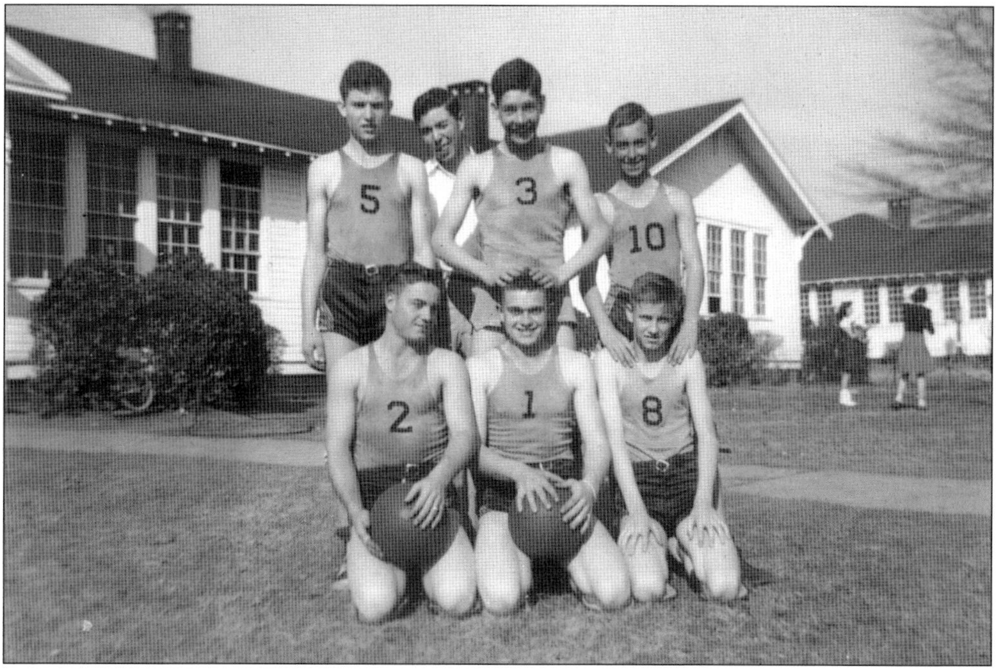

Living in a rural community supported by agriculture and the timber industry, students of Jemison High School did not initially have the opportunity to participate in organized sports because of the need to work on the farm or at the local sawmill or to attend other family responsibilities. In the years following the Depression, high school teams were organized to allow students to compete in football, basketball, and baseball. (Betty Giles.)

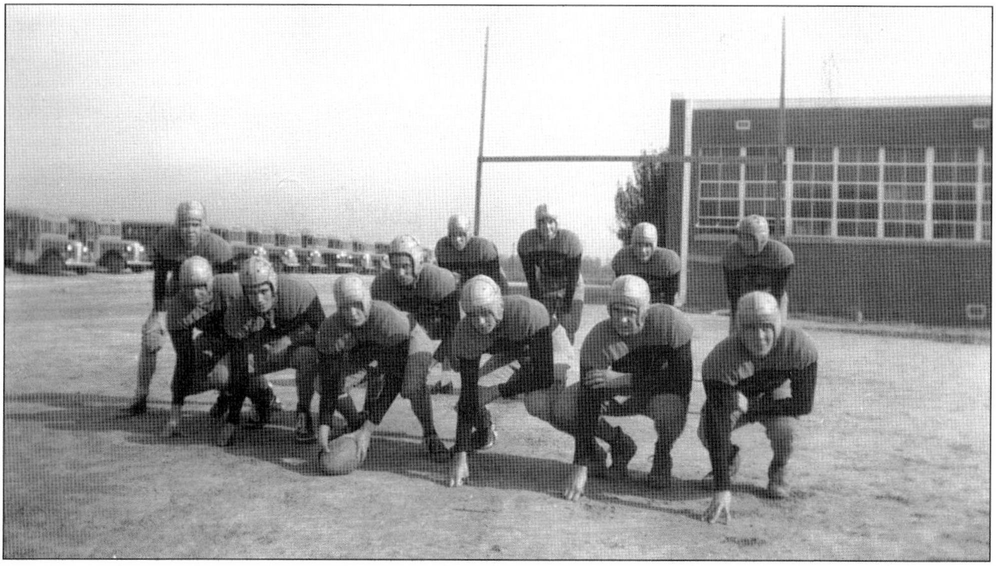

In 1947, Alton Cobb and agriculture teacher L.C. Shields organized the first football team at Jemison High School. The annual game between the Jemison Panthers and the Chilton County High School Tigers of Clanton continues to be one of the most eagerly anticipated athletic events of the year. Since 1947, the two teams have competed in more than 65 games. (Betty Giles.)

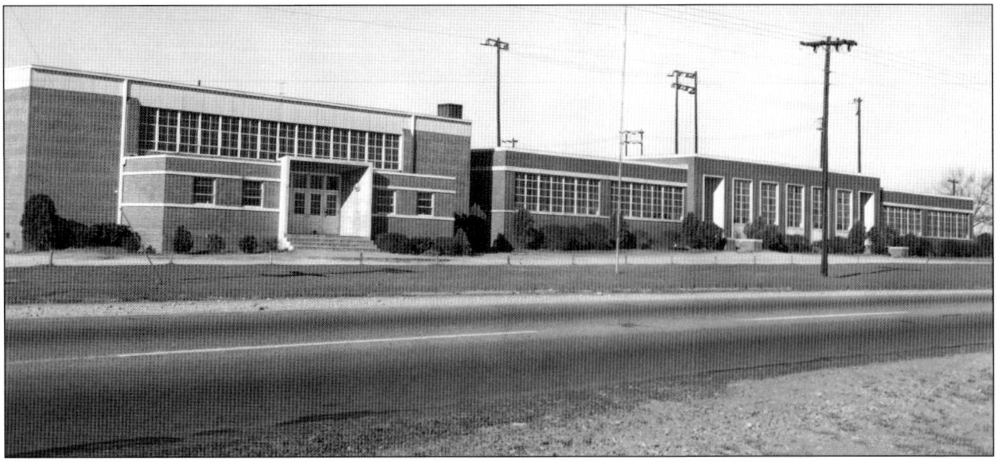

Opened to students in 1965, the new Jemison High School facility was constructed immediately north and adjoining the former high school building. Students of the elementary and junior high schools could utilize the classrooms of the former high school. The original wood-frame elementary and vocational agriculture buildings were later demolished. A new gymnasium and football field were subsequently added to the facility. (CCBE.)

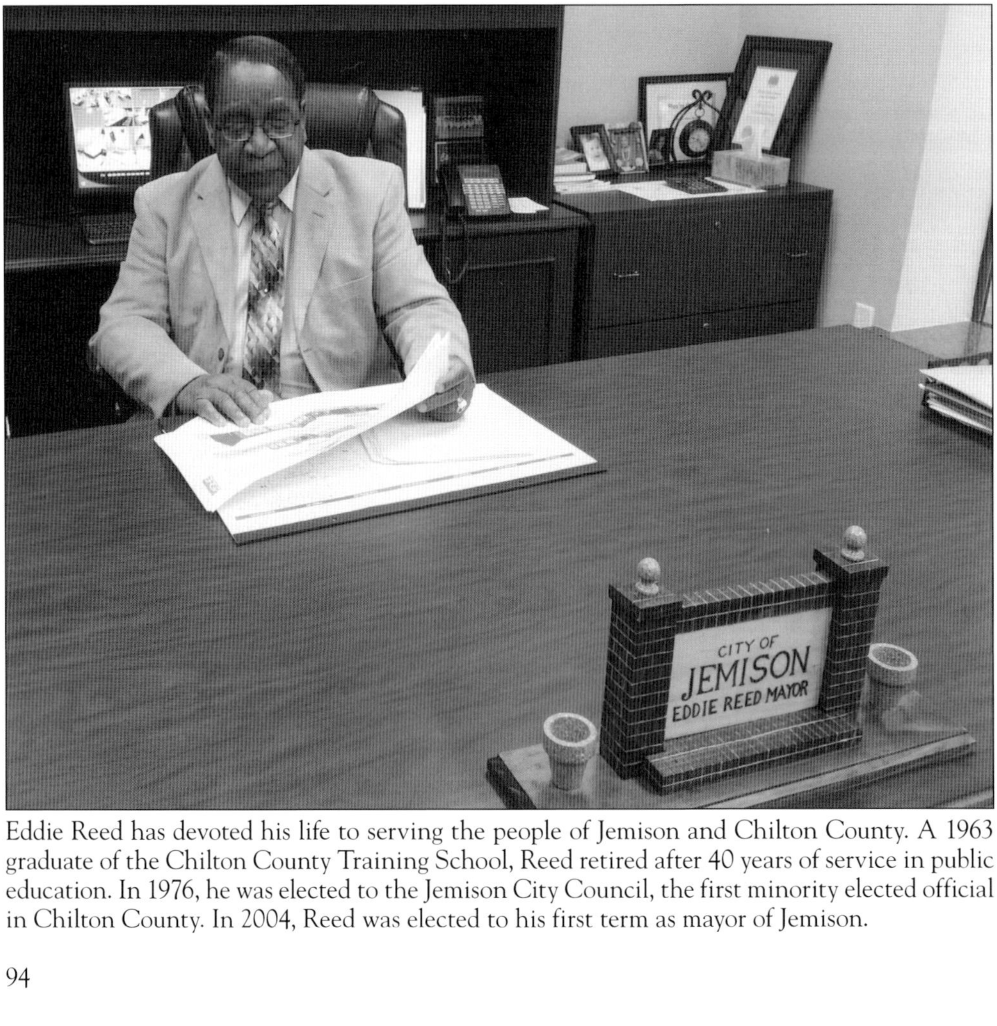

Eddie Reed has devoted his life to serving the people of Jemison and Chilton County. A 1963 graduate of the Chilton County Training School, Reed retired after 40 years of service in public education. In 1976, he was elected to the Jemison City Council, the first minority elected official in Chilton County. In 2004, Reed was elected to his first term as mayor of Jemison.

Five

MAPLESVILLE

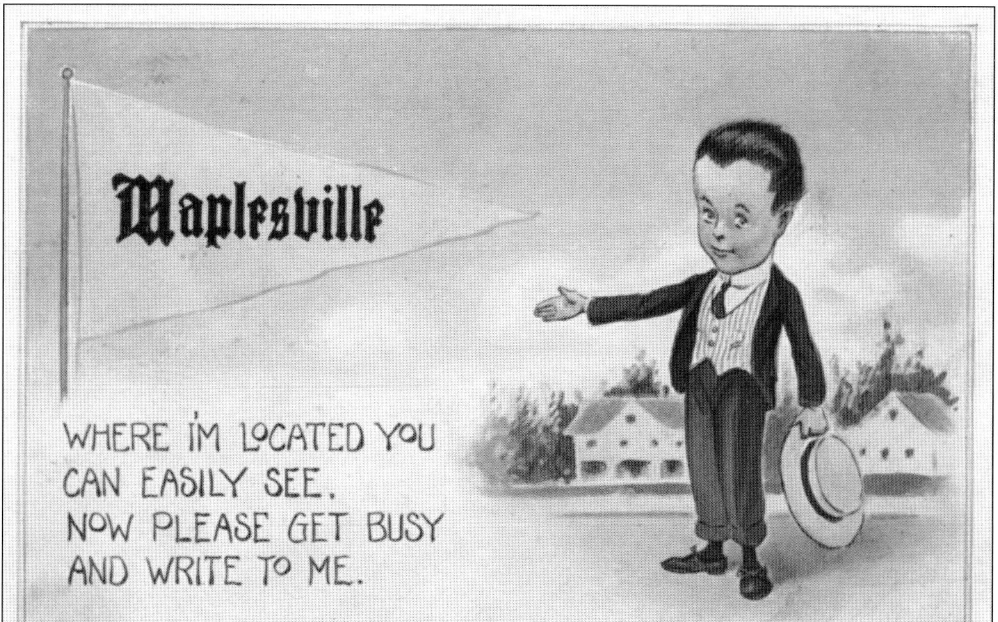

Founded in 1829, Maplesville is a town older than its county. The land that would become Maplesville has been part of four sectional divisions—Autauga, Bibb, Baker, and Chilton Counties. Originally located at the junction of two heavily traveled stagecoach routes, the town was eventually relocated three miles to the west as the railroad, a new and more efficient method of transportation, was constructed through the region. (Author's collection.)

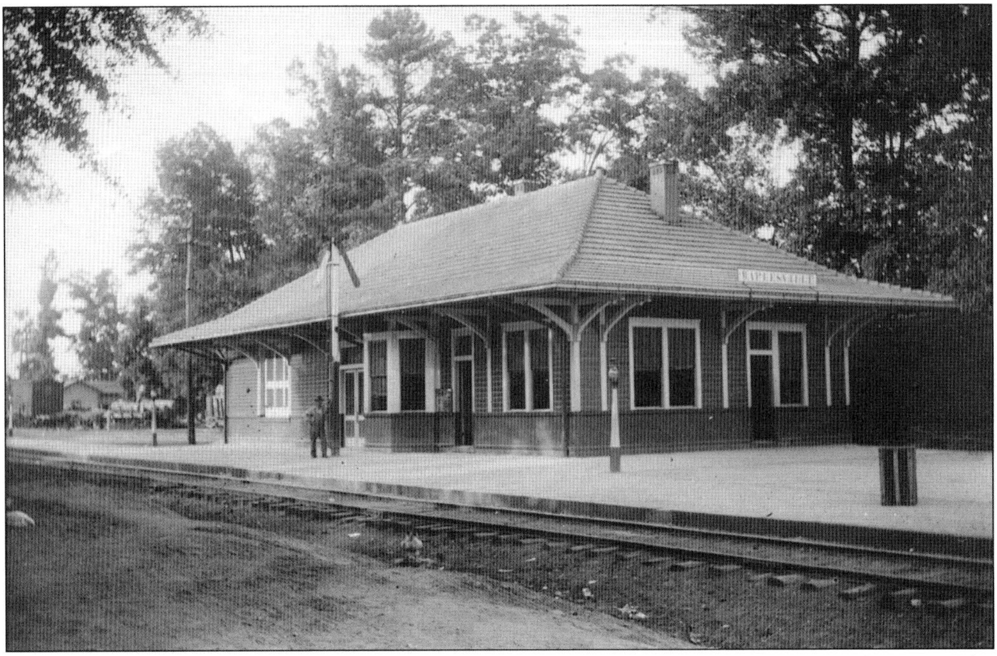

An iconic landmark, the former Southern Railway Depot is representative of the influence of the railroad on Maplesville. Originally established three miles to the east, the town was reborn adjacent to the new Maplesville Depot, which had been constructed to serve the recently constructed rail line of the Alabama & Tennessee River Railroad. (ADAH.)

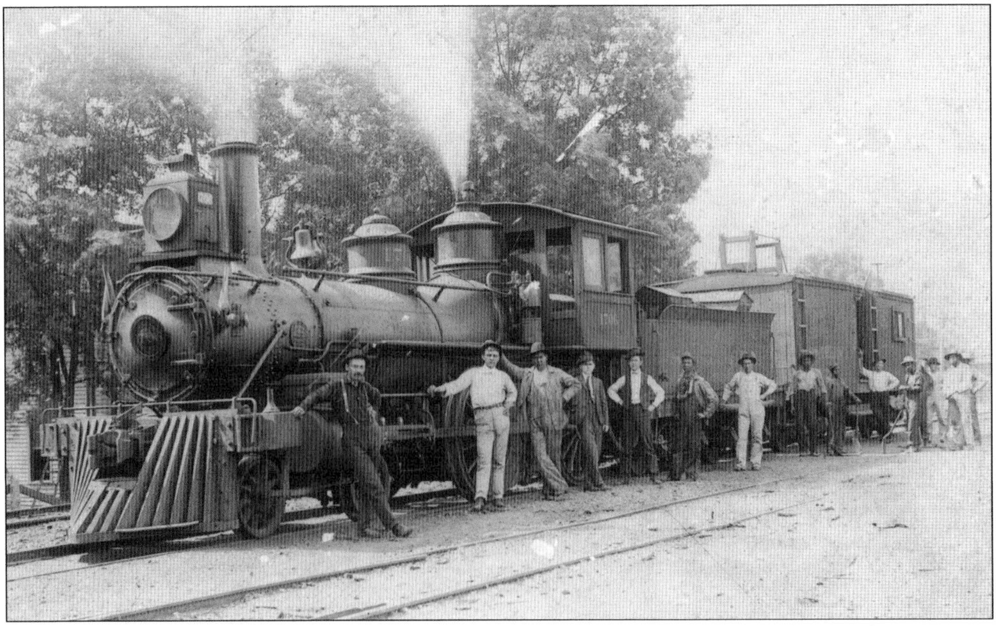

The Alabama & Tennessee River Railroad was formed in 1848 to connect Selma with commerce along the Tennessee River. In 1868, the line was redirected to Rome, Georgia, and the system became known as the Selma, Rome & Dalton Railroad. It was acquired by the East Tennessee, Virginia & Georgia Railroad in 1881, and a subsequent consolidation formed the Southern Railway System. (ADAH.)

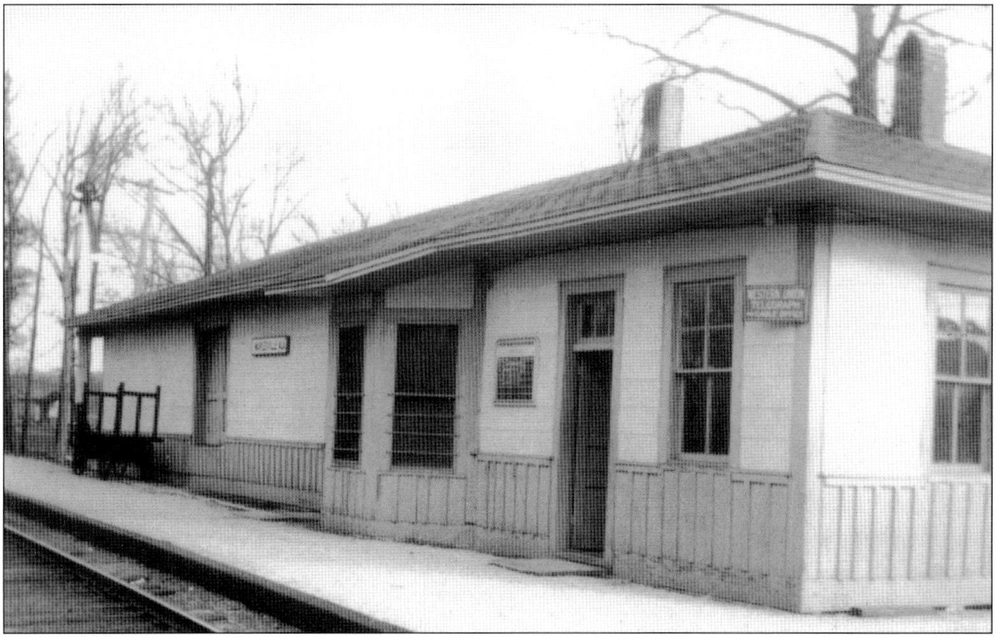

In July 1899, the Mobile & Ohio Railroad completed construction of a rail system that extended from Columbus, Mississippi, to Montgomery and intersected the Southern Railroad at Maplesville. Later known as the Gulf, Mobile & Ohio, the company constructed a depot in Maplesville for handling passengers and freight. In 1988, after standing for more than 90 years, the building was disassembled due to the poor condition of the structure.

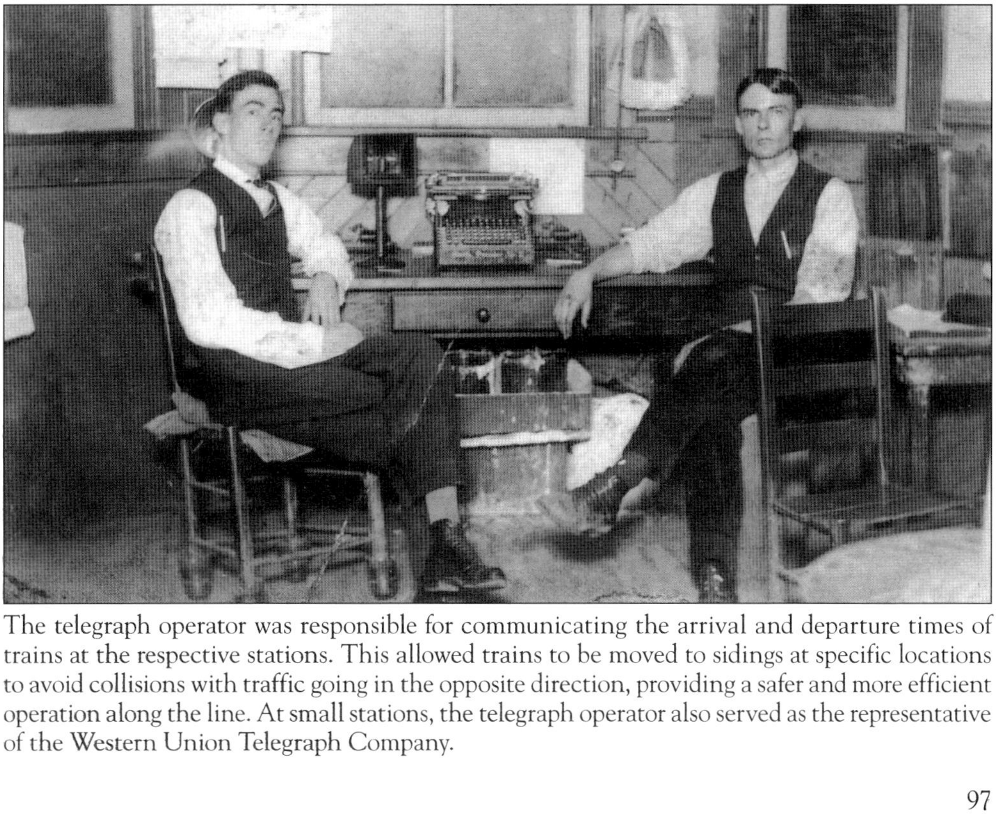

The telegraph operator was responsible for communicating the arrival and departure times of trains at the respective stations. This allowed trains to be moved to sidings at specific locations to avoid collisions with traffic going in the opposite direction, providing a safer and more efficient operation along the line. At small stations, the telegraph operator also served as the representative of the Western Union Telegraph Company.

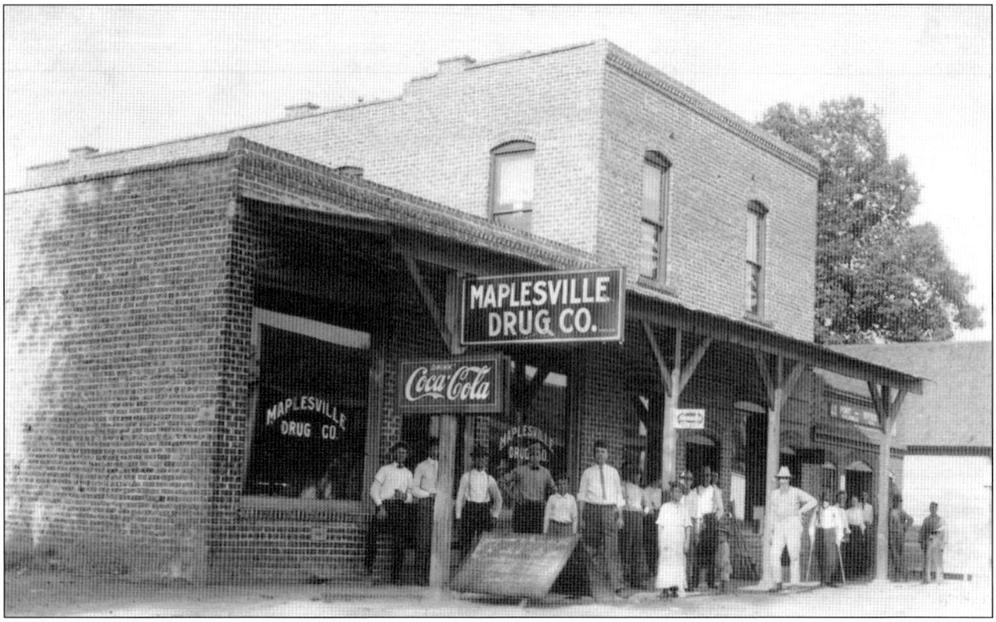

Merchants and customers take a moment from their busy schedules in the summer of 1900 to pose for a photograph in downtown Maplesville. The proprietors of the Maplesville Drug Company advertise their products on a signboard displayed along the dirt street in front of the business. The post office is located to the right of the drugstore and adjoining building.

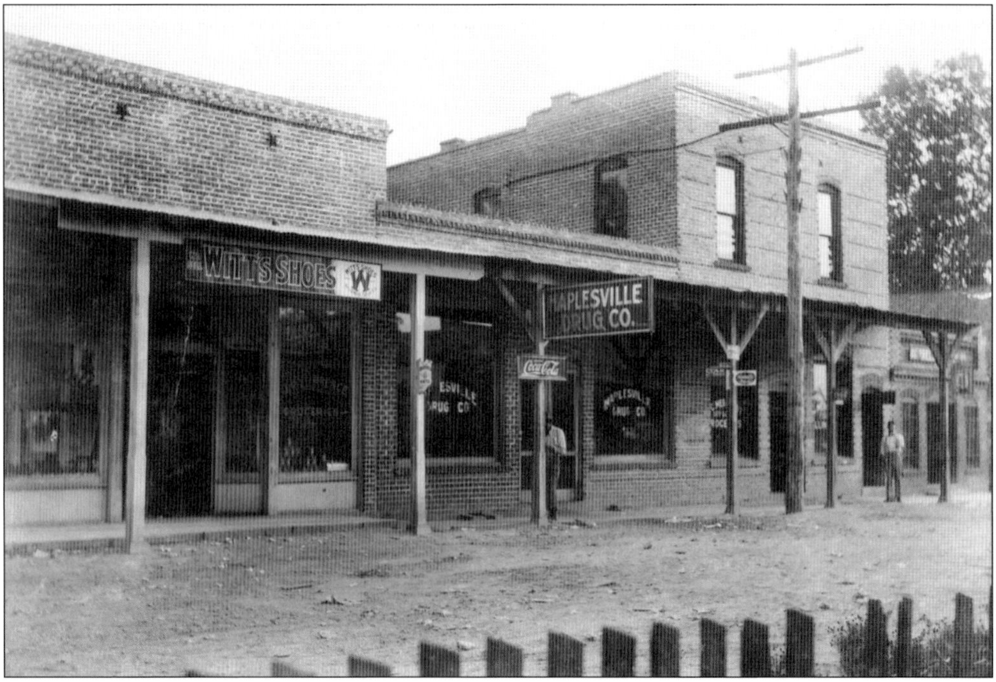

In this subsequent image, the Maplesville Drug Company has been joined by J.P. Lawrence Groceries. An advertisement outside of the building advises prospective customers that the firm sells Witt's Shoes, produced by the George D. Witt Shoe Company. Note the presence of power lines in the foreground. The town of Maplesville obtained electrical power through a cooperative agreement.

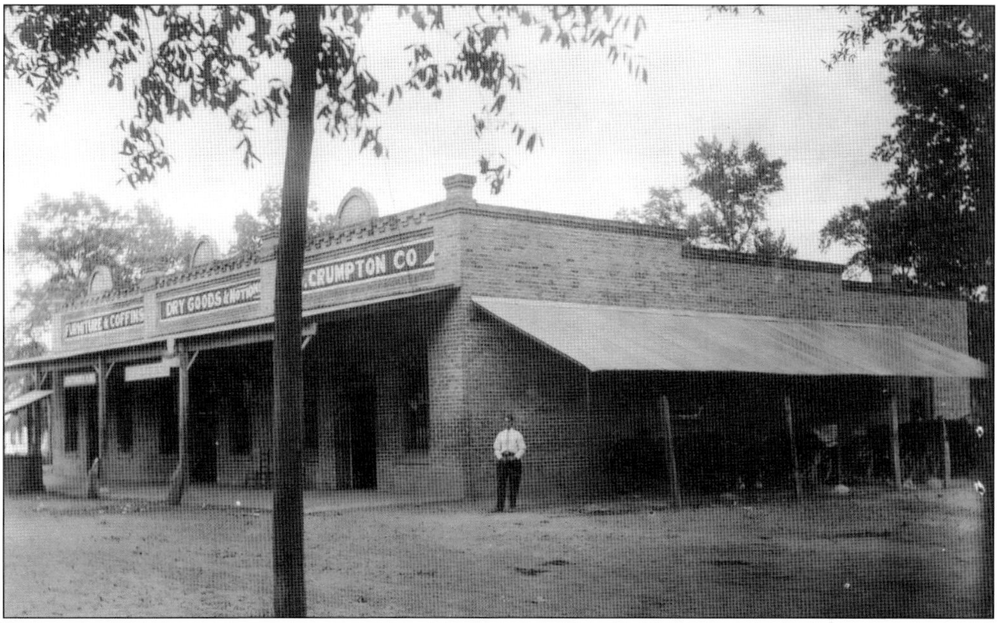

The T.U. Crumpton Company advertised as a purveyor of furniture, coffins, dry goods, and notions. Coffins were stored in a building behind the store and would be "trimmed" with exterior hardware as requested by the family or friends of the deceased. The Crumpton Company was the sole supplier of coffins in Maplesville and the surrounding area. The original Crumpton store was to the east of the Southern Railroad line.

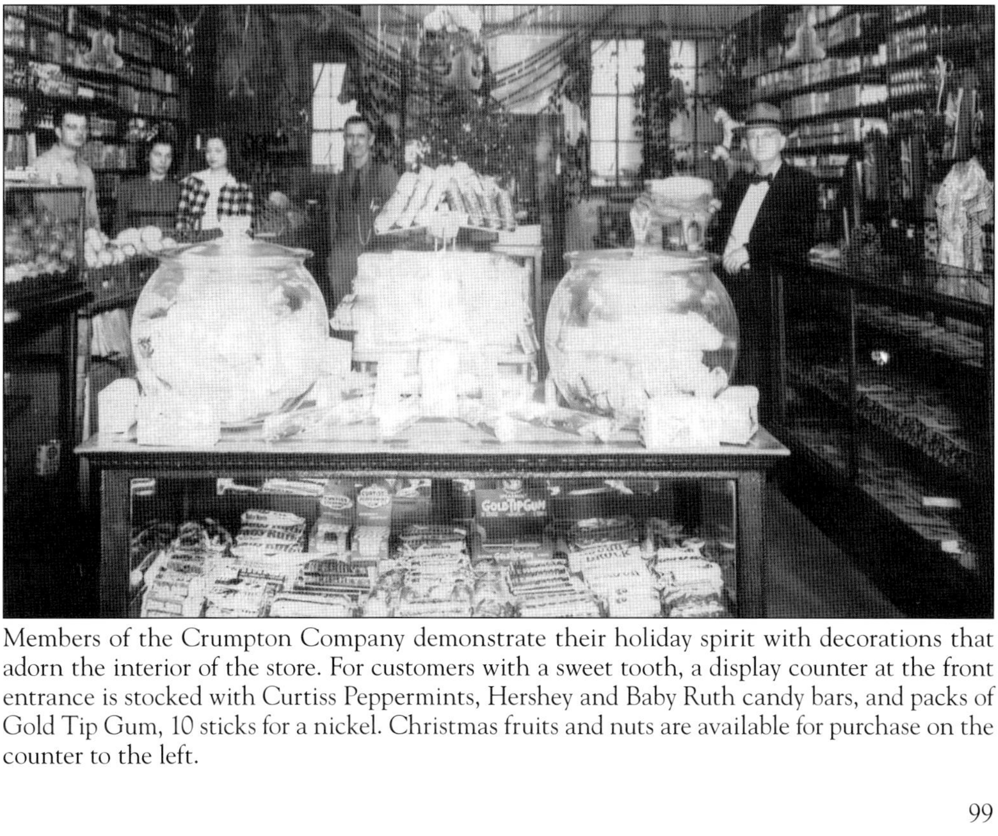

Members of the Crumpton Company demonstrate their holiday spirit with decorations that adorn the interior of the store. For customers with a sweet tooth, a display counter at the front entrance is stocked with Curtiss Peppermints, Hershey and Baby Ruth candy bars, and packs of Gold Tip Gum, 10 sticks for a nickel. Christmas fruits and nuts are available for purchase on the counter to the left.

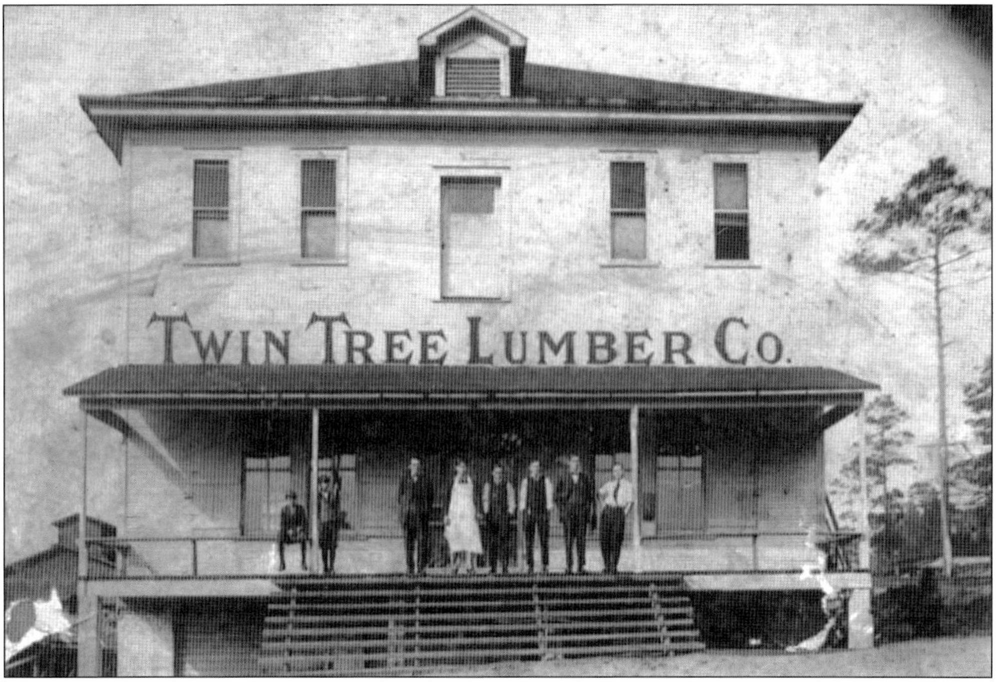

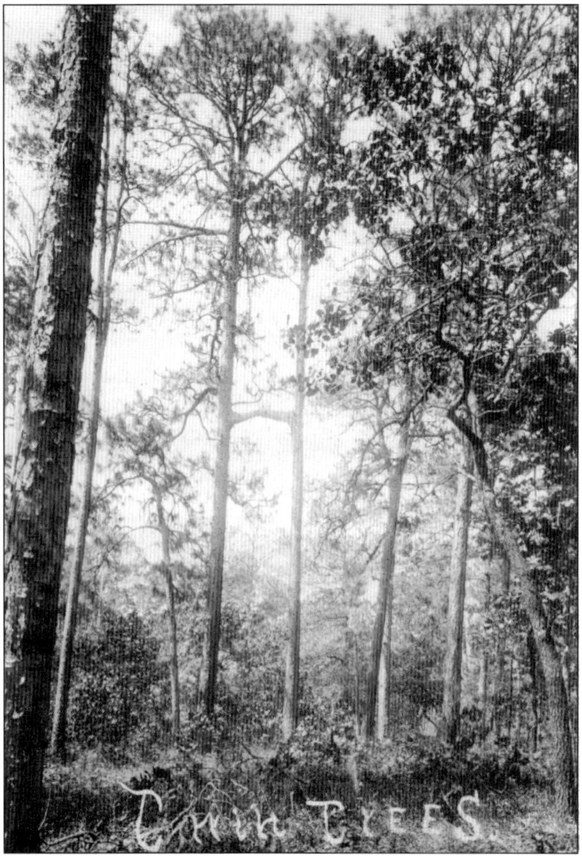

Incorporated in October 1901, the Twin Tree Lumber Company specialized in the production of longleaf yellow pine rift flooring. Like other early industries in Alabama, the Twin Tree Lumber Company was a self-contained community, consisting of the mill, commissary, hotel, and company-owned housing for employees. During 17 years of operation, the Twin Tree Lumber Company was a vital component of the Maplesville economy.

Founded by John and Edward Ensign of Buffalo, New York, the Twin Tree Lumber Company grew into a major industry and employer in an area traditionally dependant on income derived from local farms. Jobs created by the company contributed to the growth of schools, churches, and businesses in Maplesville. The name of the Twin Tree Lumber Company purportedly originated from a pair of conjoined trees discovered on company property. (ADAH.)

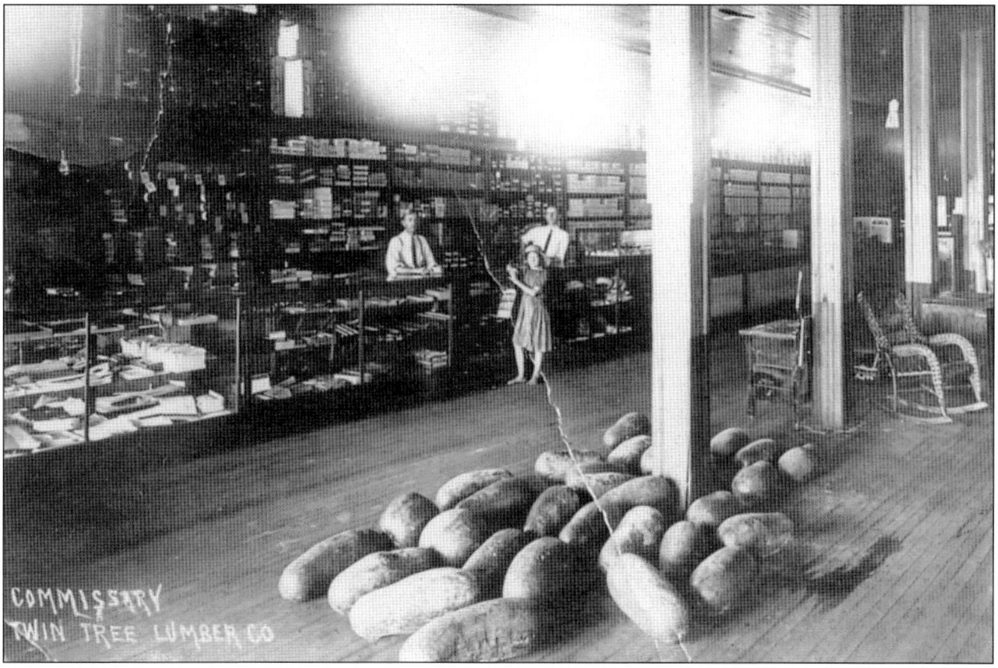

Scrip issued by the company was used by employees to purchase food, dry goods, and other items in the Twin Tree Lumber Company commissary. The scrip was a substitute for government-issued currency and could only be redeemed in a company store or commissary. Employees could exchange company scrip for currency to make purchases from other local vendors.

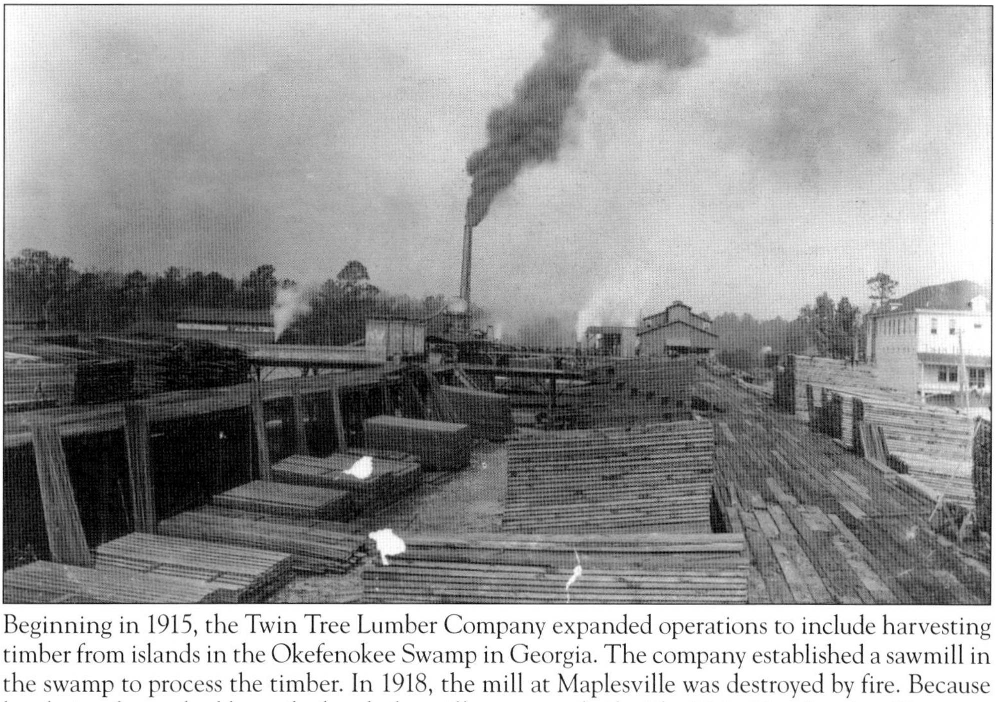
Beginning in 1915, the Twin Tree Lumber Company expanded operations to include harvesting timber from islands in the Okefenokee Swamp in Georgia. The company established a sawmill in the swamp to process the timber. In 1918, the mill at Maplesville was destroyed by fire. Because local pine forests had been depleted, the mill was not rebuilt. The Twin Tree Lumber Company was subsequently moved to Hopkins, Georgia.

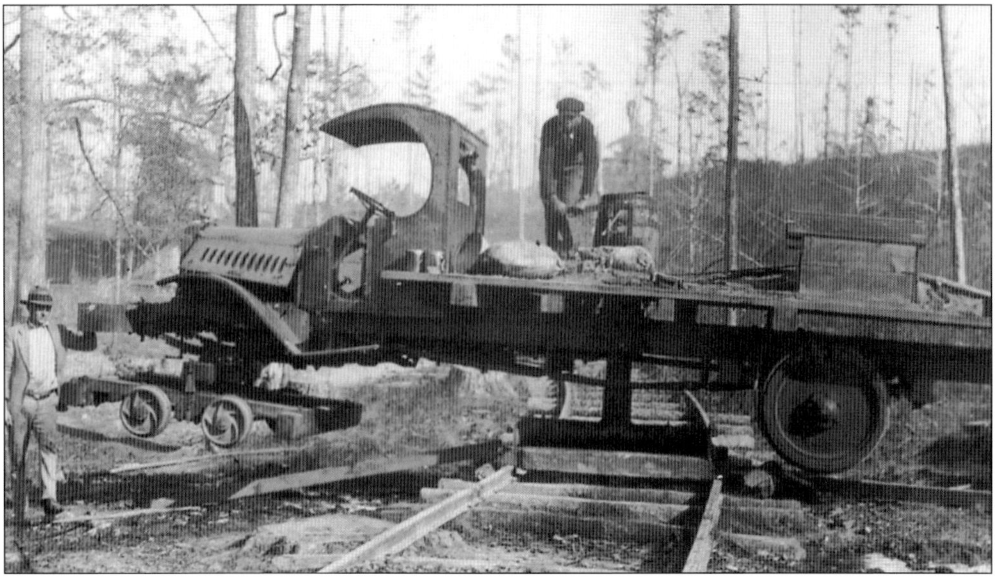

The Twin Tree Lumber Company was one of 15 timber companies operating in Chilton County from 1880 to 1925 that used rail systems as part of logging operations. Rail lines were used by logging companies in Ocampo, Jemison, Lomax, Clanton, Coopers, and Verbena. The utilization of rail spurs that joined existing main lines allowed the transport of large quantities of timber from remote locations for processing at company sawmills.

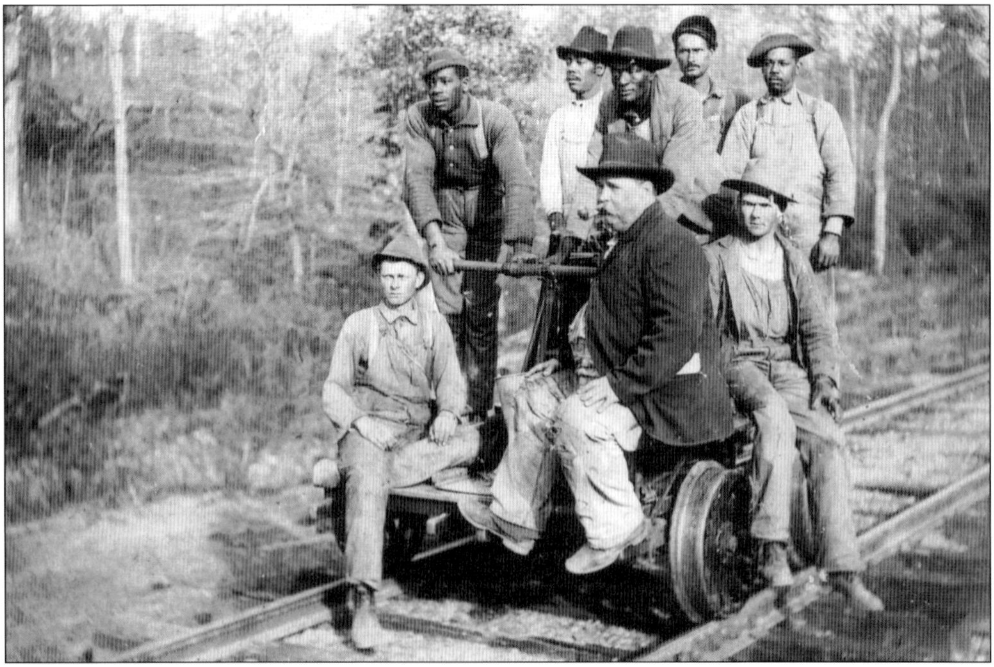

The movement of raw materials and finished products at the Twin Tree Lumber Company was dependent on the continuous operation of its rail system. Railcars would be moved along a spur to the mill or to connect with the Southern or Mobile & Ohio Railroad near Maplesville. Maintenance crews inspected and maintained the 26-mile company rail system to prevent disruptions to production.

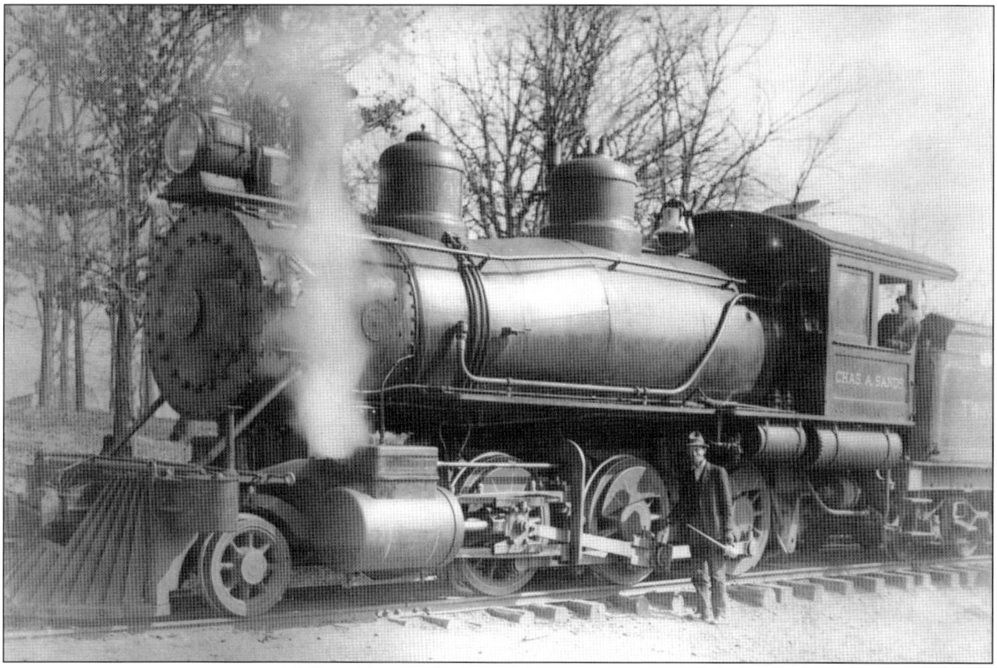

The *Chas. A. Sands* locomotive, operated by the Twin Tree Lumber Company, was produced in 1907 by the Baldwin Locomotive Works. The 2-6-0 Mogul produced sufficient power from steam converted to mechanical energy to pull 800 trailing tons. The 2-6-0 classification refers to the engine having two pilot wheels on one axle and six powered driving wheels on three axles with no trailing wheels.

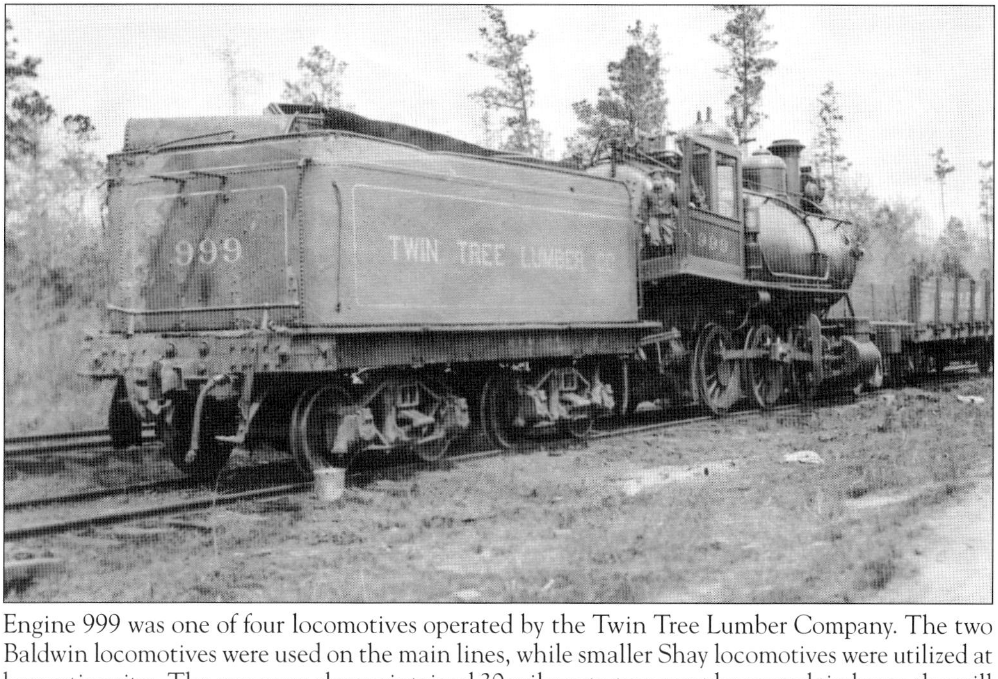

Engine 999 was one of four locomotives operated by the Twin Tree Lumber Company. The two Baldwin locomotives were used on the main lines, while smaller Shay locomotives were utilized at harvesting sites. The company also maintained 30 railcars to transport harvested timber to the mill for processing and finished lumber products to the main lines for distribution to customers.

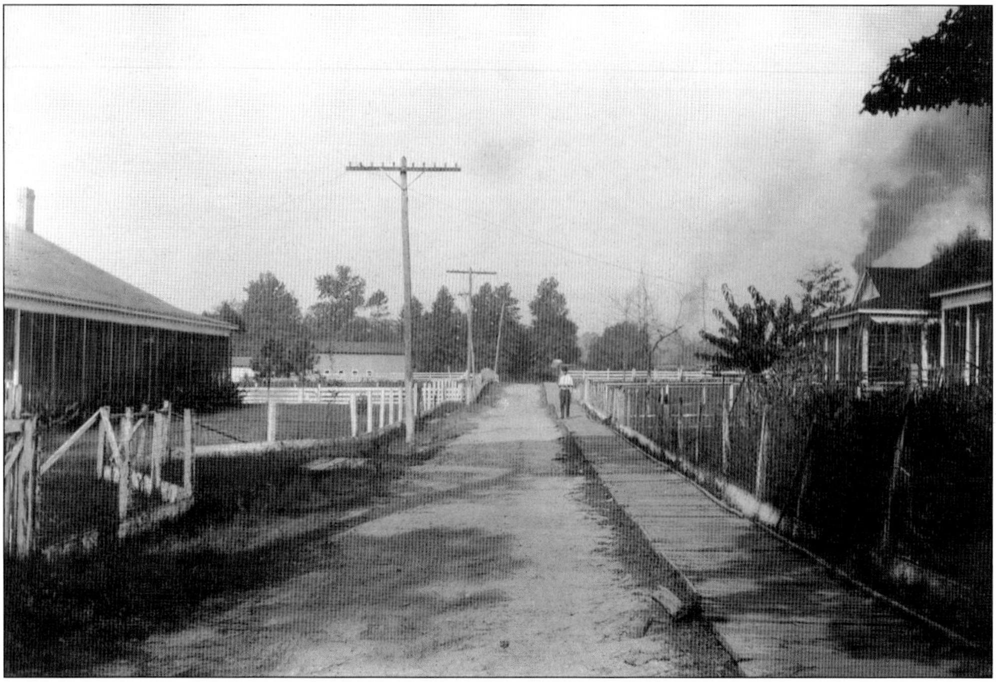

The influx of industry during the early 20th century in Maplesville resulted in numerous improvements within the community. On Sundays, residents of Maplesville could stroll along the board sidewalks to enjoy a Sunday lunch at the hotel. In November 1929, the town achieved a milestone when electrical power first became available to homes and businesses.

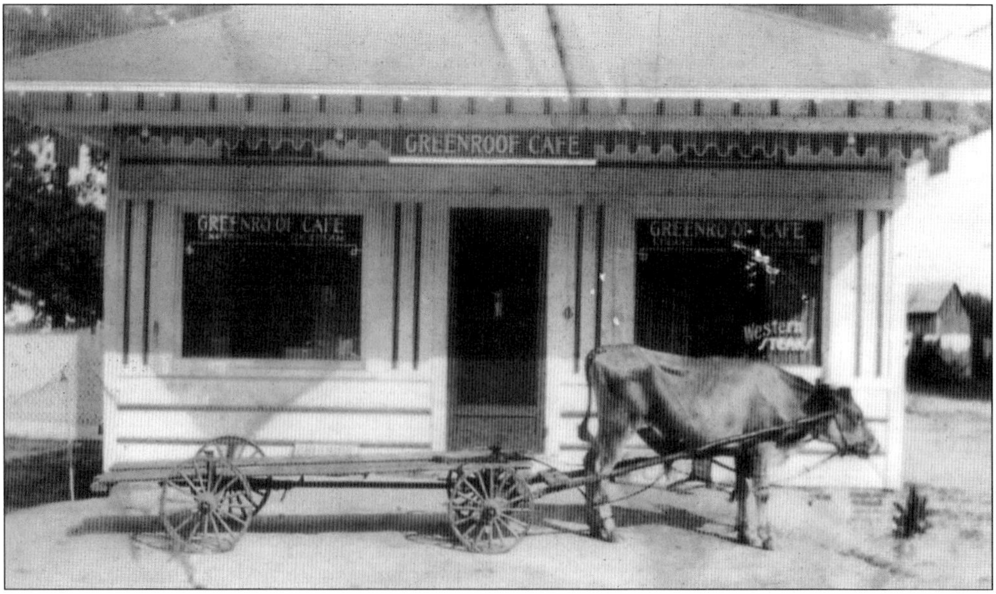

For more than 45 years, the Green Roof Café was a favorite destination for home-cooked meals and delicious barbecue. Built by Dr. H.M. Nix for his wife, Mae Potts Nix, the Green Roof was well known among bus drivers and railroad operators. With an advance order for special groups traveling on the train, Mae Nix would deliver hot meals to the depot. The porter would return her dishes on the next trip.

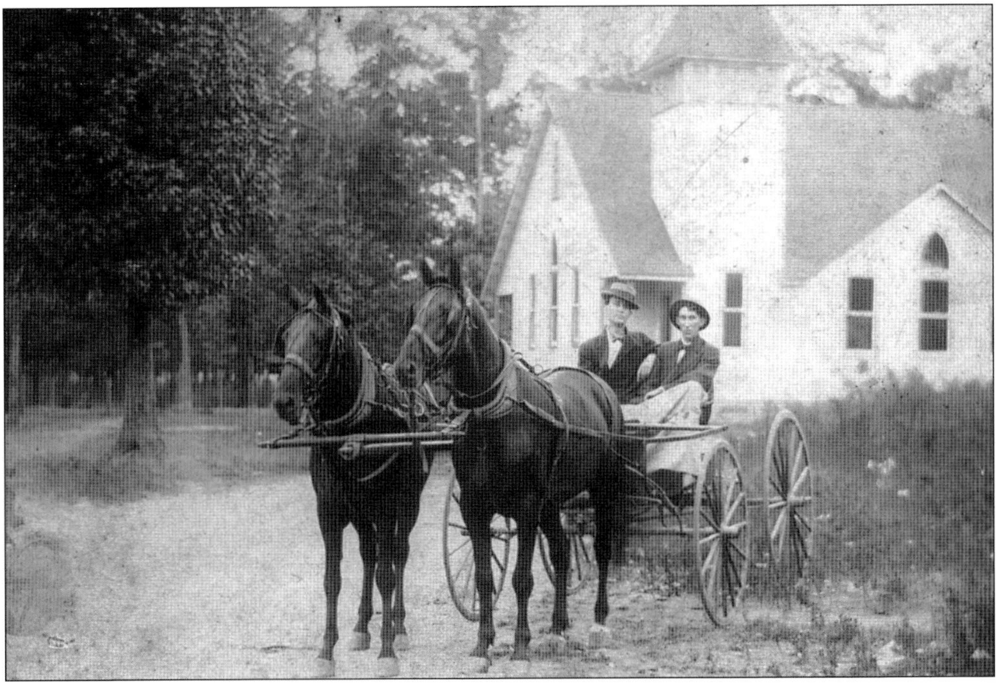

The First Baptist Church of Maplesville was organized in 1907 at a congregational tent meeting. Construction of a small frame building, erected at a cost of $3,500, was completed the following year. The church bell was obtained from the Methodist church that served Cahaba, the former capital of the state of Alabama. Early baptism services of the First Baptist Church were performed at Mulberry Creek and the Nix Mill Pond.

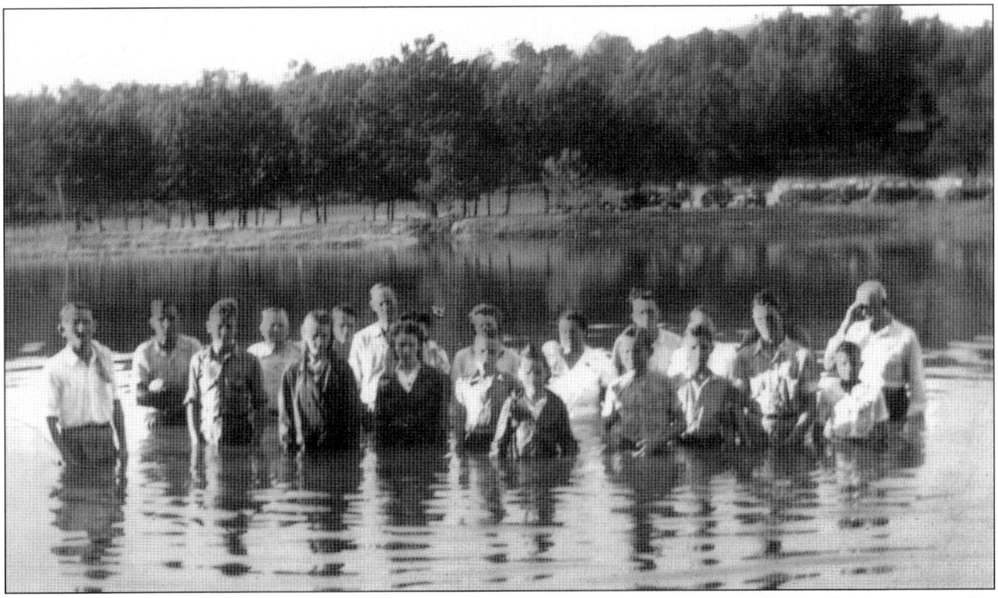

The Reverend Hymon Atcheson (left) performs baptisms in the Nix Mill Pond. Known as the "Pastor of Chilton County," Atcheson served as a Baptist minister for 63 years. On November 12, 1947, Reverend Atcheson broadcast his first sermon on local Clanton radio station WKLF; it was the station's first day on the air. He continued these religious broadcasts for 53 years.

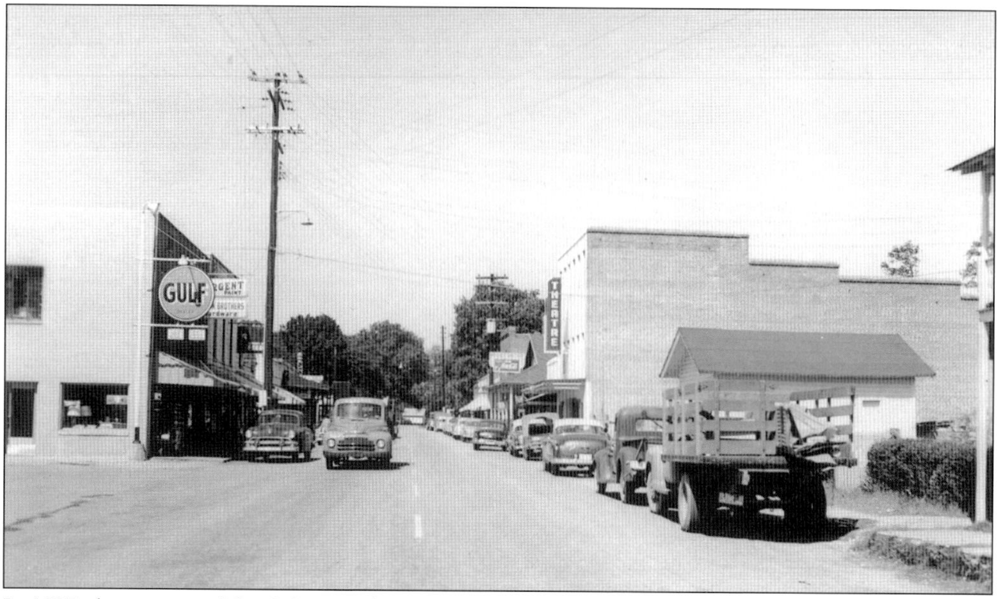

In 1937, the section of the Selma Highway, State Route 22, from Maplesville to Clanton was paved in conjunction with the Works Progress Administration. Created during the administration of Pres. Franklin Roosevelt, the WPA was a public works program designed to help alleviate the high rate of unemployment during the Depression. By 1938, paving of State Route 22 from Clanton to Selma would be completed. (ADAH.)

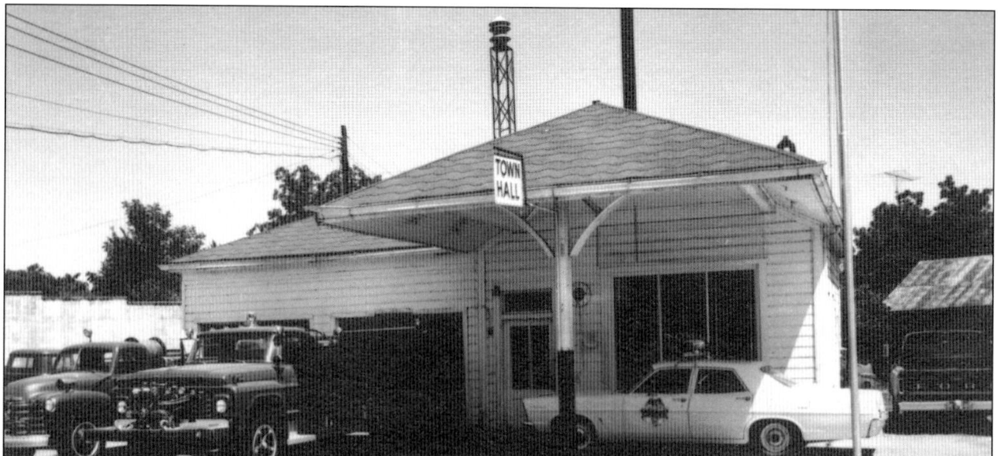

The first building to serve as the Maplesville Town Hall was the renovated J.U. Chambers Standard Oil Service Station. The building was next to the Green Roof Café on the Selma-to-Clanton Highway. The Town of Maplesville purchased the building for $12,500 in November 1952 from Dr. H.M. Nix. The building was replaced in April 1975 with a new town hall facility. (Chilton County Commission.)

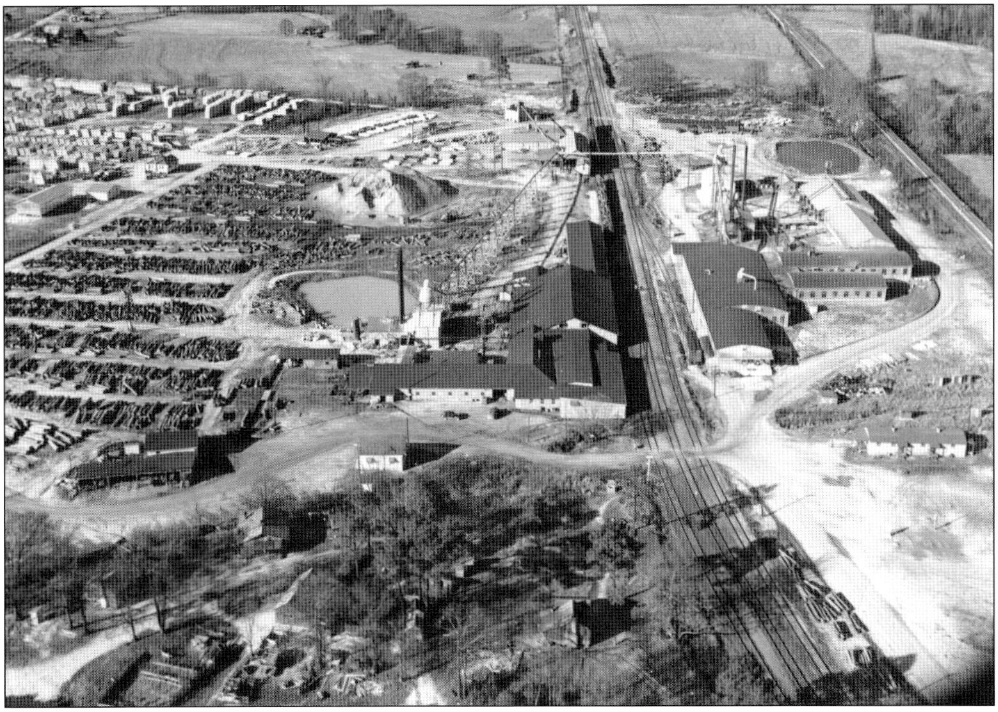

The timber industry has been a significant contributor to the economy of Maplesville. The Stremming Veneer Company began operations in 1943 and became a major employer in the community. The firm produced plywood veneer for the manufacture of household furniture and cabinets. The company ceased operations in 1958 but reopened the following year as the Thomas Veneer and Plywood Company. In 1967, the facility was destroyed by fire. (Author's collection.)

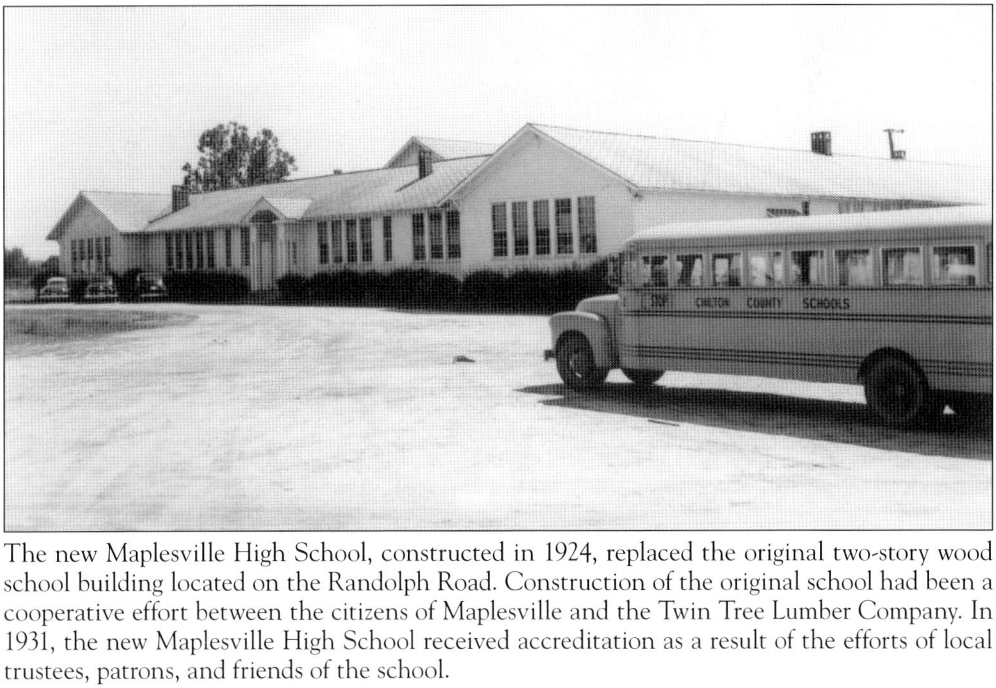

The new Maplesville High School, constructed in 1924, replaced the original two-story wood school building located on the Randolph Road. Construction of the original school had been a cooperative effort between the citizens of Maplesville and the Twin Tree Lumber Company. In 1931, the new Maplesville High School received accreditation as a result of the efforts of local trustees, patrons, and friends of the school.

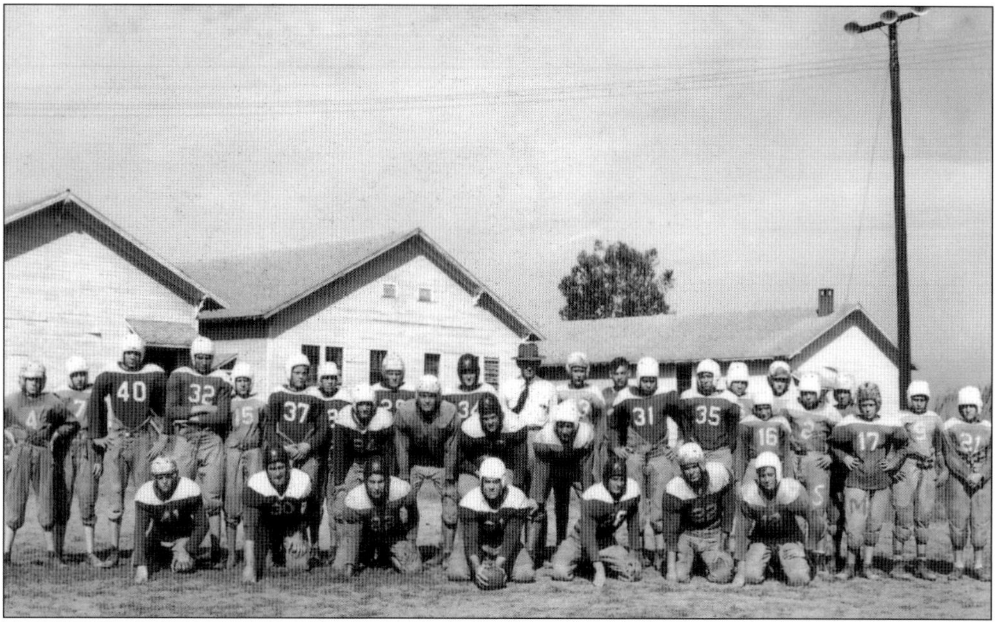

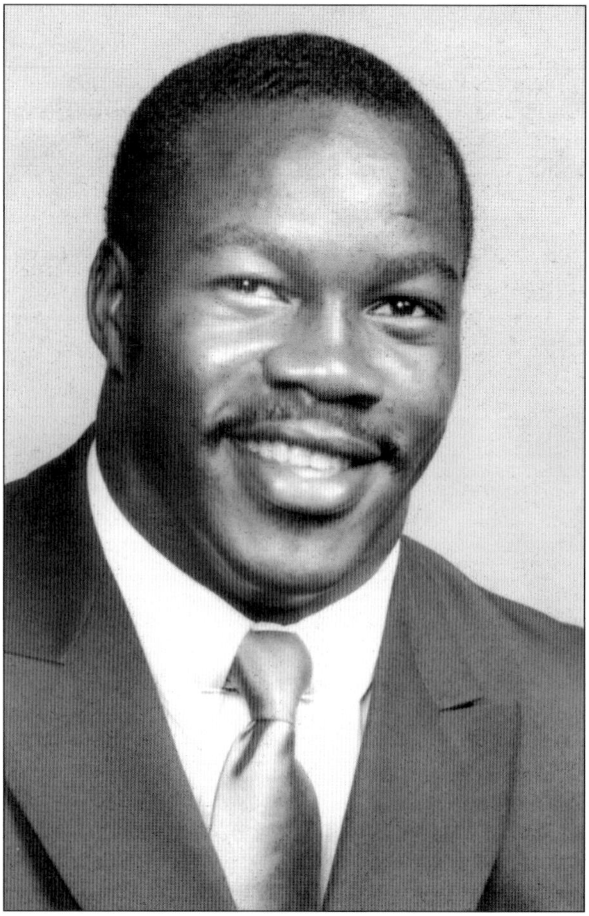

High school sports programs have always been an important aspect of life in the Maplesville community. Through the years, Maplesville High School Red Devils have excelled in football, basketball, and baseball and have earned multiple district and state championships. These achievements are proudly displayed on welcome signs in the town of Maplesville.

Thomas Lee Agee lettered in football, baseball, basketball, and track at Maplesville High School. Following graduation, Agee accepted a football scholarship to Auburn University. A four-year starter, Agee excelled as an outstanding running and blocking fullback. Selected in the fifth round of the 1987 National Football League draft by the Seattle Seahawks, Agee culminated his professional career as a member of the 1993 and 1994 Super Bowl champion Dallas Cowboys. (Auburn University Media Relations.)

Six

Thorsby

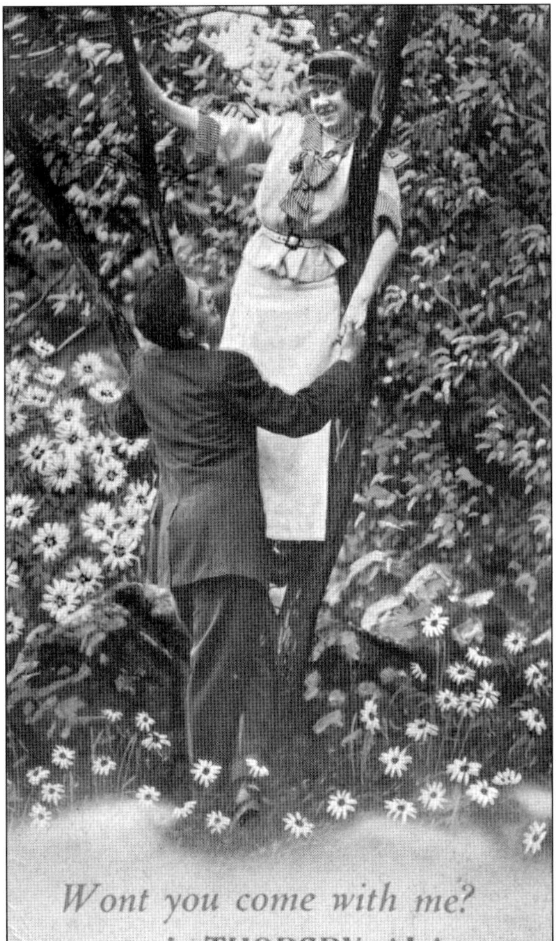

Envisioned as a community of craftsmen, musicians, and merchants, the town of Thorsby was founded in 1895 by Theodore Torkel Thorson. Seeking a mild climate and abundant farmland for the cultivation of fruit crops and vineyards, Thorson and his Scandinavian partners selected an area north of the Strasburgh depot in Chilton County. Religion, education, and economic opportunity were cornerstones of Thorson's vision for the community.

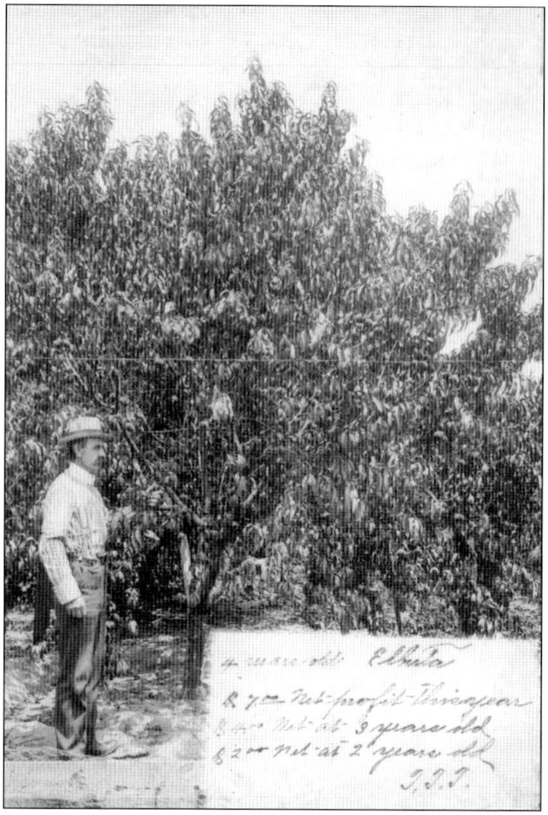

Theodore Torkel Thorson was born in November 1856 in Scandian Grove, Minnesota. As a young man, Thorson dreamed of a creating a community of fine craftsmen, talented musicians, merchants, and farmers in a region of mild climate and abundant farmland. He recruited families of Scandinavian lineage to raise produce and establish vineyards on small parcels of land in Chilton County. Thorson's dream became the town of Thorsby.

The Theodore Thorson home is an iconic structure that epitomizes the history of the town of Thorsby. This June 1900 image shows the Victorian home on the corner of Michigan Avenue and Jones Street. The design included a large tower and balcony that provided Thorson a panoramic view of the town and surrounding area. The Thorson children practiced their reading, arithmetic, and music skills on the large front porch. (ADAH.)

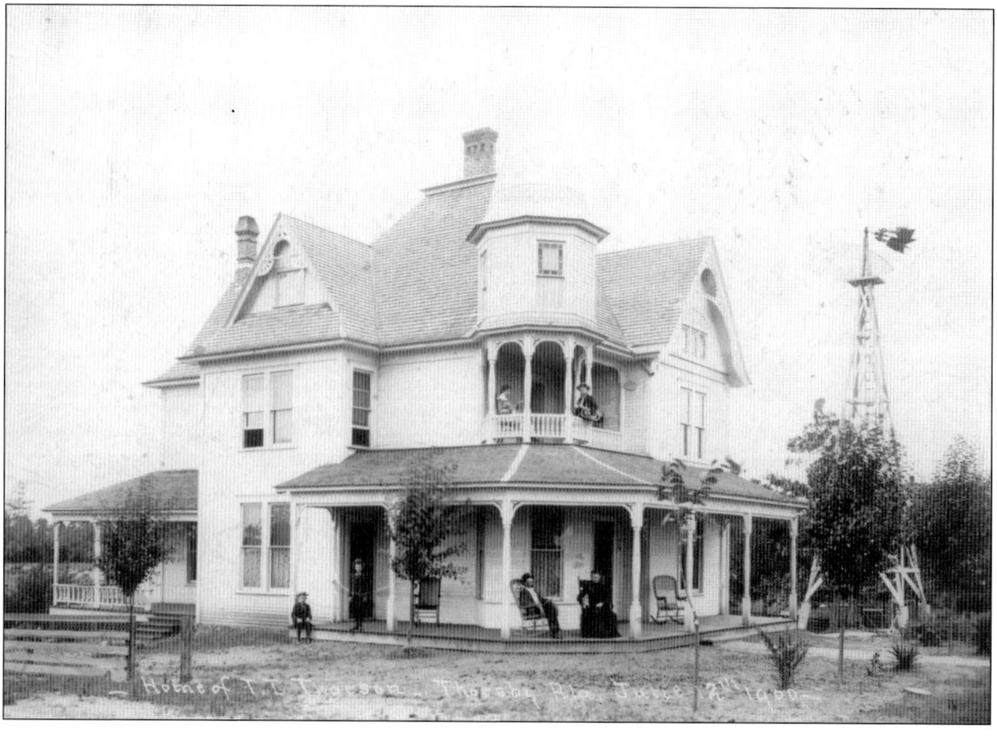

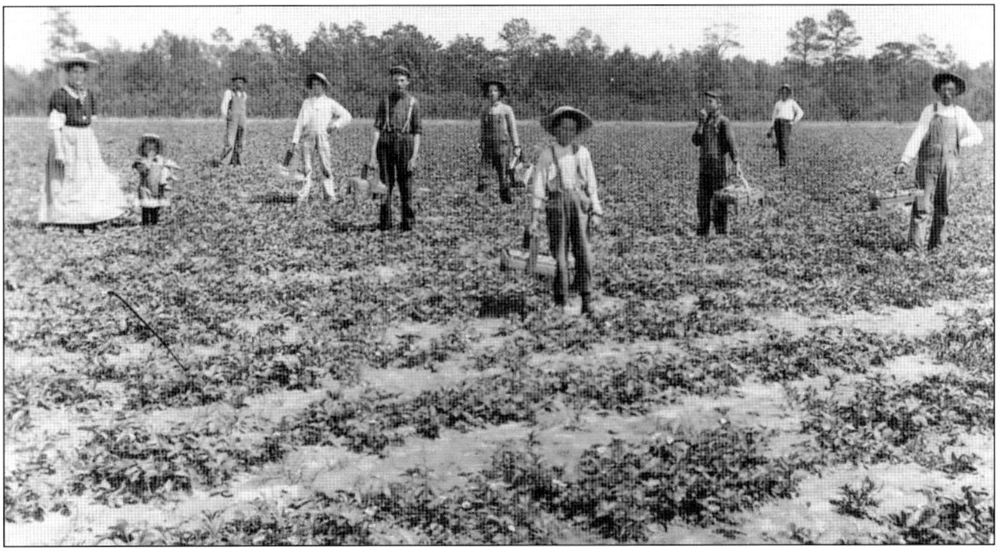

The Concordia Land & Improvement Company marketed 5- and 10-acre lots to attract Scandinavian families to settle in Thorsby to cultivate crops of fruits and berries. The produce was used locally to make wine, sold through local markets, and transported on railcars to consumers outside of Chilton County. Each summer, entire families participated in harvesting the crop.

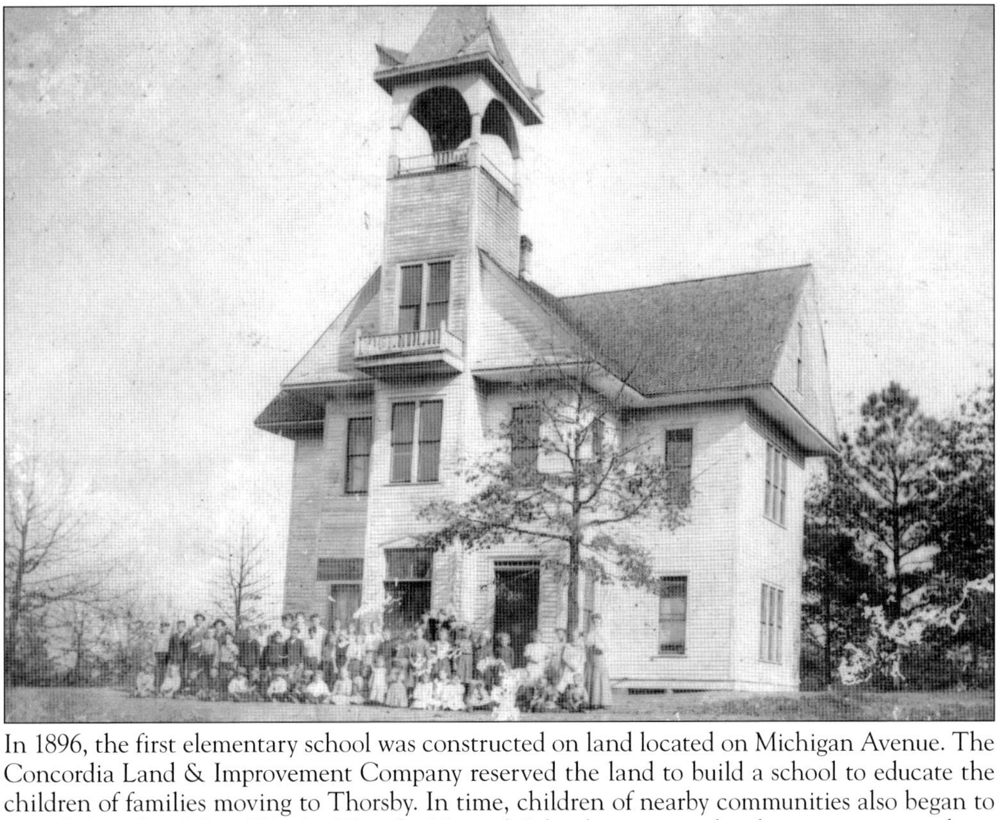

In 1896, the first elementary school was constructed on land located on Michigan Avenue. The Concordia Land & Improvement Company reserved the land to build a school to educate the children of families moving to Thorsby. In time, children of nearby communities also began to attend the school. In 1901, the Thorsby Normal School was created to better prepare students for enrollment in institutions of higher learning.

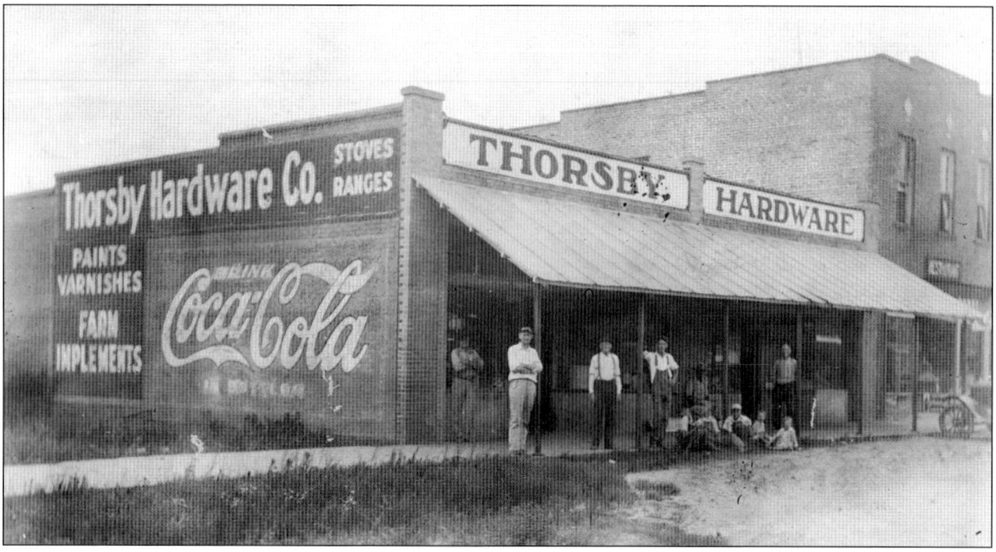

The Thorsby Hardware Company maintained a stock of stoves, paints, varnishes, and farm implements to meet the needs of its customers. At the time of this image, the store was owned and operated by J.L. and Ruben Foss. The brick exterior of the structure indicates that this is one of the buildings reconstructed after the 1914 fire that destroyed most of the Thorsby business district.

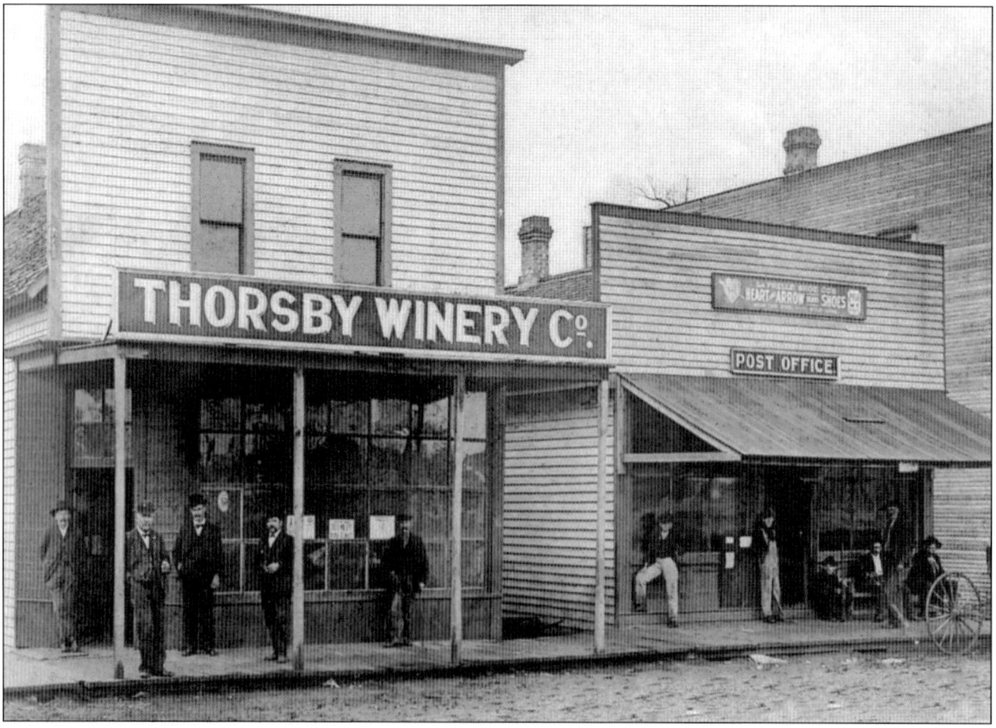

The Thorsby Winery Company used locally grown grapes to produce various types of wine. Wine production in Thorsby ended prematurely with passage of the Volstead Act in 1919, which prohibited the sale and distribution of alcoholic beverages. However, local history suggests the women of Thorsby held winemaking in low esteem and brought an end to the enterprise with an ultimatum that male winemakers found difficult to ignore.

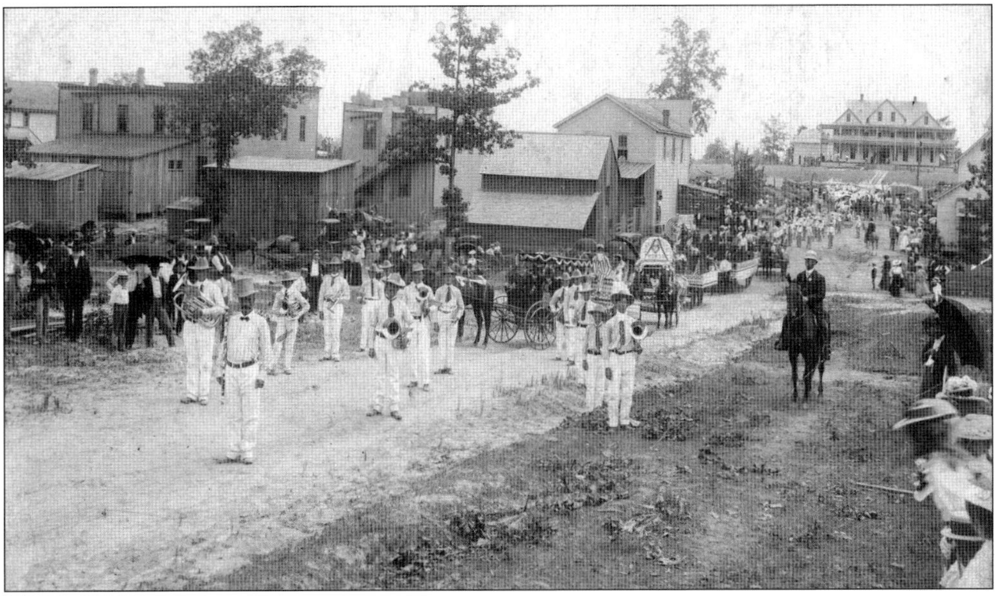

On July 4, 1900, a parade was held in honor of Independence Day and the coming of the new century. This image shows the parade being led along Concordia Avenue by the Thorsby Cornet Band. Parade floats are adorned in red, white, and blue bunting, while the second float in the parade line carries the banner of the Thorsby Normal School. The Concordia Hotel is visible in the background.

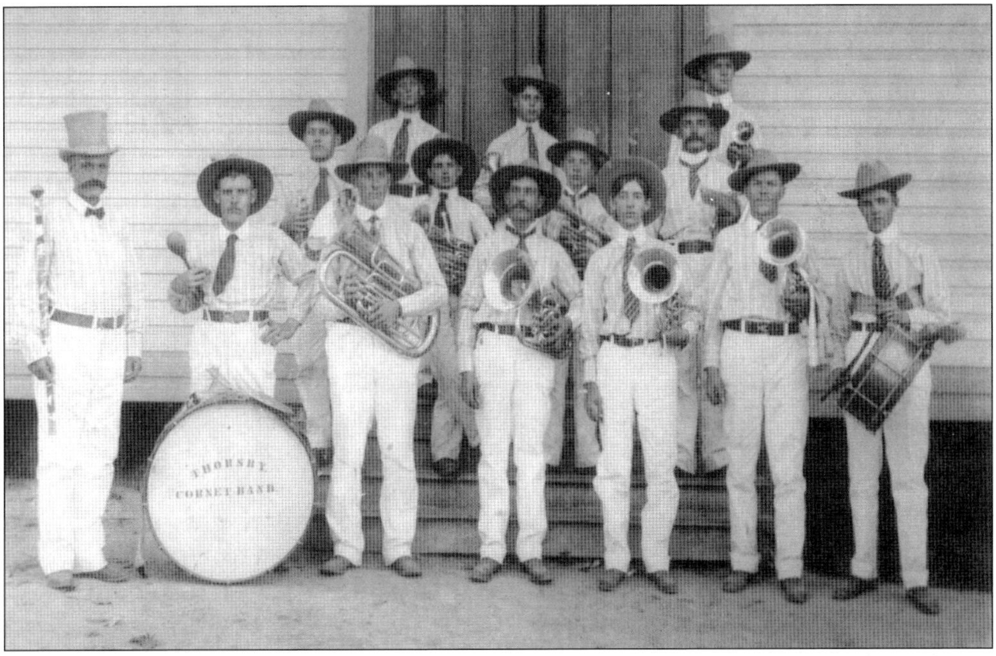

A component of the founder's vision of a community of craftsmen, musicians, and merchants, music has been an important part of the history of Thorsby. The local concert band, cornet band, and other school, church, and community musical groups have entertained residents of Thorsby and surrounding areas since the town was founded. Early bands primarily utilized brass and percussion instruments.

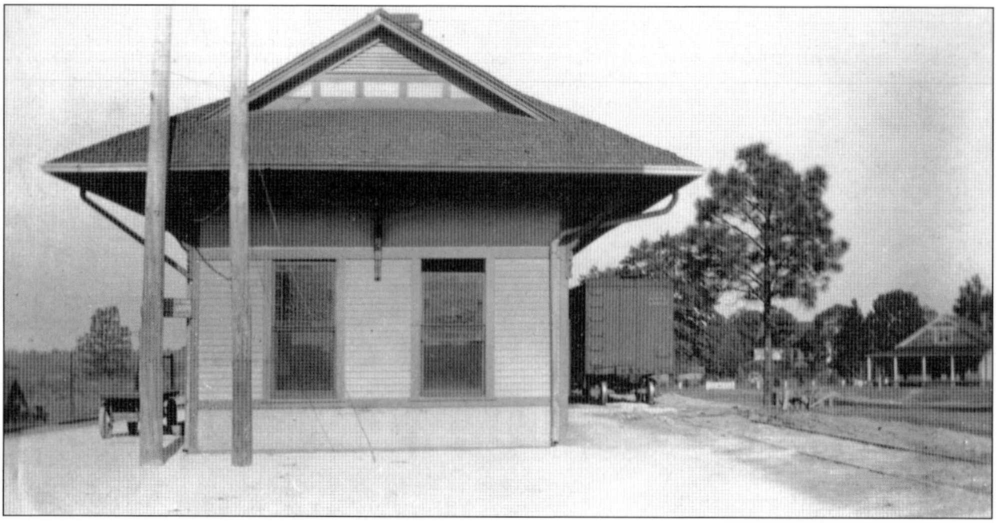

Constructed in 1897, the Louisville & Nashville Rail Depot was vital to the economy of Thorsby. The north-and-southbound rail service provided transportation not only for the residents but also for the shipment of locally grown fruit and berry products to distant markets. Other critical services included the delivery of mail and freight. In 1958, the Louisville & Nashville Railroad published a notice of intent to close the depot.

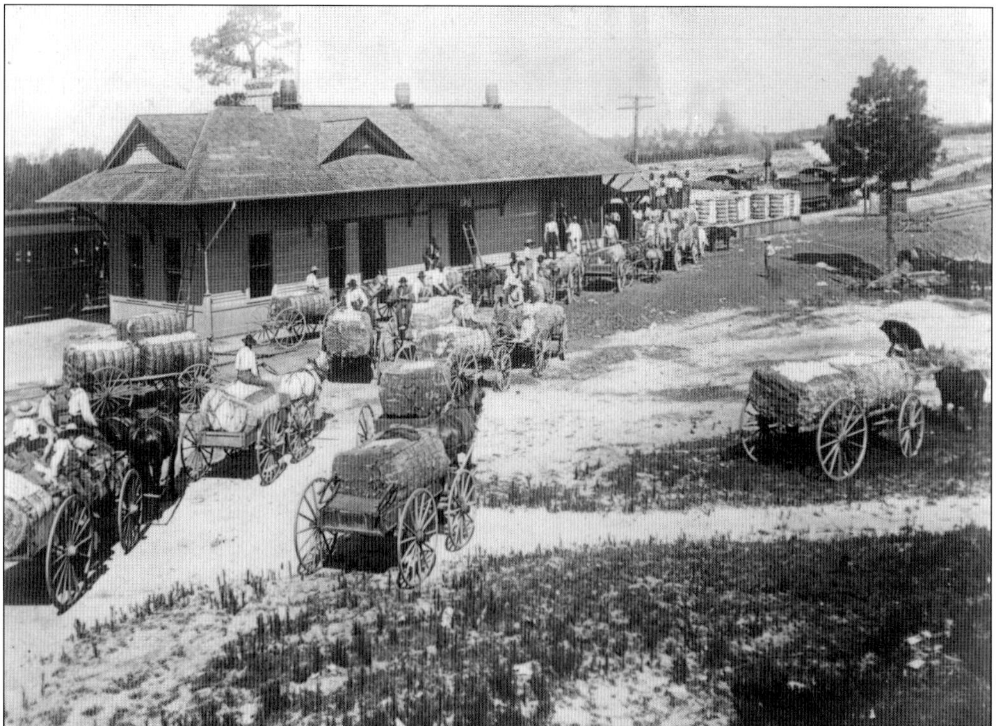

In the late fall of each year, farmers throughout Chilton County would begin to transport their cotton crop to rail depots for shipment to northern markets. To transport the cotton, farmers utilized wagons pulled by oxen, mules, or horses. While waiting to unload at the shipping platform, farmers could spend time trading gossip and discussing politics or the price of cotton or truck crops.

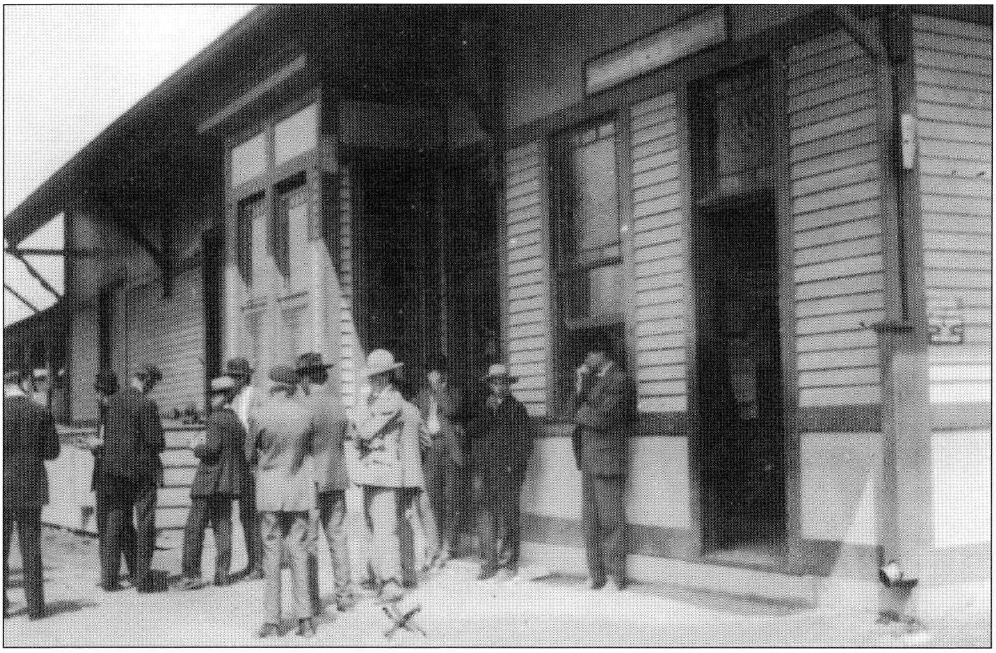

Arrival and departure of passenger and freight trains at the Thorsby Depot always generated excitement in the community. In the January 1940 timetables for the Louisville & Nashville Railroad, northbound trains are identified with even numbers (2, 4, and 6), while the southbound service use odd numbers. Overnight and sleeper service on the Louisville & Nashville system utilized more elegant names such as the Pan-American, Crescent, and Hummingbird.

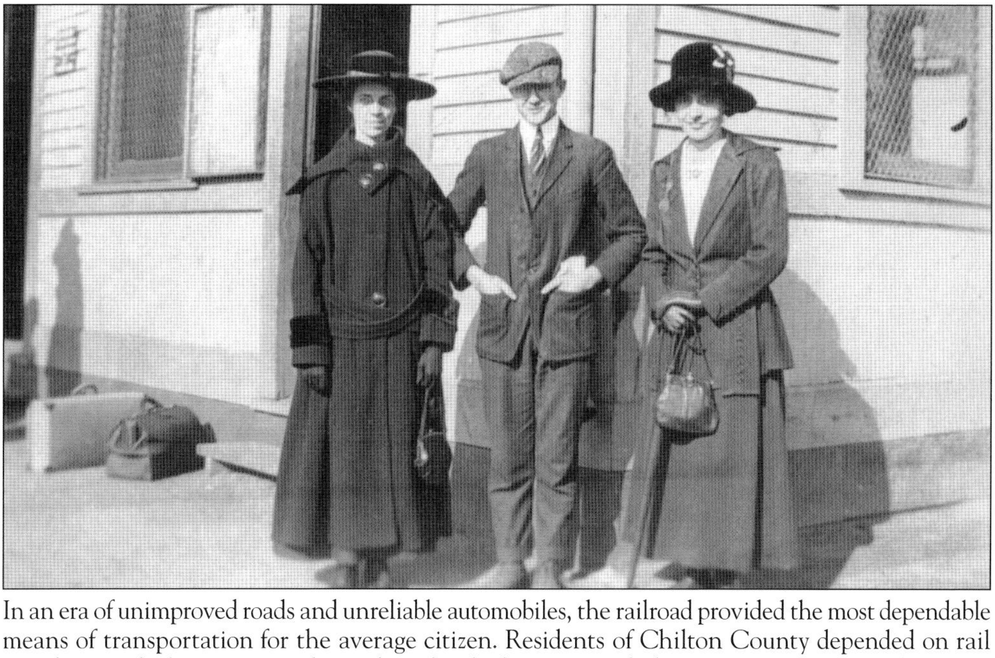

In an era of unimproved roads and unreliable automobiles, the railroad provided the most dependable means of transportation for the average citizen. Residents of Chilton County depended on rail travel not only for trips out of state but also for business and pleasure trips to Birmingham and Montgomery. Even between communities in Chilton County, the railroad provided the most desirable means of travel for families to visit friends and relatives.

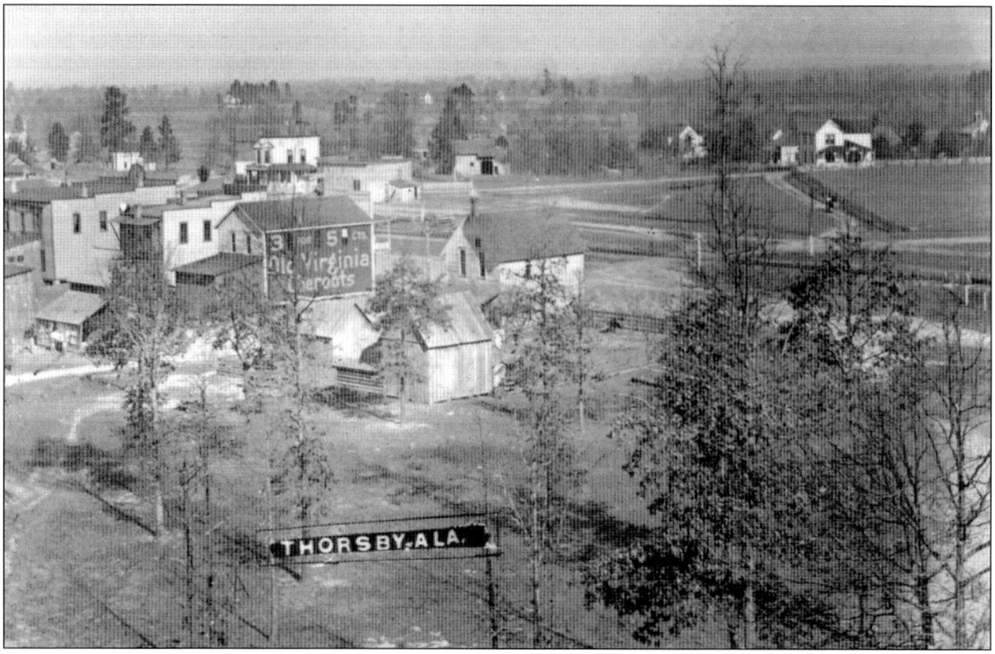

This view of downtown Thorsby shows the wood-frame buildings of local merchants. This image was made prior to the construction of the Montgomery-to-Birmingham Road. Completed in 1914, the Montgomery-to-Birmingham Road paralleled the Louisville & Nashville rail line through Chilton County. After paving was completed in 1925, the road became part of US 31, the Dixie Bee Line Highway.

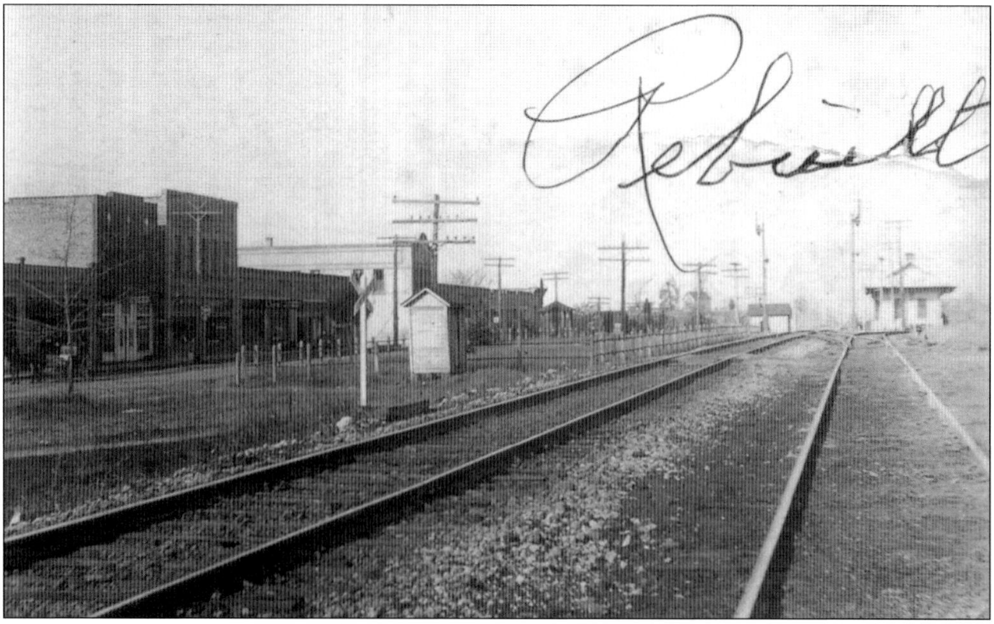

In 1914, a fire downtown destroyed several of the wood-frame buildings of Thorsby merchants. The structures were rebuilt using concrete and bricks to minimize the potential for a reoccurrence. The dual railroad tracks visible in the image were installed to allow railcars to be moved from the main line for loading of produce for shipment to markets outside of Chilton County.

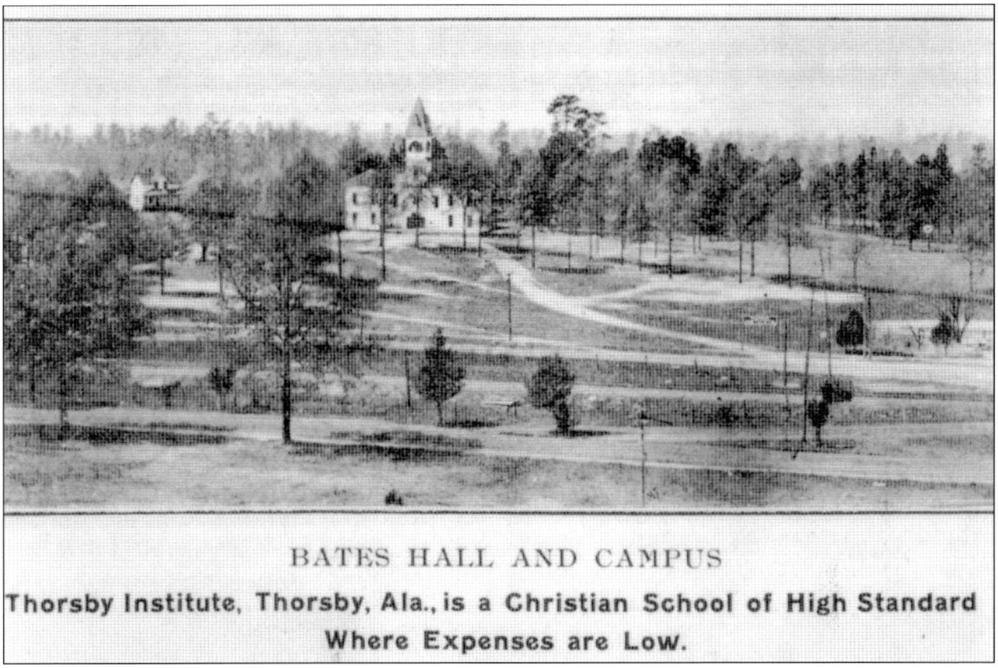

Thorsby is known as a town of churches and schools, and residents have remained dedicated supporters of both institutions. After the Thorsby Normal and Collegiate Institute was forced to close because of financial difficulties, local citizens met to form Thorsby Institute. The preparatory school was based on Christian but nonsectarian principles. Thorsby Institute became the first accredited high school in Chilton County.

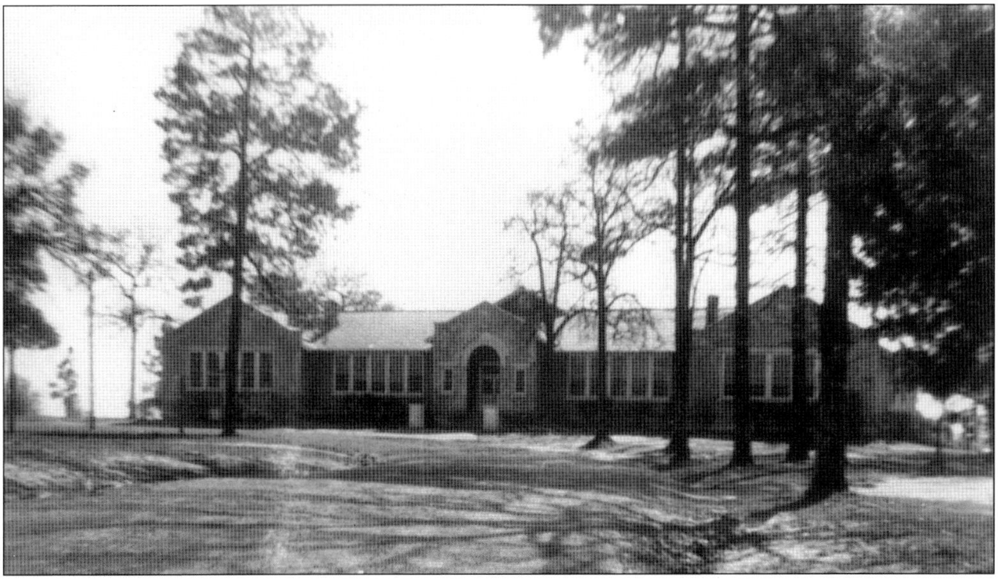

Thorsby Institute opened in September 1907 and included dormitories for male and female students. The school library maintained more than 5,000 volumes. In 1957, facing financial difficulties, the Board of Trustees of Thorsby Institute received a grant to operate within the Chilton County School System for two years. The land and buildings were subsequently deeded to the State of Alabama to be used as a high school.

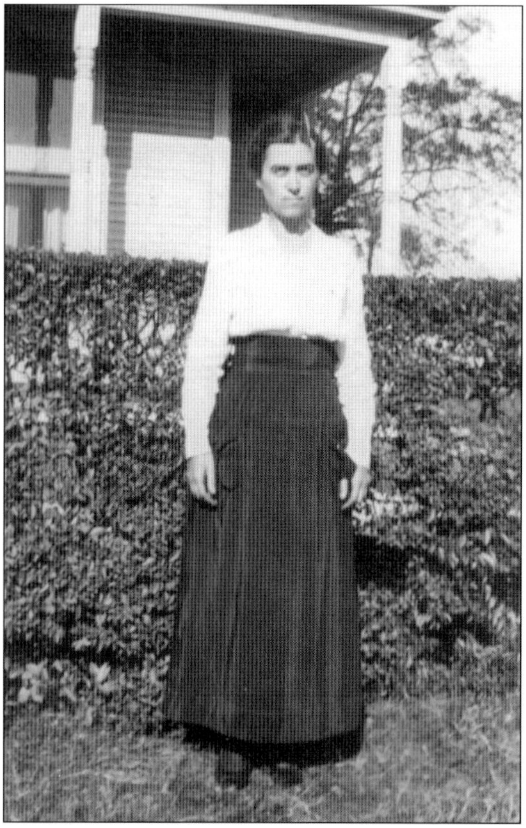

Helen Charlotte Jenkins was born on July 11, 1885, in Connecticut. After graduating from Mount Holyoke College in Massachusetts, she earned a master's degree from the University of Chicago. Fluent in Latin, Jenkins moved to Thorsby in 1907 and joined the faculty of Thorsby Institute, where she taught for the remainder of her career. The former Norwegian Lutheran church in Thorsby is named in her honor.

A high degree of scholarship, character, and experience was demanded of every member of the faculty of Thorsby Institute. From the time the school opened in September 1907, faculty members were selected on their efficiency and were members in good standing of an evangelical church. The curriculum offered the best education for students who had already conceived a serious purpose in life and who desired a useful education at a moderate price.

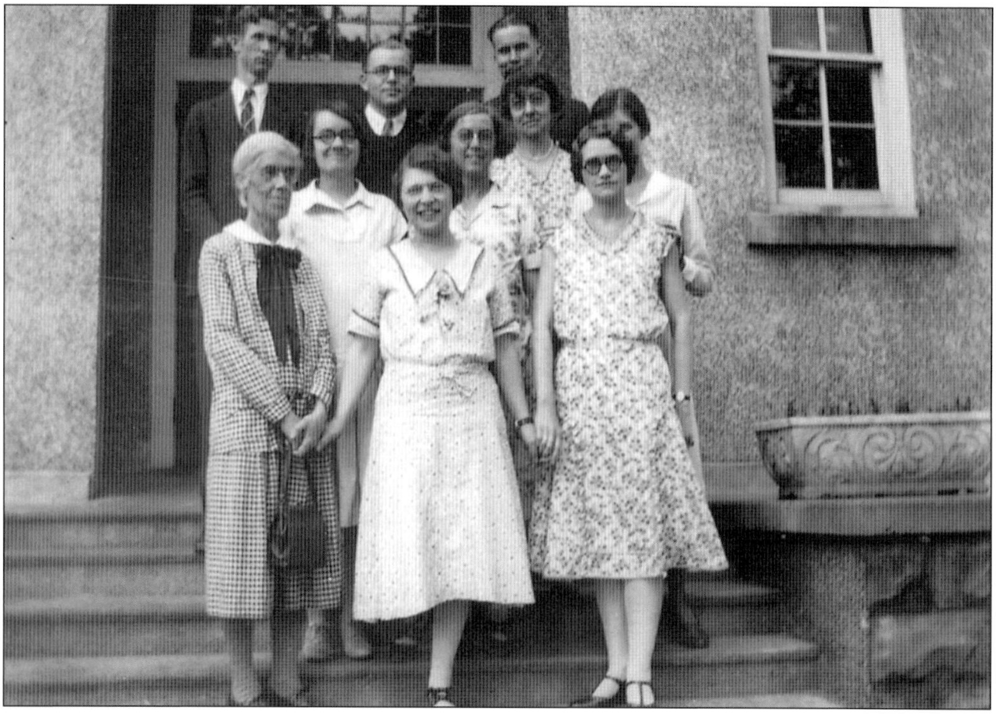

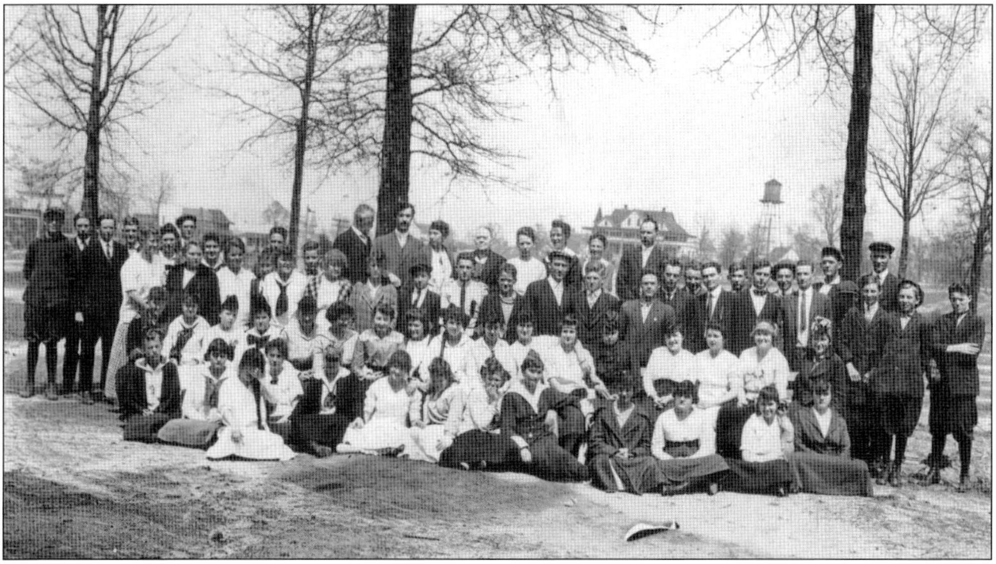

The First Annual Catalogue of Thorsby Institute states that the school was designed for young men and women of good minds and high aims. The catalogue warns that vicious or idle boys are not wanted. The former Thorsby Hotel was purchased for use by the institute and converted into a dormitory for young women. The original dormitory for female students is visible in the background.

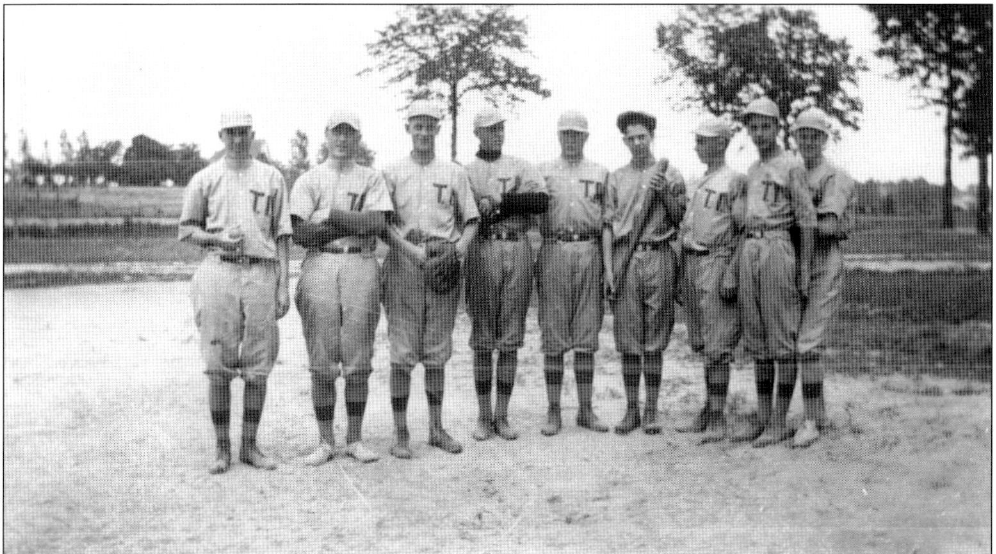

Students at Thorsby Institute were encouraged to participate in various types of athletics. The baseball team competed with other teams in Chilton County. If a game was scheduled outside of Chilton County, the team would often board the Louisville & Nashville Railroad at the Thorsby Depot for transportation to the venue. A goal of Thorsby Institute was to field strong teams to represent the school.

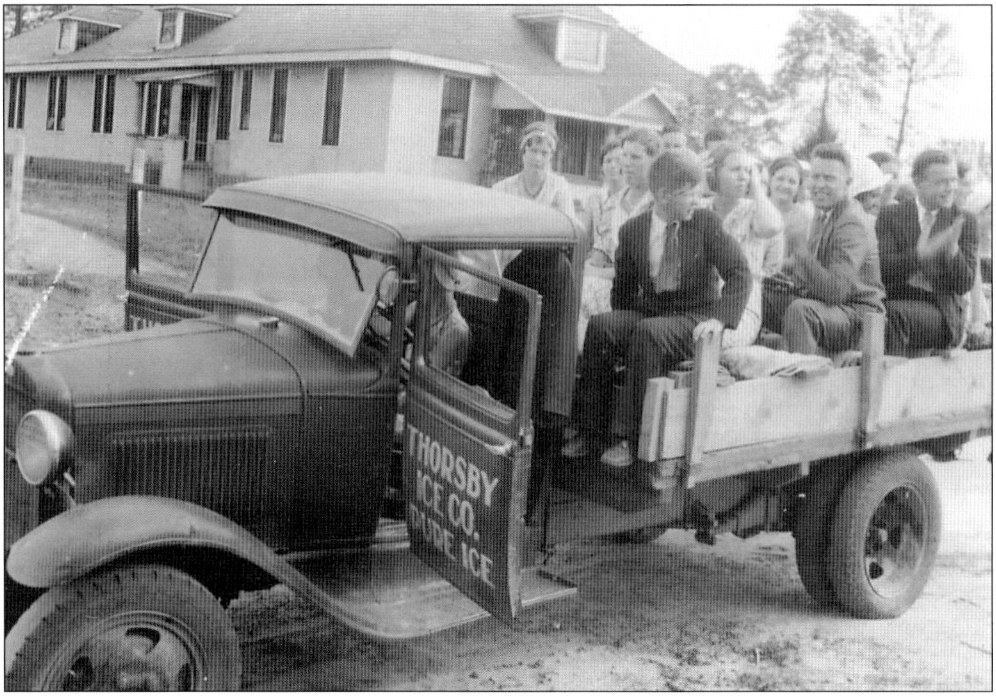

Life at Thorsby Institute was not all work and no play. The school and local churches sponsored social and other activities for students. To a significant degree, the lives of students and residents of Thorsby were intertwined, as local citizens provided continuous support for the school, faculty, and student body. Sunday afternoon picnics were a popular activity for students, even if they had to borrow an ice truck for transportation.

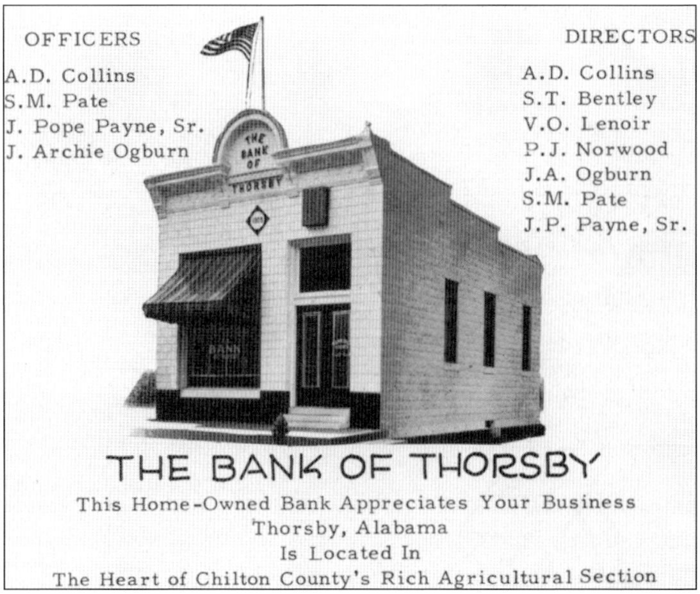

Founded in 1909, the Bank of Thorsby was advertised as being in the heart of Chilton County's rich agricultural section. The home-owned bank served the financial needs of residents, businesses, and especially truck growers. Bank officer and director Archie Ogburn served as the first chairman of the Chilton County Peach Festival. The building is currently being used as the Thorsby Historical Preservation Museum. (Douglas and Janice Cleckler.)

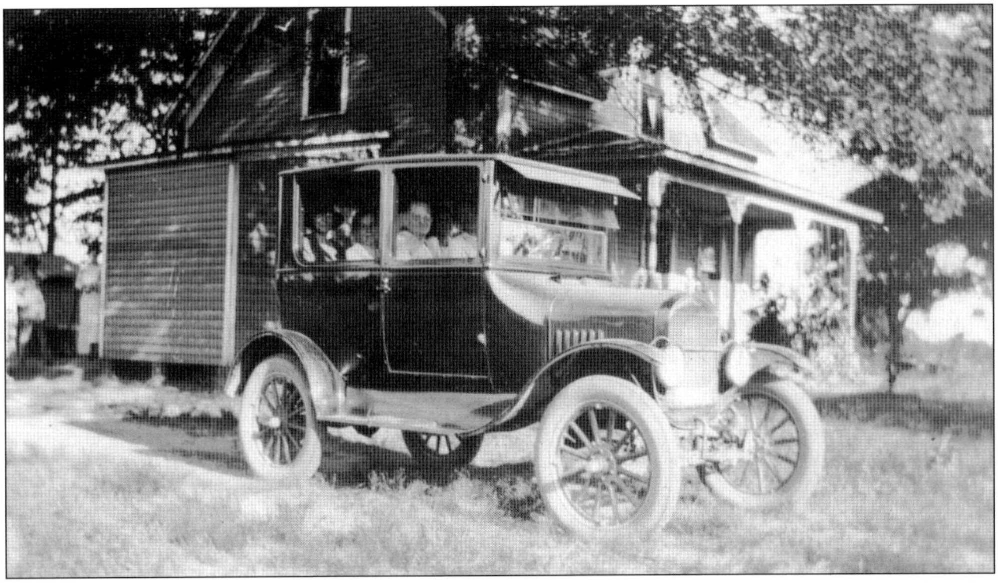

The Montgomery-to-Birmingham Road linked Verbena, Coopers, Clanton, Lomax, Thorsby, and Jemison. The convenience of automobile travel allowed residents to avoid the schedule restrictions of the railroad. Businesses along the Montgomery-to-Birmingham Road flourished with the increasing popularity of the automobile, while the railroads began closing depots along their routes.

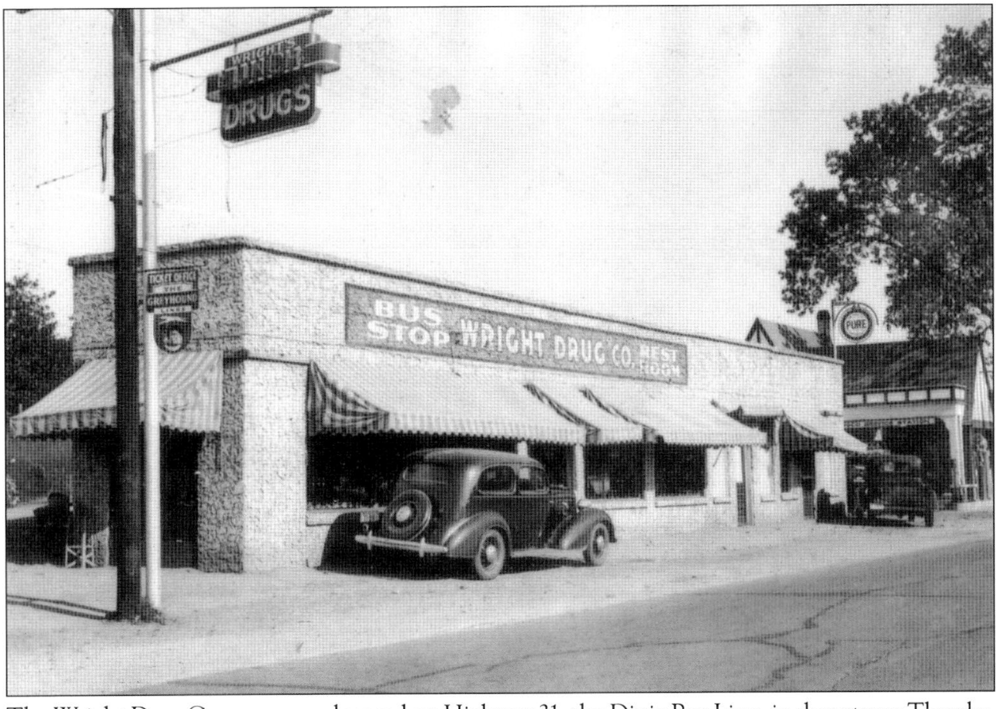

The Wright Drug Company was located on Highway 31, the Dixie Bee Line, in downtown Thorsby. Like other businesses in Chilton County, the Wright Drug Company benefitted from its proximity to the highway. The business also served as the Greyhound bus station, serving a mode of travel that contributed to the demise of passenger travel on the Louisville & Nashville Railroad.

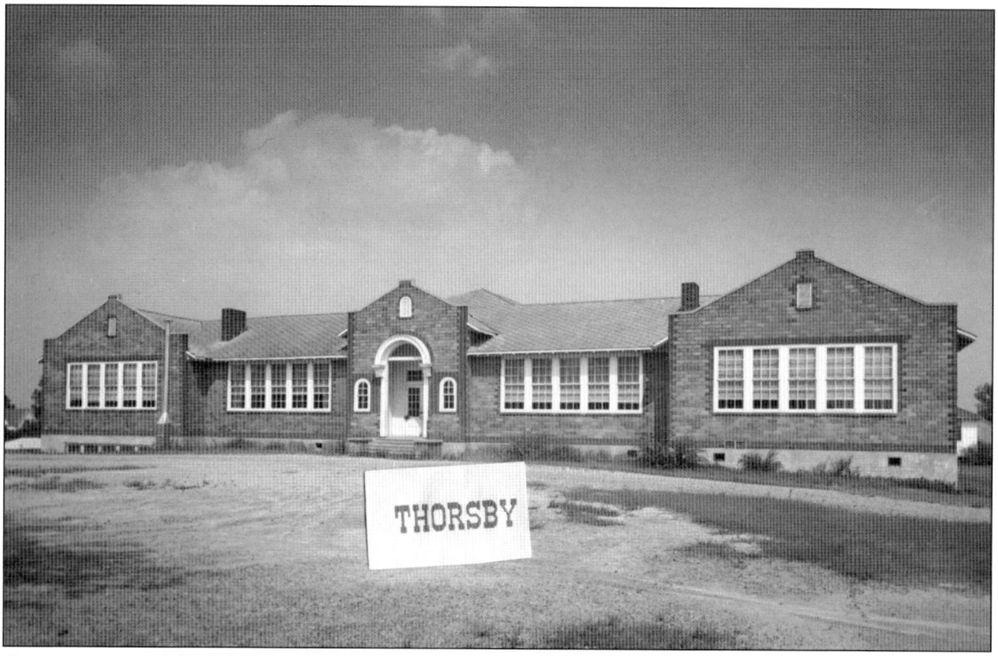

Construction of the Thorsby Public School began in 1924 on a five-acre parcel at the intersection of Jones Street and Illinois Avenue. The school was for students in first through ninth grades. The basement of the building afforded additional space for training students in trade skills. The facility was closed in 1975 after serving as the Thorsby Elementary School.

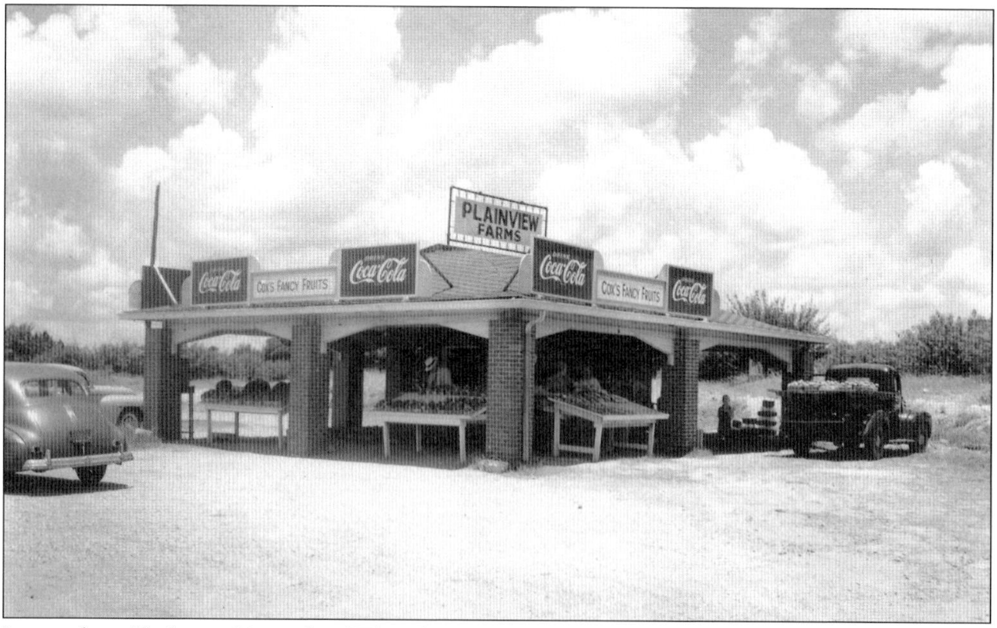

Located on Highway 31 south of Thorsby, Cox's Fancy Fruits was a popular curbside market operated by Enoch and Maude Cox. Offering a variety of fresh peaches, watermelons, strawberries, and other produce, Cox's Fancy Fruits enticed transient and local travelers on Highway 31 to stop and take advantage of the opportunity to acquire some of the best fruits and vegetables produced by Plainview Farms. (Chilton County Extension Service.)

Seven

VERBENA

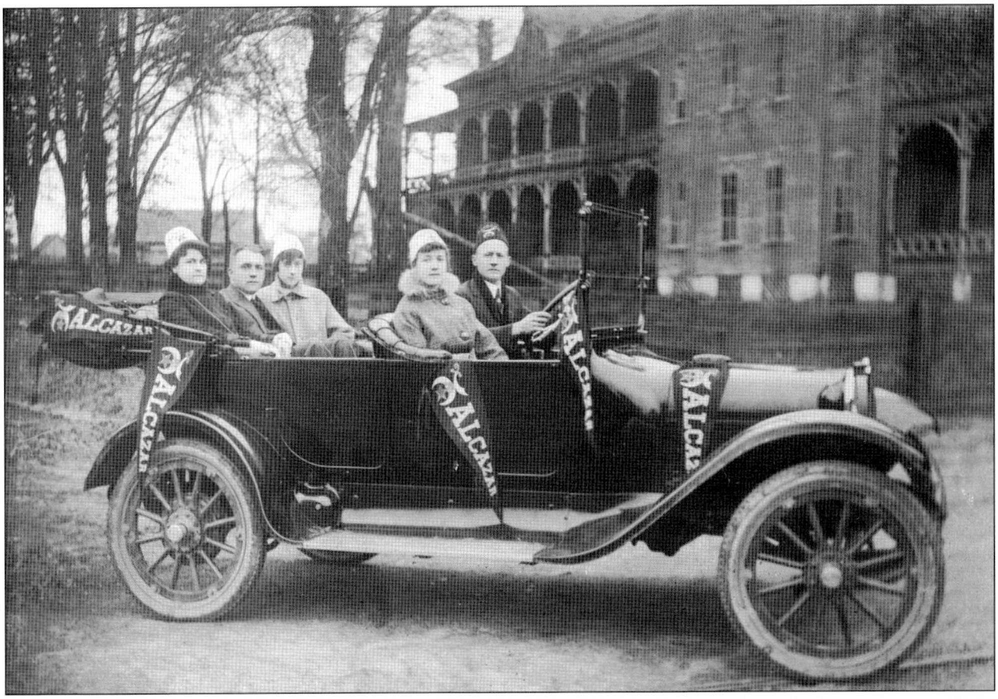

Described as having the advantages of an altitude well above sea level with fine water and no mosquitoes, the town of Verbena provided priceless features of health and comfort for residents and tourists. The town was originally known as Summerfield, but the name was changed in recognition of an abundance of the verbena plant native to the region. In January 1976, Verbena was listed in the National Register of Historic Places. (ADAH.)

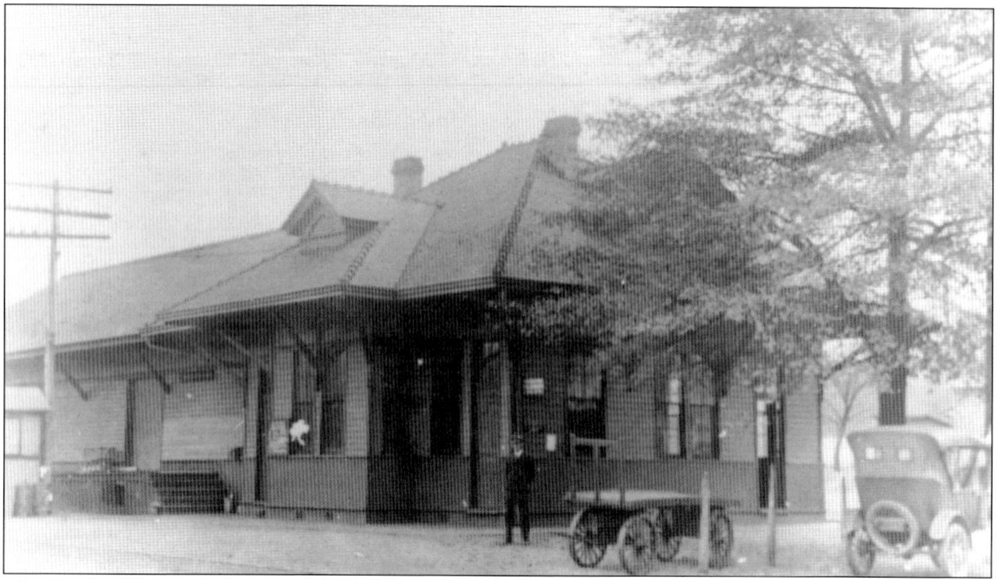

The convenience of travel by railroad provided a means for prosperous residents of Montgomery to escape the oppressive summertime heat of the city to enjoy the cool, fresh air prevalent in the higher elevations of Verbena. A haven for the well-to-do of the Montgomery River region who sought refuge from recurring epidemics of yellow fever, Verbena became known as a town born of this often fatal disease.

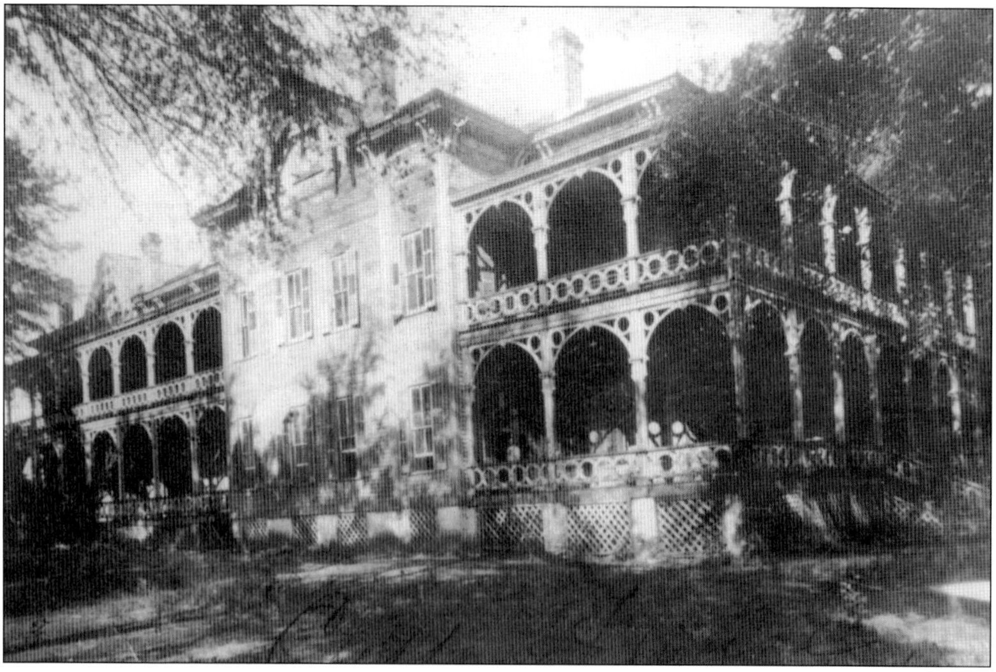

Constructed in 1882, the Clifton House Hotel was a large, two-story structure surrounded by open porches that allowed guests to enjoy the clean, fresh air of Verbena. Even though they may have been to Atlantic City or abroad to Europe, the summer season was never complete for affluent families of the Alabama Black Belt until they visited the Clifton House. In 1922, the structure was destroyed by fire.

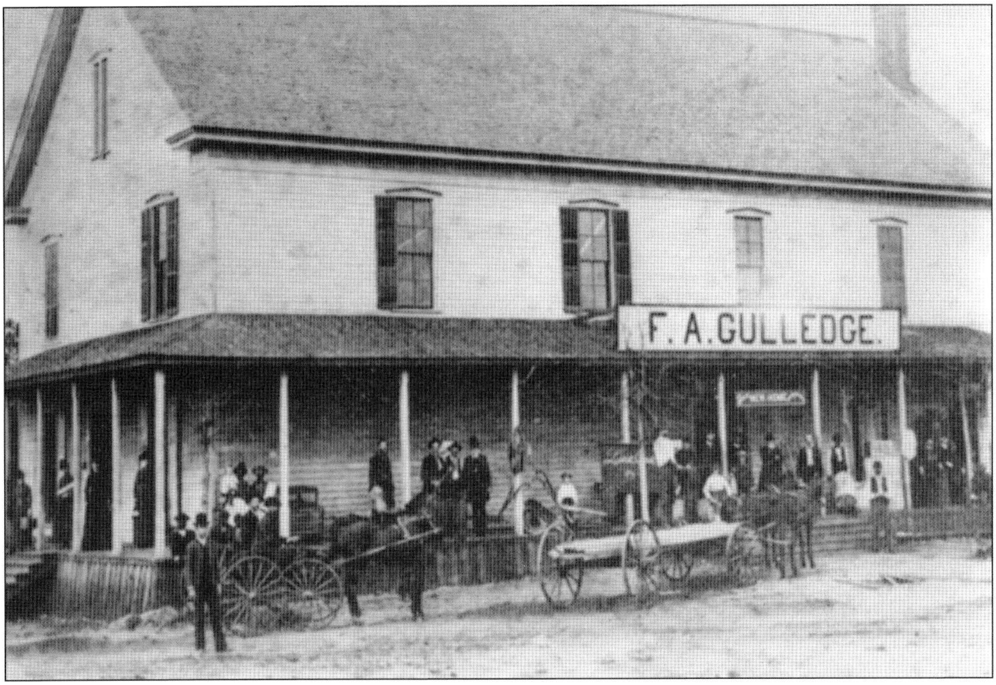

Established in 1876, the F.A. Gulledge store remained in continuous operation for 82 years, making it the oldest business in Chilton County. The general merchandise business supplied residents of Verbena and the surrounding area with farming, homemaking, and other products. William Gulledge, son of founder F.A. Gulledge, closed the business in 1958 upon reaching 83 years of age.

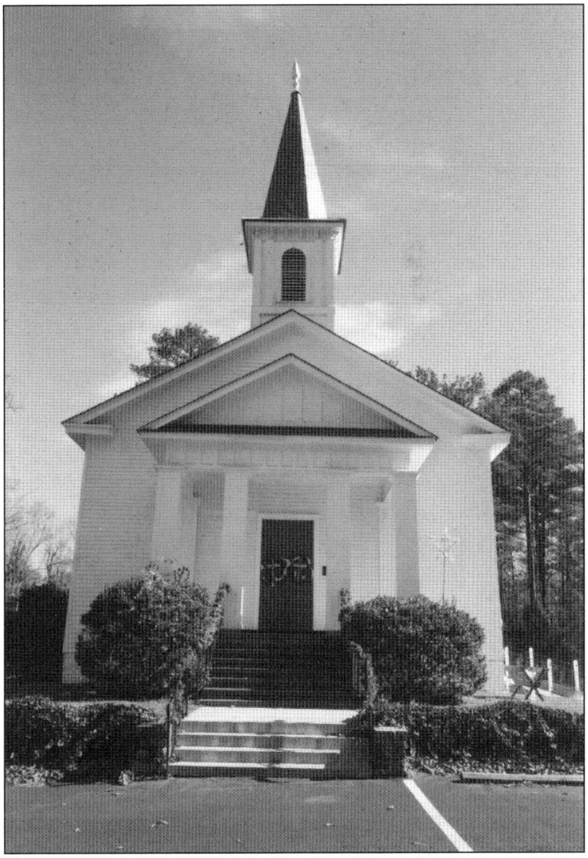

Organized in 1871, the 11-member congregation of the Verbena United Methodist Church first met in a small house that also served as a school. In 1875, the congregation established a fund to purchase four acres of land for construction of a permanent place of worship. Completed in September 1876, the white frame building was the first church constructed in Verbena.

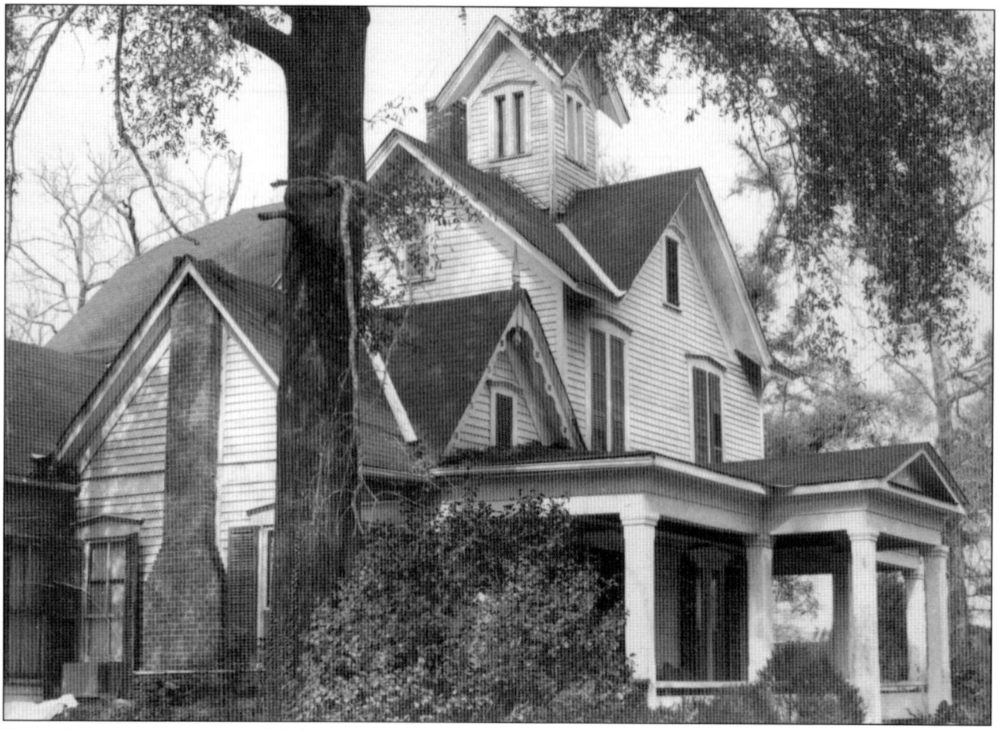

Early literature describes Verbena as a quiet town where a gentle wind causes the leaves of the oak trees that shade the town to sigh one of those sighs of content that a person breathes after a good meal, a good sermon, or well-rendered piece of music. Oakside, a stately home located on the Louisville & Nashville Railroad, was surrounded by majestic oak trees and gardens.

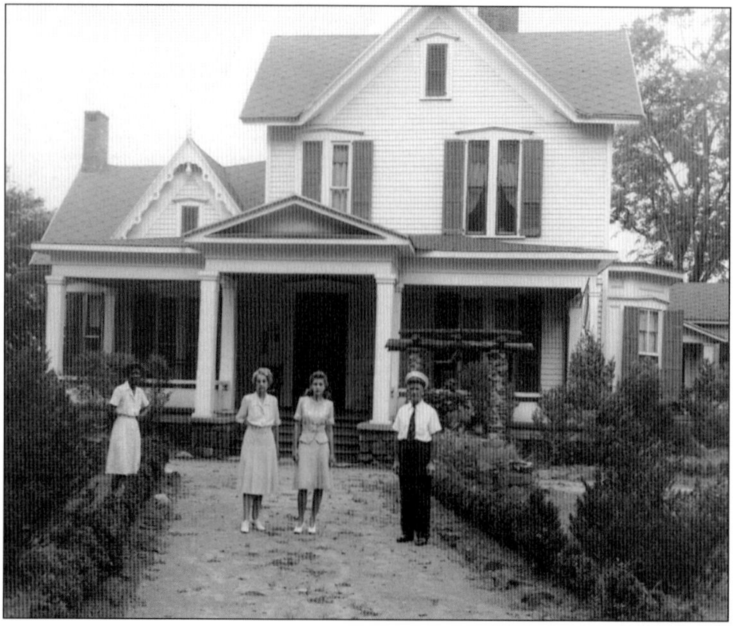

From left to right, Lizzie Baldwin, Mary Lee Gibson, Gertrude Gibson, and Sidney Lanier Gibson pose for a photograph in front of Oakside, the Gibson home in Verbena. Sidney Lanier Gibson was the nephew of poet, author, and musician Sidney Lanier. Gibson was also a talented writer and published poems each week in the *Union Banner* newspaper. Oakside was constructed in 1875 by Maj. Joseph Carr Gibson.

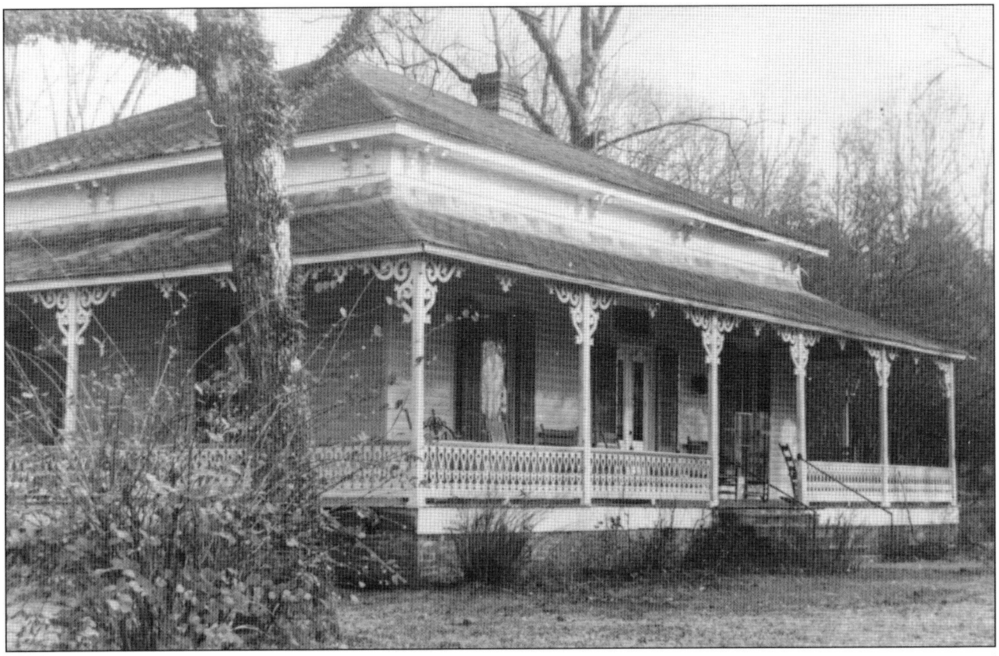

Each summer, Verbena became a mecca for Montgomery families who made the town home until the first frost of the fall eliminated the scourge of yellow fever and made it safe to return to the capital city. Many of those who came to Verbena during the summer decided to make the town their permanent home. By 1890, Verbena had become the largest community in Chilton County.

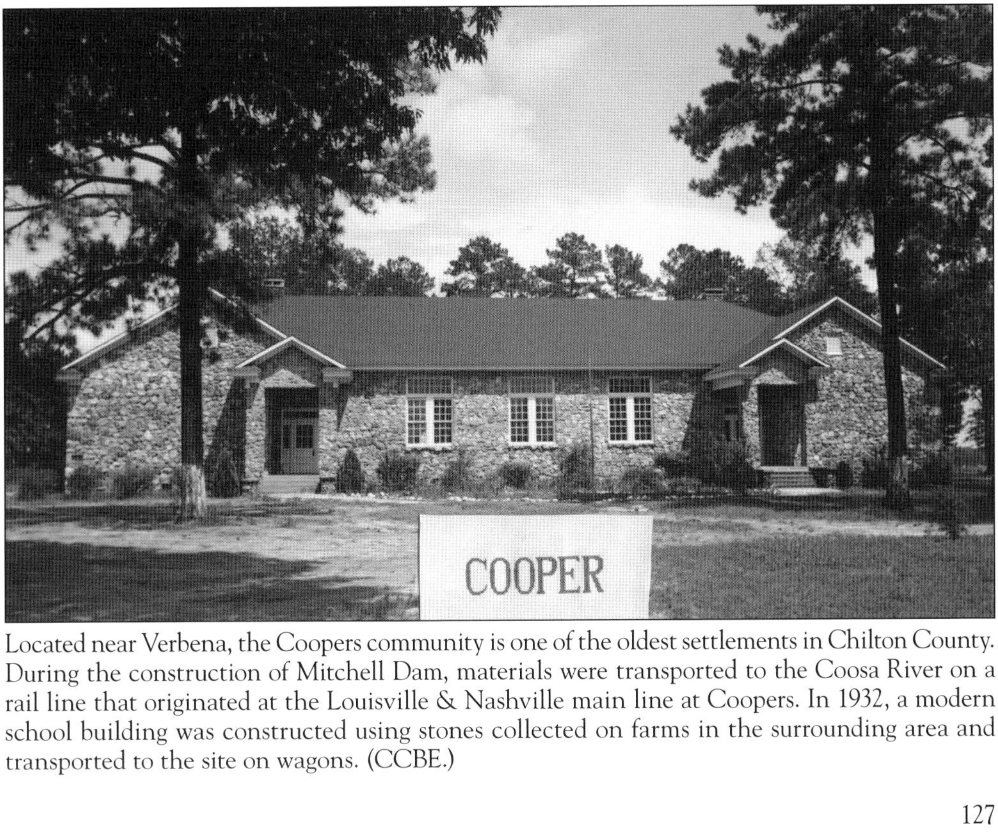

Located near Verbena, the Coopers community is one of the oldest settlements in Chilton County. During the construction of Mitchell Dam, materials were transported to the Coosa River on a rail line that originated at the Louisville & Nashville main line at Coopers. In 1932, a modern school building was constructed using stones collected on farms in the surrounding area and transported to the site on wagons. (CCBE.)

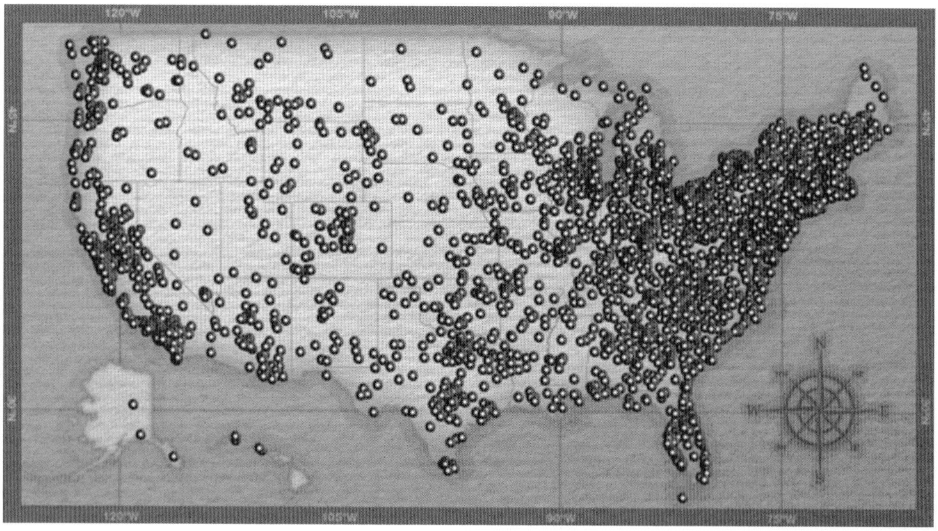